IRISH MANAGEMENT INSTITUTE

When, in the 1950s, industry was thin on the ground and self-faith was low, the newly founded IMI gave companies a framework for managing. It taught managers techniques they had not known before — and how to apply them. It has continued to create in wider society a sense of awareness of management, of the centrality of management and management education to economic development. Most importantly, but more difficult of measurement, it contributed to the attitude of can-do that has brought Ireland's industrial economy from there to here.

ABOUT THE AUTHOR

Tom Cox has worked with Irish business organisations for almost forty years. He was part of the team that led the development of the IMI for a quarter century from 1960, gaining a close knowledge of the personalities who brought the ethos of modern management to Ireland. From 1984–96, he was chief executive of the Dublin Chamber of Commerce, helping it to adopt a new role in the economic development of the capital. In the 1990s, he carried out economic development assignments in central Europe, and elsewhere, for the European Union and the United Nations Private Sector Development Programme. He is a director of a number of companies and serves on some voluntary bodies.

THE MAKING OF MANAGERS

A History of the Irish Management Institute
1952–2002

Tom Cox

Oak Tree Press

Cork

Oak Tree Press
19 Rutland Street,
Cork, Ireland
http://www.oaktreepress.com

© 2002 Irish Management Institute

A catalogue record of this book is
available from the British Library.

ISBN 1 86076 240 9

Printed in the Republic of Ireland by Colour Books Ltd.

CONTENTS

MESSAGE FROM PRESIDENT McALEESE

The Irish Management Institute has played a major part in the developing Irish economy, through its many education and training programmes, tailored to suit the requirements of Irish industry. The Institute's achievements stand as a tribute to the many who have worked with, and in, the IMI to impart knowledge and skills to managers and leaders and to the future drivers of Irish business.

Without that calibre of management, it would not have been possible to aspire to, much less sustain, the strong economic position we have enjoyed in recent years. Across all social sectors a professional discipline and commitment is evident: people are prepared to work long hours, to take risks, to hold their nerve, to work towards a vision.

The IMI has contributed much to that vision. In an ever-changing global economy, where the sands are constantly shifting, it has been ready to break new ground, to change, to take new directions when they were required. That alertness to change has been at the heart of the Institute's enduring success. It has helped it endow generations of Irish managers with the skills and the confidence to open doors to the new, prosperous Ireland we have achieved today.

Mary McAleese

MARY McALEESE
PRESIDENT OF IRELAND

FOREWORD

Barry Kenny
Chief Executive
Irish Management Institute

I am delighted to have the opportunity to introduce a history of the Irish Management Institute fifty years after it was founded. I can vividly recall my feelings on taking charge in 1995 — a certain ambition to make my own mark, tempered with an awareness of the central role played by the IMI in developing the modern Irish economy and a consciousness of the weight of history and tradition.

I think Tom Cox has done a marvellous job in writing this history. He shows us the vision of the founding fathers, and the unstinting voluntary work of the first council and board to give reality to this vision. While in its early years the IMI was independent, Government and EU support was essential to bring about the major development phase of the Institute's activities. I would like to acknowledge the role of those key public servants in Dublin and Brussels who showed their confidence in the vision and worked in partnership with the IMI to deliver its goals.

We owe a particular debt to our customers — the many thousands of managers who have attended our programmes and seminars down the years. And to the faculty and staff of the Institute, who have developed the ability to seamlessly organise and deliver high-quality management development interventions. While participants will see breezy and confident presentations, which may look effortless, we ourselves are fully aware of the hard work and personal commitment required. I should also recognise the great contribution from practising managers, who give generously of their time to address our conferences, events and briefings, and also to bring the lessons gained from cutting-edge practice to our programmes.

I have, of course, a particular interest in the role played by my predecessors, once styled *director general*, and now *chief executive*, in steering the Institute through a period of change and development. I am sixth in succession — not a bad total for fifty years.

All in all, I can look back with pride on the contribution the IMI has made in creating a cadre of confident and capable Irish managers with a global outlook. I have had the privilege of leading the Institute through a process of change, when we have returned to our original independence from subsidy, and developed as a market-facing centre for management development. I look ahead with confidence, happy that we are on the right path, and that, in all likelihood, another fifty years must go by before history will judge our plans and strategies again.

Barry Kenny
May 2002

Perspective

Kevin Kelly
Chairman
Irish Management Institute

The writing of a history to mark the fiftieth anniversary of the founding of the IMI provides an opportunity for reflection, as well as the possibility of looking ahead.

For anyone with an interest in the IMI, or in the evolution of today's cadre of highly competent, flexible, and externally focused Irish managers, Tom Cox's history makes interesting reading.

For the first decade of its existence, the IMI acted as an institute of managers, with visiting speakers, networks to exchange experience, and a brief to stimulate the provision of management education in universities and third level institutes. We were starting from a low base, and had much to do.

From 1962 on, the Institute became directly involved in the provision of management development, and became a major player in its own right. The IMI grew, and with support from its members, Government and the EU, expanded rapidly and built the much-admired National Management Centre in Sandyford.

Today, the Institute has achieved operational self-sufficiency, and operates as a high-quality centre for management development working intimately with its client businesses. History does not stand still, and I have no doubt that the IMI of 50 years' time will be quite different.

The mission of the IMI is, as it always has been, to improve the practice of management in Ireland. As the provision of development and training services by commercial organisations has grown, the Institute must continue to position itself at the leading edge of current practice.

The core competence of the IMI is its expertise in adult learning, its ability to work with practising managers to develop their skills and expertise. The Institute of tomorrow will focus on development rather than training, with the research resources to identify global best practice in management, and adapt and apply this practice in an Irish context, to help deliver improved performance for our member organisations.

A faculty with recognised international expertise will deliver intensive, residential development programmes in our Sandyford campus and beyond, acknowledged as partners by leading organisations in developing the expertise and skills of their key strategic resources, their people.

In this, our fiftieth anniversary year, we have the opportunity to reflect and take pride in the achievement of our predecessors, and at the same time work with the management and staff of the Institute to press ahead. For, in the words of Robert Frost, we have

"promises to keep and miles to go before we sleep."

Kevin Kelly
May 2002

ACKNOWLEDGEMENTS

I had better declare a vested interest: this is the story of an organisation that I worked with for almost half of its life, from 1960 to 1984, sharing its aspirations and from close quarters observing its development during its formative decades. I knew almost all its founders. I hope that being "in the family" has not contaminated the objectivity that you, the reader, has the right to expect.

Jim Byrne, secretary of the Institute, persuaded me to accept chief executive Barry Kenny's trusting invitation to undertake this history to mark this year's Golden Jubilee of the Institute's foundation. Barry and Jim sustained me through the project. I am grateful to them.

In compiling the story, I have drawn heavily on the files and memories of two surviving founders of the Institute, Michael Dargan and Michael MacCormac. The latter, with Louden Ryan, John Murray and Geoffrey McKechnie, were my main pathfinders through the development of management education in UCD and Trinity College. I am grateful to the Institute's first director, Paul Quigley, for preparing excellent notes for me. I am indebted to Ivor Kenny, director-general from 1963–1982, for his vivid memory, not only of the events but of the people, and especially for allowing me to plunder his extensive contemporaneous account of the 1972 merger attempt with the Confederation of Irish Industry. I turned often to Noel Mulcahy on the evolution of the young Institute's teaching philosophy and the development of its remarkable international network, and to Breffni Tomlin for Chapter Twelve.

I have drawn much from the hours of discussion with IMI staff, past and present. I thank them for their great generosity and patience. Their input to the making of Irish managers has been — and is — crucial; I regret that it has been possible to record here only a hint of the scope and depth of their achievements, individually and collectively.

I thank Dr T.K. Whitaker for sharing his unique perspective on how dependence and despondency were displaced by hope and vision. Sir Anthony O'Reilly was generous, not only with his time, but in sharing his monograph on the four ages of the Irish economy. I am grateful to Judge Roderick Murphy and the family of the late Denis A. Hegarty for access to his papers; to Noel MacMahon for his recall of the National Joint Committee for the Human Sciences and their Application in Industry; and to the late John Gallagher, director general of the Institute of Public Administration, who let me see an unpublished memoir by the late Tom Barrington on the founding and early development of the IPA. Tony Prendergast and Harry Hannon helped with lore on Sir Charles Harvey; Jim O'Donnell with his wise counsel on pitfalls to avoid; John Corcoran shared his thesis on management development. Donal Nevin helped me on trade union history, as did Eamonn Cahill on the Irish National Productivity Committee's mutation to the Irish Productivity Council, and Arthur Gibney on the genesis of the design of the national management centre. Dermot Egan read a late draft and made several useful comments.

I thank Margaret Fulcher who guided me through the Institute's archive and helped me in many aspects of the work; Vivienne Adams for planning and organising interviews and cheerfully processing several drafts; Kieran McLaughlin, Hannah Dyas and Michelle Griffin for their valuable help at the pre-publication phase; Elaine McMahon and her colleagues in the Institute's excellent library; Alex Miller for his prompt sourcing of books; Alan Cox for his insightful and constructive inputs; and Brian Langan for his welcome editorial hand-holding.

Finally I must say something about the gender issue. For much of the early history of the Institute, management was assumed to be a male preserve and, indeed, it was. Many of the sources quoted in the book, therefore, use the male pronoun when referring to managers. It jars.

Tom Cox
May 2002

I dedicate this book to Nóirín with great love and gratitude for her enduring encouragement

CHAPTER ONE

THE CONTEXT

The postman negotiating the backroads of Ireland, delivering letters from America, eagerly awaited dollars pressed inside, may have been unaware of the effect he and his whirring bicycle were having on the national economy. But, at the mid-point of the twentieth century, "emigrants' remittances" were a prominent feature on the external payments side of the annual Budget and played not a small part in keeping home fires burning.

In 1950 Ireland was still a young state, unsure and tentative, haunted by the ghosts of the Civil War; a country on its own, grappling with many issues and, as the first post-colonial nation of the twentieth century, without models to follow. Resources were pitifully scarce — the only external largesse being that same "money from America". Agriculture, the economic backbone, was primitive enough. The smallholdings on which it was based may have kept body and soul together but generated precious little wealth. Britain dominated the Irish economy: it called the shots on prices for agriculture and was the source of most industrial products.

The lack of opportunity bred a sense of hopelessness in the young. The crowded primary school was as far as many of them got in education. Then, there would be a year or two helping at home, following the fortunes of the local GAA team but, too soon, for too many, there would be the one-way ticket to England, America or Australia. An entire class might emigrate within a few years of leaving school. Large numbers of young men and women saw their future, not in Dublin, Cork or Galway but in Liverpool, Coventry and Kilburn.

The year the Irish Management Institute was founded, 1952, the government, urgently in need of cash, imposed increases even on such staple fare as bread, butter, sugar and tea. Average annual income per head of population was $400, less than half that of Britain and one-fifth that of the United States. T.K. Whitaker, on his 85th birthday,[1] recalling the mid-1950s, described the country as having been "enveloped in a palpable cloud of despondency", with exports of industrial goods still accounting for only six per cent of total exports. Michael Dargan, one of the founders of the IMI, also recalls the emptiness of the time, in particular the absence of any economic vision. State jobs — in the Civil Service, teaching, the Garda — were keenly contested. Local manufacturing, where it existed, was barely surviving in a depressed home market. In the cities, there were jobs in retailing, fuel distribution, bakeries and, for the lucky ones in Dublin, a prized career in Guinness's, Jacobs or the banks. The professions were narrowly based and did not offer much opportunity for the modest outflow of the universities. Tourism was stagnant after a post-war boom "consisting largely of British tourists seeking a good meal".[2]

Right from its foundation, the State was heavily dependent on imports. It lacked manufacturing capability for consumer goods, agricultural equipment and food processing. In the mid-1920s the first Cumann na nGael government imposed a modest number of measures to help local manufacture. The Fianna Fáil government in 1932, in its first Finance Act, erected an extensive protective wall of tariffs and quotas behind which a wider industrial base might be nurtured. Importers and distributors were encouraged to establish industries to replace imports with local manufacture. This regime was backed by the Control of Manufactures Acts which required that these enterprises had to be at least 51 per cent Irish-owned. The radical policy was applauded, albeit with a caveat or two, by no less distinguished an authority than John Maynard Keynes who told an audience at the first Finlay Lecture at University College, Dublin, in April 1933:

---

[1] Whitaker, T.K. (2001), "We Have Come a Long Way — But We Still Have a Long Way to Go", *The Irish Times*, 8 December, p. 10.

[2] Kennedy, Kieran A. and others (1988), *The Economic Development of Ireland*, London and New York: Routledge.

If I were an Irishman I should find much to attract me in
the economic outlook of your present government towards self-sufficiency.

The outbreak of World War II endorsed the prudence of that policy, which was driven by a formidable duo: Sean F. Lemass and
John Leydon. Lemass, decisive and determined to tackle the
State's economic deficit, was Minister for Industry and Commerce,
the only cabinet member with a business background. Leydon, his
chief adviser and policy enforcer, was, at 37, five years Lemass's
senior, intellectually strong and of independent mind. He had already impressed in the Civil Service with his grasp of economics.
When Lemass became minister, he straightaway appointed Leydon secretary of the department. What followed was one of the
most innovative periods in the history of the state as the challenges
of growth were met with unique and imaginative solutions.

Industrial jobs created from the 1930s to the 1950s were almost
entirely the fruits of the Lemass/Leydon axis. They helped nurture
an industrial ethos in Ireland. Factories appeared, not just in cities
but in small towns where they drew their workers from neighbouring villages and small farms — Pierces of Wexford, Irish Alumin-
ium in Nenagh, Irish Ropes and Newbridge Cutlery in Co Kildare,
Carrigaline Pottery in Co Cork, Arklow Pottery in Co Wicklow,
Currans Enamelware in Clonmel and others. Consumers may have
complained for a time about quality, reliability and price, but there
is no evidence of deliberate exploitation by manufacturers of their
protected position. Most companies struggled with a chronically
depressed home market and, during the Emergency, as it was
called, with raw material shortages.

Welcome as these fledgling industries were, only a small minor-
ity of the unemployed found work in them. Those who did so could
not expect much in terms of career growth. Almost all were from
rural, non-industrial backgrounds. The lack of any formal training
left them unprepared for careers in business. It was difficult for
them to relate to the pace and practices of industry. British expatri-
ates managed much of Irish business. Even the brightest local recruits were inhibited by their unfamiliarity with the industrial ethos
and would aspire at most to the lower-level managerial positions.

The Lemass/Leydon strategy was two-pronged. Where private enterprise was unwilling or unable to invest in areas of strategic national importance, the state would step in to establish agencies, industries and trading companies which would develop the infrastructure and exploit natural resources. Generally these state-sponsored bodies — at one time as many as 50 — were under direct ministerial/Civil Service control. They included the Electricity Supply Board, the Irish Sugar Company, Bord na Móna, Shannon Airport Development Company, Bord Iascaigh Mhara, the Industrial Development Authority, the Industrial Credit Company, Córas Trachtála and various insurance companies. They helped fill in the sparse economic infrastructure.

Garret FitzGerald, in a 1961 study of state-sponsored bodies for the Institute of Public Administration, noted that, while many were set up in the 1930s, the greatest number appeared in the immediate post-war years which he described as "a period of transition from a siege economy to a normal peace-time economy". In six years (1946–52) about 15 were established, including the Industrial Development Authority (1950), the export agency, Córas Tráchtála (1951) and the grant-giving Foras Tionscail (1952). Later, Lemass[1] said the leadership and example of the semi-state bodies set standards of performance that inspired private enterprise to greater achievements and helped build up confidence in the country's future. They were, he said, "a very important factor in the nation's growth".

By the mid-1950s, as Europe recovered from the war, some of its states began to regroup into larger, potentially more powerful economic coalitions — the Coal and Steel Community and, later, the European Economic Community. These developments triggered in Ireland a gathering realisation that its policy of protectionism could no longer be sustained. Manufacturing companies would have to face a tough new environment. Ireland's challenge — daunting at the least — was to galvanise what was still a pre-industrial, isolated economy, to the degree that it could contemplate membership of a wider economic bloc. This could not be done without a seismic shift in the national temper — from an attitude of dependency to one of self-confidence. The story of the Irish Management Institute is part of that transition.

---

[1] By then Tánaiste as well as Minister for Industry and Commerce.

CHAPTER TWO

TWO GROUPS, ONE GOAL

Michael Dargan came from Ballivor, County Meath. His father was a farmer and butcher who inculcated in his son an early appreciation of the relationship between effort, shrewdness and achievement. The boy was given two bullocks to prepare for market. Whatever price they made, he could keep, preferably for re-investment in a further enterprise. When the fair day arrived, the boy battled with the "tanglers", getting what he thought was a top price for his bullocks. He got a sharp business lesson, though, when his father told him they had been resold up the street at a handsome premium.

Dargan's first job, in the Civil Service, included a beneficial stint as private secretary to the Minister for Posts and Telegraphs. But business was where he wanted to be. In the 1940s he joined Aer Lingus as staff and services manager. He spent time in New York establishing the company's North Atlantic service. Through contacts in US airlines and the industry's regulatory bodies he was introduced to the American Management Association (AMA) and the Conference Board of America — both pioneers in management training.[1] He joined both and was introduced to a stream of data on how management worked and how managers' performance could be improved — a treasury of seminars, books, analysis and research unavailable in Ireland.

---

[1] Following a visit to the AMA in 1954, Captain J.M. Feehan, writing in the third edition of *Irish Management* (July–August 1954), noted that the "management movement in America" was then forty years old, having been formed in 1923 through the amalgamation of the several of the pioneering groups.

Returning home, he was determined to do something about bringing this resource to Irish managers. He and others — T.P. (Tommy) Hogan, managing director of Plessey Ireland Ltd., electrical manufacturers; Colm Barnes, partner in a knitwear business, C. & R. Barnes; Dr L. Dillon Digby, director of Pye Ireland Ltd., radio and electronics manufacturers — formed an action group to get something done. Hogan was a prominent industrial entrepreneur involved in a number of ventures. He had the ear of Sean Lemass. He chaired the group which also included a young advertising tyro, Peter Owens of Domas Ltd., advertising agents; Louis O'Brien, general manager of the paint manufacturers, Walter Carson & Son (Dublin) Ltd.; Liam Boyd, sales manager for Ireland of Trans World Airlines; Michael Fitzpatrick of Fitzpatricks Footwear; Dermot O'Flynn, the general manager of J.J. O'Hara & Company Ltd., builders merchants; and T.C. Wade, personnel manager of Esso.

Through his Conference Board and AMA memberships, Dargan provided the committee with information, articles and reports on the state of the art. They would meet in the upstairs offices of Domas at 76 Grafton Street and it was there they decided to form an organisation to promote the cause of better management in Ireland. According to Dargan:

> We thought initially about a study group through which we would develop our own knowledge of management subjects. But we decided to aim higher and form a wider association for people interested in the subject of management, an Irish Management Institute.[2] An inaugural committee was formed under the chairmanship of Hogan and we provided ourselves with rather natty notepaper which bore that title.

What sort of organisation would this Irish Management Institute be? It would, according to Hogan's committee, "promote the science of management in all its aspects; provide guidance and educational facilities for management personnel; collect and disseminate knowledge of management problems among its members with a view to improving management practice". It would seek to create "a collegiate framework for managers to

---

[2] Dargan suggested the name.

meet and exchange experience" through conferences, lectures and study groups. It intended to facilitate contact with senior civil servants, rare in industry at the time, and it would distribute information about management techniques and practices.

On 31 March 1952, Hogan wrote to a number of prominent businessmen looking for their support:

> This letter is addressed to you in the belief that there is an outstanding need in Ireland for an organisation to promote the science of industrial management. It is felt that, whereas other aspects of our industrial revival have been catered for by existing organisations, no attempt has yet been made to stimulate interest in the very important subject of management methods. It is further felt that an increase in our industrial productivity can be achieved by application of up-to-date management methods in our industries.

There was a good reaction and arrangements were made for a meeting of interested people in the Shelbourne Hotel on 1 May.

Coincidentally, Sean Lemass and his Civil Service advisers in Industry and Commerce had also been concerned at how far Ireland was lagging in relation to this new discipline of management. The department had done some research of its own, spurred by a circular from the Organisation for European Economic Co-operation (OEEC), touting a European Institute of Management. Lemass asked Leydon to bring in the heads of the commercial state bodies, some leading private sector business people and academic economists to meet him. The meeting took place in the department's Kildare Street offices on 23 April 1952. Lemass was recovering from an operation, so it was his cabinet colleague, Frank Aiken, Minister for External Affairs, who received the visitors and introduced the officials — John Leydon, secretary of Industry and Commerce, his assistant secretary, J.A. Cassidy, and J.J. McElligott, secretary of the Department of Finance. J. Dolan, an assistant principal, took the minutes.

All the leading semi-state bosses were there: Dr J.P. Beddy, chairman of both the Industrial Development Authority and the Industrial Credit Company; C.S. (Todd) Andrews, managing director of Bord na Móna; R.F. Browne, chairman of the ESB; T.C. Courtney,

chairman of CIE; and the general manager of Aer Lingus, Jeremiah
F. Dempsey. The private sector was represented by Sir Charles
Harvey, assistant managing director of Guinness; and a director of
the National Bank, Sir Cornelius Gregg. James J. Davy, partner of
J. & E. Davy, spanned both sectors — leading stockbroker, chairman of the Gresham Hotel, vice-chairman of Merchants Warehous-
ing, director of Hammond Lane Foundry and acting chairman of
the Irish Sugar Company. Academia was represented by the re-
nowned George O'Brien, Professor of Political Economy and the
National Economics of Ireland (to give him his full title). Given the
topic, Sir Charles Harvey had asked permission to invite from
London Sir Hugh Beaver, the head of the Guinness company, who
happened also to be chairman of the five-year-old British Institute
of Management (BIM).

Aiken spoke of the Government's concern to see "the greatest
possible increase in industrial production". The constraint was not
a shortage of capital and labour but weaknesses in "the technique
of business management". He offered the Government's blessing
on the work and handed the meeting to Leydon, who opened with
a formal question to the assembly: "Is there a necessity in this
country for the provision of facilities for education in business
management?"

Having got his formal affirmative, he put it to the group that
there was, indeed, an urgent necessity to strengthen management
across the board, not just in business but also in the utilities, government and local administration. He pointed to the superiority of
the United States in management education and to the strong demand in American industry for the graduates of the 600 colleges
then offering degrees in business management to over a quarter of
a million students. He said that the colleges' aim was to integrate
management theory with practice and to provide the next generation of managers with a basic foundation in the humanities.

Ireland had to catch up. How? Leydon had already pondered
the question. First, he was in no doubt that the Government should
keep out of it. Who, then? Not industry. He was not very flattering
to the visitors — if the initiative were left to business, it would not
happen: Irish business interests had "not yet reached the stage
where they would accord such a development the necessary
measure of support". So, if not government or industry, who?

Leydon's preference was the universities. He accepted that management, as an academic subject, might be outside the scope of university education "as the term is normally used in this country". He was not proposing a purely academic approach — it would have to be practical too; there would need to be close links with business. He offered the model of the Harvard Business School with its courses for practising managers.

Sir Hugh Beaver was cool on the universities. In England, he said, there was, as yet . . .

> . . . no acceptance of the thesis that business management contained a sufficiently high intellectual content to justify an ad hoc faculty at a university or the conferring of a specific degree in the subject.

This, coming from the chairman of the British Institute of Management, showed the gulf separating the British from the US attitude to the new discipline.

Sir Hugh drew a distinction between pre-career learning, leading to a qualification, and study by practising managers of management techniques. In England, the emphasis was on "the acquisition of as much knowledge as possible within the industry", with some attendance at postgraduate university courses, although the latter, in his view, "must be driven by business interests who must press the universities — and not vice versa". Unless this happened, the chance of success was "meagre". Leydon, although impressed by Sir Hugh's conviction, was not yet prepared to surrender his preference for the universities and suggested that a committee of businessmen could advise them. But the die was now cast and the meeting sided with Hugh Beaver.

The sole academic, George O'Brien, cool on the suggestions, confined himself to remarking that his university, "which is in receipt of grants from public money" had "an obligation to co-operate if such is desired". The only reason he was there, he said, was to pick up some pointers for the B.Comm, currently under revision. As recently appointed Dean of the Faculty of Commerce, he wanted to lessen the theoretical bias of the degree in favour of "more practical subjects such as accountancy". He saw an opportunity to garner views from the potential "consumers" of his graduates.

His request drew some trenchant responses. Jim Beddy — an erstwhile part-time lecturer on the course — said that business generally was "apathetic" about recruiting B.Comm graduates. He implied that the curriculum was irrelevant and that the only way to remove the apathy was by a restructuring of the course. James Davy put it more diplomatically, mentioning that "there was a suspicion hitherto that the universities were too academic"; for that reason, more managers were recruited from the ranks of chartered accountants. The commerce curriculum needed to be broadened. Todd Andrews was positive about the output of the universities, particularly engineering graduates, many of whom joined Bord na Móna as managers. He was clearly happy with the product and suggested that the commerce degree could do with input from the engineering faculty. O'Brien's fishing expedition was rewarded and he agreed to circulate for comment his draft syllabus with copies of comparable curricula from other universities.

As the meeting reverted to the main theme, a clear divergence of view emerged between the two most powerful civil servants of the period, Leydon and McElligott.

J.J. McElligott, secretary of the Department for Finance, saving his powder until last, said that "any instruction in business management should be intensely practical and not imposed by government or the universities, but should spring from industry". Not only that, business should also pay! He bluntly told the visitors that industry was already well cosseted with protective tariffs and quotas. Indeed, he blamed this for apathy in relation to the standard of management, comparing Irish firms unfavourably with industry in the US and Britain, where real competition demanded efficiency. Nearer home, "the state and semi-state bodies have come to be by far the biggest units", implying that they were more alert to the benefits of good management than the private sector. He revealed that experts in O&M[3] had been appointed to the principal departments of the Civil Service, and "resort has also been had to the services of a British firm of business consultants".

---

[3] Organisation and method: later, work study and, later still, industrial engineering.

The Kildare Street meeting formally concluded that facilities for the education of managers were badly needed in Ireland and they were unlikely to be provided without co-operation between business and the universities. It was left to a sub-committee of Harvey, Beddy and Andrews to define the nature of those facilities. George O'Brien volunteered the services of someone from his department. He also promised to recruit a representative of Trinity College. Leydon proposed that the Department bow out of the process to avoid giving an impression of state manipulation. This was not well received. After protestations that it could be disastrous to the project, Leydon succumbed and promised continuing departmental co-operation.

The department was aware, probably through Lemass, that T.P. Hogan's group was promoting an "Irish Management Institute". R.F. Browne, chairman of the ESB, was asked to make contact with Hogan to let him know what had gone on in Kildare Street. This was the first step towards the fusion of the two groups.

A week later, around the corner in the Shelbourne, the meeting arranged by Hogan's group presented their proposal for an Irish Management Institute. The cross-section of business leaders who attended agreed that the project should proceed at once. Soon afterwards, Hogan was invited to St. James's Gate to meet the "business management committee" of Sir Charles Harvey's group to explore how they might work together.

CHAPTER THREE

TOSÚ MAITH

The meeting in St James's Gate took place on 19 May, Sir Charles Harvey in the chair. He had the stamp of his station — major general, retired, distinguished service as brigade commander in the Indian army during the war; later, military adviser-in-chief to the Indian State Forces. Senior officers were in demand by industry for man management after the war. Lord Iveagh, chairman of Guinness, invited Harvey to be a director of the company. He was posted to Dublin as assistant managing director in charge of personnel, then numbering several thousand. He was Guinness's last director-in-residence in 98 James's Street, the company's elegant Georgian house, across from the brewery. A tall, rangy figure, with a clipped, patrician manner, he was never less than courtly in pinstripes or tweeds. He had a habit of referring to everyone by surname only. Authoritative, confident, he could charm when necessary — valuable qualities when it came to merging the energies of two disparate groups seeking the same end, not an easy mission in Ireland.

T.P. Hogan was more reserved, respected for his acumen and achievement. An engineer turned entrepreneur, he enjoyed the adventure of originating and leading a variety of industries. He was appointed to a number of state boards, including, in time, the chairmanship of CIE. Professor Michael MacCormac — a co-founder of the Institute — finds it difficult to assess Hogan's contribution to the IMI project:

He was less effective than Harvey in groups and in chairing committees. But he was there when he was wanted and he was close to Lemass.

Harvey was flanked by J.P. Beddy, Todd Andrews and Professor George O'Brien. O'Brien brought with him Paddy Lynch, a former senior civil servant, who lectured in economics at UCD. George A. Duncan, professor of political economy, TCD, had been invited but sent his apologies. Hogan was accompanied by members of his group — Dargan, Barnes and Digby. Denis Greene, a solicitor and director of Dollard Printing House, was also there.

The meeting was brisk. After a few introductory remarks from Sir Charles, T.P. Hogan said his committee considered that they had, in fact, already established "a very modest Irish Management Institute" without having "worked out any definite scheme in detail". He offered the view that it would be "advantageous if the ideas of both bodies could be co-ordinated". This brought the meeting to the heart of the matter. All agreed that the committees should merge. And that was it: there was no need to refer the decision, as both sides came to the meeting with full powers. Instead, those present formed themselves into a "merger committee" to carry the project forward. They adopted the Hogan group's name, Irish Management Institute. A sub-committee was nominated to define the aims and objectives of the institute and report back quickly so that a formal proposal could be put, first, to the Minister for Industry and Commerce and, later, to a public meeting.

George O'Brien, smarting, perhaps, from the vigour of the B.Comm criticism at the April meeting — although he was one of its greatest critics within the university — proposed that the universities drop out at this point. The businessmen assured him that, on the contrary, their involvement was important. Relenting, he offered to make available someone from his department. Paddy Lynch, his first choice, declined on the basis of commitments. He then nominated Michael MacCormac, a lecturer in his department. MacCormac, an alumnus of the commerce course, was, as it transpired, an excellent choice: he was the only member of the faculty with a serious interest in business studies, a regard fuelled by a postgraduate course at the London School of Economics.

The sub-committee was asked to:

- Define the objects of a management body, having regard to the existing proposals for a management institute, and the relationship of such a body with the universities and other educational bodies;

- Outline the most effective form that the organisation might take in order to achieve these objects: the scope and conditions of membership; structure; methods of providing facilities offered (e.g. lectures, discussions, conferences and information); and finance;

- Report on the most appropriate means of securing the support and assistance of trade and industry, together with professional bodies and organisations in related fields;

- Act as an advisory body on business education until such time as the institute was established.

The sub-group, expanded by some co-options in the interim, met for the first time at the Industrial Credit Company's offices on St Stephen's Green, on Monday morning, 26 May 1952. They were all there: Sir Charles Harvey, chairman, and T.P. Hogan, vice-chairman, with Beddy, Greene, MacCormac, and John J. Walsh — a full-time executive in the Industrial Development Authority who joined at the suggestion of his chairman, Beddy, the latter taking a back seat at that stage. Also there was Denis Hegarty, general manager, Dublin Port and Docks Board, invited because of a keen interest in the subject. Michael Dargan[1] was in his familiar role as secretary.

Sir Charles's command style comes through in the minutes: he "expressed his confidence that the committee would, by addressing itself to the terms of reference, be able to report back without delay". It was in the committee's hands "to ensure, by energetic action, that the institute would be successfully founded".

---

[1] Michael Dargan was responsible for carrying out decisions of the committee, attending to administrative detail including, subsequently, preparations for the inaugural meeting of the Institute in December 1952. Because of this workload, Aer Lingus provided him with an additional part-time secretary, Ms C. Whyte, who dealt exclusively with IMI affairs. After Ms Whyte left, the files were mislaid, a loss greatly lessened by a set maintained — and subsequently presented to the IMI — by Michael MacCormac.

To start them off, the committee was able to review work already done: the scope of the proposed institute as defined by Hogan's committee; draft terms of reference prepared for Harvey's group by Beddy; and a set of objectives for the institute, drafted by his colleague, Walsh. There was also Hogan's letter to business leaders some time previously telling them about the project.

The committee had no particular model in mind for the proposed institute. There was a ready connection to the British Institute of Management through the strong presence of British companies and managers in Irish manufacturing and through the presence of the chairman of the BIM at the meeting in Leydon's office. Later, a BIM council member, F.C. Hooper, would be invited to address the IMI's inaugural meeting. So, as their discussions developed, the working committee probably had sight of the memorandum, articles of association and organisational structure of the neighbouring institute.[2] Sir Charles Harvey later told the inaugural meeting that the committee had looked particularly at countries close to Ireland's state of development, such as Norway, South Africa and Australia. Certainly, material from the Australian Institute of Management had an influence on the early shape and activities of the IMI. But the structure that emerged was mainly the result of a review of Ireland's needs, rather than a model transplanted from elsewhere.

The first meeting agreed the aims of the Institute. Its objective would be clear, unambiguous and singular: to raise the standard of management in Ireland. It would:

- Stimulate interest in management problems and techniques;

- Act as a medium for the exchange of information on management, and provide a reference library;

- Examine problems of management, particularly in relation to Irish conditions;

- Organise educational media such as lectures, conferences and discussions;

---

[2] During the first decade of the Institute's life, the link with the BIM was strong; its director-general, John Marsh, was a frequent visitor to Dublin and a speaker at many IMI functions.

- Encourage the provision of facilities within industry for training in management;

- Co-operate with the universities, technical schools and other educational bodies in the development of business courses for students at all levels and encourage business concerns to give members of their staffs the opportunity to attend such courses;

- Provide a common meeting ground for persons exercising managerial responsibilities;

- Establish liaison with professional and specialist bodies, both in Ireland and with management bodies abroad;

- Invite and encourage the interest and co-operation of organisations in related fields.

The objective and, indeed, the methodology have stood the test of time and are testament to the intellectual focus the founders brought to their task in discouraging times. There would be two main categories of membership — corporate and individual. The Institute would also offer associate membership to interested non-managers and affiliate membership to "specialist organisations and other bodies or persons concerned with management".

The solicitor, Denis Greene, was the expert on organisation. He proposed a three-tier committee structure headed by a council of 24 elected members. An executive committee of between six and nine, elected by members but reporting to council, would be responsible for financial administration and employing staff. The third tier would consist of "advisory panels for various purposes as required". Greene's model was adopted. His advice was that the inaugural general meeting should be asked to approve a simple constitution for the first year, the option of forming a limited liability company to be left for a later stage.

Having disposed of the institute's objective, outline structure and legal status, the committee concentrated on outputs. These would happen gradually — a library and information service, for instance, could develop only after recruitment of staff; but short courses and conferences could be organised by a sub-committee reasonably quickly and run in association with specialist organisations. Popular subjects of the period were time-and-motion study, market research, and budgetary control. Longer educational courses could follow with the co-operation of educational institutions. Publication of proceedings at meetings, reports of study groups, information bulletins and even a journal could follow in due course.

First, however, there was the recruitment issue: staff would need money — £1,000 a year for the senior appointment and £300 for a typist. Other costs brought the budget for year one to £3,000, to be funded by membership dues. A schedule of subscriptions was agreed, based on size of company: 25 guineas for companies with over 2,000 employees, reducing to three guineas for firms with fewer than 50 people and two for individuals. Founding committee members were asked to look for commitments from their own companies and from any contacts in big businesses such as banks and insurance companies, so that the inaugural meeting could be told that a lot of the funding was already in place.

The working committee responded well to Sir Charles Harvey's call for speed. They completed their business in three meetings, presenting a six-page report to the merger committee before the end of June. It was well received. George O'Brien suggested that it be forwarded to John Leydon without delay. Before doing so, however, Todd Andrews — who as head of CIE was later to replace "Nelson's Pillar" on the destination signs of Dublin buses with "An Lár" — proposed that the title Irish Management Institute be given also in the Irish version. He offered the formula Foras Bainistíochta na hÉireann, which was adopted and is still in use.

The agreed report went to John Leydon to be put to a full meeting of the two initiating groups. Confident of a positive outcome, the committee asked Michael Dargan to prepare promotional material and, with J.J. Walsh's help, to make arrangements for an inaugural meeting.

There were still many who considered the proposed institute of doubtful practicality. This was apparently true even in the heart of the business establishment. Harvey asked Sean Lemass if he would talk to the leading business organisations — the Federation of Irish Manufacturers (FIM), the National Agricultural and Industrial Development Association (NAIDA) and the main chambers of commerce — in advance of the inaugural meeting, to secure their goodwill.

Leydon invited members of both the original groups to Kildare Street on 30 July. They included Harvey, Hogan, Dargan, Beddy, Greene, Hegarty, Walsh, Owens, Barnes, Boyd, Courtney, Dempsey, Fitzpatrick, Lynch, O'Brien, O'Flynn, and Wade. Frank Lemass, general manager of CIE, was also included. Leydon was there, as was C.M. Fitzgerald, assistant secretary of the Department of Finance, representing McElligott. The Tánaiste, Sean Lemass, entered. He told them that he and the Government were delighted at the progress and complimented them on pooling their resources. The fact that the initiative had come from business showed its growing awareness of the need for better management. "The chances of prospering are advanced on this account", he said, adding that this "good start" needed to be followed by a continued and sustained effort. He referred to the way the merger committee had helped the UCD economics faculty revise the commerce degree[3] and urged the universities to keep in touch with business and with the Institute — they had a function of leadership as well as one of instruction, he said. Before leaving, he assured the group that he would happily talk to the business organisations as requested and looked forward to presiding at the inaugural meeting.

When he had gone, the meeting approved the report after a paragraph-by-paragraph scrutiny. Now that the merger was complete, the main committee was re-titled the "provisional committee". It was given power to co-opt and would guide the process until the Institute came into being and elected a council. Another group would produce a promotional pamphlet on the institute. It would also prepare a list of invitations to the inaugural meeting, arrange speakers and venue. Tommy Hogan would chair that committee. The duo in charge of the logistics of the inauguration, Michael Dargan and J.J. Walsh, were joined by Michael Mac-Cormac and Louis O'Brien. The advertising expert, Peter Owens, was in charge of press and publicity.

The *tosú maith* (good start) referred to by Lemass was complete.

---

[3] Changes were, as a result, introduced in the degree; economics was included and less relevant subjects dispensed with.

CHAPTER FOUR

ARMED AT ALL POINTS AND READY FOR ACTION

What impresses most about the events leading to the inauguration is the sustained energy of the project. Meetings were frequent, the work onerous and the attendance record impressive. The
members of the newly styled provisional committee were, of course,
well known to one another; it was the same as the merger committee,
with a few omissions: Todd Andrews, Colm Barnes, George O'Brien,
Dillon Digby and George Duncan had withdrawn.

In August, the group approved a brochure to promote awareness of the institute and help raise money to cover the inaugural
expenses. It was a simple eight-page booklet titled:

INFORMATION FOR MANAGEMENT
by Businessmen

Widely distributed, it recounted the genesis of the institute — the
coincidental emergence of two groups with similar aims, the
merger, the Government's blessing. It described the institute's objective and listed the organisations with which the founders were
associated. The benefits of membership were outlined, including
special courses promised by the universities. It assured readers
that, even if the organisations listed were all Dublin-based, the institute would cater for the whole country. And, then, an exhortation:

> Management institutes have been set up in other progres-
> sive countries and the benefits they confer on individual

businesses and the nation are accepted. We feel sure that
you will agree that business in this country should be
equally well served and that an Irish Management Institute will fulfil a widely felt need. Your interest and help are
confidently requested.

The brochure appealed to companies to send donations to Sir
Charles Harvey at St James's Gate to defray the exceptional expenditure of the first year. The top corporate membership rate had
been increased from 25 to 30 guineas, an indication of the growing
confidence of the promoters.

The committee then turned its attention to arrangements for the
inauguration. Everything was planned with care: the staging of the
meeting — who would be on the platform, who would speak and
for how long. Not surprisingly, given his prominent role to date,
Sir Charles Harvey was the unanimous choice to chair the event.
Lemass would launch the Institute. A prominent English businessman would describe how the British Institute of Management
had benefited British industry. The president of the Associated
Chambers of Commerce would be invited to speak — briefly. An
invitation to the president of the principal industry organisation,
the Federation of Irish Manufacturers, was deferred until Lemass
reported on his promised meeting with the federation.

The inauguration was confirmed for Tuesday 9 December 1952
at 3.00 p.m. The Aberdeen Room of the Gresham Hotel was
booked. It was "noted with pleasure" that it would be free of
charge. The formal resolutions were drafted by Denis Greene,
who is remembered by Michael MacCormac as a key member of
the founding group and not just for his legal acumen:

> He did a lot behind the scenes and was among the princi-
> pal people driving the project at the time. He did all the
> legal work. But he was more than just the lawyer; as a di-
> rector of Dollards, the printers, he had plenty of practical
> business experience. He did a lot of thinking about the
> way in which we should go forward.

Sir Charles duly got word from John Leydon that Lemass had seen
the three business bodies. The news was good. The Tánaiste had
urged support for the Institute and all three, according to Leydon,

"seemed to be quite enthusiastic about the proposal". The way was now clear to invite D.D. Frame, president of the FIM, to speak. Davy Frame was a man of considerable influence in industry affairs. His company, Hammond Lane Foundries Ltd., was a landmark industry in Dublin, dominating the Irish structural and fabricated steel sector. His association with the new project was important.

Despite its excellent work, the sub-committee planning the details of the event had its wings clipped over a news item in the papers on Saturday, 18 October. *The Irish Times* headed the item:

"SUPPORT FOR MANAGEMENT INSTITUTE"

The report was positive: plans for the inauguration were well advanced; promises of support had been received from "business firms in all parts of the country"; the universities were co-operating; and the project enjoyed "the encouragement of the Minister for Industry and Commerce who would preside at the inaugural meeting". The Institute, it was pointed out, would be "completely Irish" but would exchange information and ideas with similar organisations elsewhere.

The sub-committee was probably quite pleased at the coverage, assuming that, having been given the press relations role, they were within their brief in getting on with it. Not so. Members of the senior committee were not pleased. At a meeting two days after publication, Jim Beddy ominously asked for clarification of the sub-committee's terms of reference.

The contentious item was probably the final paragraph of the report:

> In view of the general aims of the Institute, it is possible
> that the industrial trade unions will be asked to become
> affiliated members.

Hogan defended his sub-committee's initiative. Nevertheless, it was decided that, in future, the minutes of his committee would be circulated so that views could be expressed "on the intentions of the sub-committee in matters of importance". Approval could be assumed only in the absence of any comment after two days.

Nominations to the council and executive committee were given a lot of thought to ensure sectoral and geographic representation. A prepared panel of names would be put to the attendance with the suggestion that the panel be elected *en bloc* as a council to act for an initial period of one year. This would give the provisional committee some control in seeing to it that the new council included significant non-Dublin industries like Arklow Pottery, Waterford Iron Founders, Waterford Glass, General Textiles (Athlone), Irish Ropes (Newbridge), Hygeia (Galway), Irish Tanners (Portlaw), J. & L.F. Goodbody (jute manufacturers, Offaly and Waterford) and the prominent Cork companies Seafield Fabrics and Dowdall O'Mahony. The prominent non-Dublin-based academics, Professors John Busteed, UCC, and Liam O Buachalla, UCG, would be asked to allow their names to be included. The Federation of Irish Manufacturers, the National Agricultural and Industrial Development Association, and the Association of Chambers of Commerce would be invited to nominate representatives.

The first council was now taking shape. It included the provisional committee, other members of the original merger committee, and nominees of the companies, associations and universities listed above. During November, Sir Charles and his secretary, Miss E.G. Boyd, were busy writing to the agreed panel inviting their participation in the council:

> It is intended that the Council will be a governing body and will rely on the Executive Committee for the general administration of the Institute. As far as I can foresee, therefore, the demands on the time of its members will not be heavy.

The provisional committee addressed the delicate territorial question: all-Ireland or just the south? The BIM was asked if there was any sensitivity about the IMI promoting itself across the Border. It immediately gave the Irish institute *carte blanche* to the North, saying that it saw no prospect of being able to deal with the needs of Northern Ireland in the foreseeable future.

Meetings were now weekly, with the sub-committee working day-to-day on the minutiae of the inauguration. On 24 November, the order of business was agreed for the December inauguration.

The platform party comprised the Tánaiste, Sean Lemass, Sir Charles Harvey, John Leydon, T.P. Hogan, Michael Dargan, Professors George O'Brien, George Duncan, John Busteed and Liam O Buachalla, and the presidents of FIM, NAIDA and the Association of Chambers of Commerce. F.C. Hooper, managing director of Schweppes Ltd., would represent the British Institute of Management.[1]

The Lord Mayor of Dublin would also be on the platform. The first citizen, Alderman Andrew Clarkin, was also a businessman. In fact, during his mayoral term, he was the butt of Myles na Gopaleen's column in *The Irish Times* over the prominent, but permanently stopped, clock on his Pearse Street coal distribution premises.

Stewarding duties were allocated among members of the committee. Michael MacCormac and J.J. Walsh would direct council members to the first two rows of seats. To ensure that the proceedings could be heard, Louis O'Brien had charge of the public address and Denis Greene was nominated to "duties at the end of the hall, including a signal to speakers on voice reception". Sir Charles would greet the Tánaiste, the Lord Mayor, John Leydon and F.C. Hooper. Tommy Hogan would look after the other guests. Denis Hegarty would escort the Tánaiste from the meeting.

Space was booked in the four dailies on Friday, 5 December, for the notice of meeting:

Irish Management Institute

A public meeting will be held at the Gresham Hotel on Tuesday, 9 December 1952, at 3.00pm to establish an Irish Management Institute. The object of the Institute will be to further the science and practice of business management.

The meeting will consider proposals based on a report prepared by a Committee which was appointed by a representative group of business undertakings.

An Tánaiste, Mr Sean Lemass, has kindly consented to preside.

All persons interested in the subject are invited to attend.

---

[1] Leydon, Busteed and O Buachalla were unable to attend.

The provisional committee could now, for the first time, lift its horizons beyond the inaugural meeting. The new executive committee would meet on 15 December 1952 at 14 St Stephen's Green to agree an advertisement for an "organising official" and consider a programme of events. The council would not meet until early February. Regarding the "organising official", there was a suggestion that, to get things going, the executive consider secondment of a civil servant. Given the pledges of support from Lemass and Leydon, this would have been easy to achieve. But the provisional committee ruled it out. If advertising did not produce a suitable candidate, a secondment would then be considered — but from business. Meanwhile, the management of finance needed to be put in professional hands. Michael MacCormac, an accountant, was prepared to take it on, despite the workload he already carried on the sub-committee.

The day before the inauguration, the provisional committee met for a final review. Michael Dargan handed out his list of executive committee nominees — the provisional committee plus five prominent businessmen: D.D. Coyle of Hygeia, Galway; James Davy, J. & E. Davy, stockbrokers; Jack Eason of Easons, newsagents and book suppliers; Sir Cornelius Gregg, a director of the National Bank; and R.D. Lord, Seafield Fabrics. The list would be proposed from the floor by R.F. Browne of the ESB, seconded by P. Lenihan, managing director of General Textiles.

The inaugural meeting was an outstanding success. At three o'clock on Tuesday 9 December 1952, over 600 businessmen, eager to see this new management organisation launched, crowded the Gresham's mirrored, elegant Aberdeen Room, a popular venue for dinners and society balls. For the inaugural meeting, the piano and music stands of the Neil Kearns Gresham Orchestra were pushed backstage and replaced by a long, green baize-covered table. Chairs, three microphones, and water jugs completed the set-up. The rather compact stage left little elbowroom for the 11 dignitaries.[2] Michael Dargan, honorary secretary, and George O'Brien sat at either end of the table. Facing the audience were Professor Duncan, J. O'Keeffe (the Association of

---

[2] See the photograph section.

Chambers of Commerce), P. Moylett (NAIDA), T.P. Hogan, vice-chairman, the Lord Mayor, Alderman Clarkin, the Tánaiste, Sean Lemass, Sir Charles Harvey (chairman), F.C. Hooper, representing the BIM, and Davy Frame.

Sir Charles welcomed the packed house and introduced the platform party. Lemass rose and in his gruff style told the entirely male audience that Irish industrial development was entering a critical phase. Hitherto, the limited objective was to meet home demand for consumer goods, previously imported. This had been achieved by eliminating or severely restricting foreign competi-tion. The free market's "price test of competitive efficiency" did not apply. In a few sentences, he sketched the background to protection and listed its practical effects. Early progress was easy and rapid because the industrial base had been so low. The public had turned a blind eye to some inefficiency and accepted higher prices for home-produced goods so as to secure greater and more diversified employment.

> Almost everybody was willing to give the new Irish indus-trial projects a fair chance to get started; to give their managements time to get organised; to acquire experi-ence in production methods suitable to our circumstances and to train personnel in technical processes, in the con-fident expectation that, when all the disadvantages arising from lack of previous experience have been overcome, Irish industry will prove itself capable of achieving as high a level of efficiency as industry anywhere else.

That phase had ended, he said. In many industries, the limits of expansion within the home market had already been reached and plans were in train to bring the remaining industries to those limits in the early future. The Irish public was no longer tolerant of inefficiency, no longer willing to allow protective measures to be used to cloak defective organisation, obsolete equipment and techniques, or a level of costs which was "unnecessarily and avoidably high". Signalling a future of free trade and sterner com-petition, the Tánaiste painted a challenging scenario. He warned non-exporting industries that they, too, would have to reach the highest standards of efficiency if they wanted to hold onto their home markets.

Those responsible for the direction of our industries will
have to face up to a new situation in which security in the
home market is no longer to be regarded as their right,
but as a privilege for which they must continuously qualify
by the high character of their leadership.

He described the movement to create an Irish Management Institute as an acceptance that the quality of management in Ireland
was capable of substantial improvement — indeed, that further
progress in industry could not happen without it. This, he said,
called for an organised effort, beyond the capacity of individual
firms. He criticised Irish industry for having taken so long to demand adequate management education and training facilities:

Perhaps an undue reliance on the assumed permanence
of protective measures might have blunted the keenness
of managers and relaxed their effort to acquire efficiency.

He stressed the urgency of filling the knowledge gap and also
cautioned against direct importation of management education
models from other countries, pointing out that "our national circumstances have had no exact parallel elsewhere". Irish solutions
for Irish problems! His speech signalled, unambiguously, a sharp
change in the government's policy on industrial development:
protection was out; free trade was the way of the future:

The aim of efficient business management everywhere is
to secure maximum production at the lowest cost per unit,
to develop markets for the whole potential output and to
manage labour relations so as to eliminate causes of unnecessary friction and to maintain a happy atmosphere in
all parts of the organisation. In this country, national needs
require us to stress also the further aim of developing export trade, to break out of the protective shell of the home
market and win new markets abroad, which will permit
industrial expansion to proceed and the national economy to acquire greater strength.

We are forced to depend, to a greater extent than most
other countries, on achieving a higher degree of efficiency at all levels of factory organisation, but very particularly at the top. Problems created by the smallness of

our population and the necessarily limited size of our industrial units, make it clear that some hard thinking will
have to be done if we are to find remedies suitable to our
circumstances.

What might the new institute offer? First, recognition of the fact that
the most effective, practical training in management could be provided only within industry. This could be complemented by educational and academic courses at undergraduate or postgraduate
level in the universities. Envisaging future MBA courses, Lemass
proposed "special courses for men who had already had some
practical experience in business affairs". He went on:

> But while the importance of using university graduates in
> business management can, is and should be stressed, it is
> equally important that young men entering business
> without the advantage of university training should also
> have the opportunity of qualifying for higher responsibili-
> ties. It is these opportunities which the proposed man-
> agement institute will provide.

The universities were not spared:

> If our business leaders are open to criticism . . . it should also
> be said that, heretofore, our universities appear to have
> adopted a passive attitude, not apparently regarding them-
> selves as having any function of leadership in this field.

On the other hand, he singled out for praise the evening classes on
business studies at UCD and "the very well conceived courses in
business techniques that are being provided by the Dublin Vocational Educational authorities".

Pointing out that raising the standards of management needed a
united effort, Lemass urged all businesses to co-operate by sending

> their executive personnel, and young men who are poten-
> tial executives, to the courses and discussions which the
> Institute might organise. It will pay worthwhile dividends
> even from a commercial viewpoint. It cannot fail to benefit
> the nation in all its activities.

Lemass's reputation as a tough-minded, practical politician was high among business people, regardless of their politics. His support for the management institute was, therefore, invaluable to the promoters and was certainly a major factor in motivating them to progress the project as speedily as they did. On inauguration day, the Irish Management Institute could not have wished for a better or more eloquent initiation.

Sir Charles Harvey thanked the Tánaiste and began his address with a (not exactly stylish) definition of management:

> The art, science or practice of utilising personnel or materials to the best advantage in the production of goods or the provision of services of adequate quality with the maximum economy of materials, labour, time, money and fuss.

He took his audience on a tour of developments in management training, beginning with the paradigm of management organisations, the American Management Association, established in 1923. Nearer home, and much more recently, he instanced the British Institute of Management which had been established on the recommendation of committees appointed by the Board of Trade. The founders of the IMI had looked closely at countries closer to Ireland's population size and state of development — Norway, South Africa and Australia. They had been impressed by the Australian Institute of Management, which may have provided the nearest prototype for the early IMI.

Sir Charles described the sort of institute his fellow managers could look forward to. There would be study groups, meetings with internationally famous experts. There would be an annual management conference, lasting a few days, with "intensive discussion and lectures", providing the ideas and stimulus for the work of the Institute throughout the ensuing year. Some events would focus on specialist aspects of management, like marketing and personnel. Study groups would examine problems specific to the Irish context. Eventually, there would be a library/information service and, if finances permitted, a journal. He told them that the new institute hoped to sponsor business-related courses in the universities and the vocational schools. UCD had already revised its commerce course for undergraduates to include input by industrialists. These lectures would be open to members of the IMI. UCC was in contact with the Cork Chamber of Commerce and the Cork branch of the Federation of Irish Manufacturers for the same purpose.

He described the proposed committee structure of the institute and the plan to appoint a full-time "organising secretary". The major-general behind the business suit stirred as he told "the troops" that the meeting would be required not only to approve the formation of the Institute but "to issue it, as it were, armed at all points and ready for action". A resolution would be put to the meeting to appoint a caretaker council and executive committee. The latter, he said, would comprise the existing provisional committee, reinforced by "certain well-known men of affairs". Both committees would retire at the end of 1953 and a draft constitution would be submitted for the approval of members. On the subject of finance, he reported that £1,850 had been contributed towards the expenses of the first year and appealed for sufficient members to ensure an adequate annual income. The Institute had the special needs of smaller businesses very much in mind, so he urged them also to join.

F.C. Hooper, who was also a writer and broadcaster of repute on management topics, brought fraternal greetings from the BIM. He spoke about the role of the manager and the constituent functions of management. Today, he said, they were embarking on a long-term project. Expectations of a quick and measurable payback on subscriptions would represent "an improper view about an institute of management". He cautioned that the Institute should not trespass on fields already catered for by the professional associations. He concluded with the observation that the new institute would help gain an appreciation of the manager's wider role in society.

Sir Charles Harvey paid tribute to T.P. Hogan and his leadership of the group that initiated the notion of an Irish Management Institute. Hogan described the categories of membership and joined in the appeal for members, again exhorting small firms everywhere in Ireland to see the Institute as a centre for advice and help. He hoped that "provincial members will be able to spare the time to take an active part in the affairs of the Institute and lend it a national atmosphere in the widest sense". The venture was wished Godspeed by the spokesmen for the business establishment,

Frame, Moylett and O'Keeffe, all pledging the support of the significant bodies they represented.

The speeches had lasted an hour. Sean Lemass invited the meeting to proceed to inaugurate the Institute by formally assenting to the following resolution:

> RESOLVED that this meeting, representative of organisations, firms and individuals in Ireland whose activities cover a wide field and who are interested in raising the efficiency of management, recognising the necessity for an Irish institute of management hereby constitute themselves as Foras Bainistíochta na hÉireann — the Irish Management Institute — and that it is further resolved that:
>
> a) until the 31 December 1953 the institute shall initially function on the basis of the report of the working committee dated 2 July 1952;
>
> b) the council shall submit to a general meeting of the institute to be held not later than 31 December 1953, a draft permanent constitution for the institute;
>
> c) the first council shall be empowered to appoint auditors who shall hold office for the same period as the council.

The resolution was passed by acclamation and the IMI came into being.

His work done, Lemass gave way to Sir Charles, who explained the procedure for electing the council and executive committee. He asked permission to propose the election of a council consisting of a prepared, representative list of business people and nominees of the educational bodies. He called on the chairman of the ESB, R.F. Browne, who was sitting at the front of the hall, to propose, first, the election of the executive committee who would, *ex officio*, be members of the council. Browne, consulting his list, stood and proposed as arranged the election of the members of the provisional committee *en bloc*:

> Sir Charles O. Harvey, assistant managing director, A. Guinness Son & Co. (Dublin) Ltd. (chairman); T.P. Hogan, managing director, Plessey Ireland Ltd. (vice-chairman); Michael J. Dargan, staff and services manager, Aer Lingus

Teoranta (hon. secretary); Dr J.P. Beddy, chairman and managing director, Industrial Credit Co. Ltd., chairman, Industrial Development Authority; Denis Greene, Roger Greene & Sons, solicitors, and director, Dollard Printing House Dublin Ltd.; Denis A. Hegarty, general manager, Dublin Port & Docks Board; Michael J. MacCormac, lecturer, Department of Commerce, University College Dublin; Louis O'Brien, Walter Carson & Sons (Dublin) Ltd.; J.J. Walsh, member, Industrial Development Authority . . .

Four "prominent industrialists", were added who, said Browne, were representative of industry and commerce nationally:

. . . D.D. Coyle, manufacturer, Galway; James Davy, Stockbroker, Dublin; J.C.M. Eason, chairman, Eason & Son Ltd. and Sir Cornelius Gregg, director, National Bank Ltd.

He confirmed that, if elected, all were willing to serve. P. Lenihan of General Textiles seconded Browne's proposal, which was carried unanimously. The next business was the election of a council. This time, Sir Charles proposed the list — an impressive panel of people prominent in manufacturing, commerce, industrial development, financial services, transport and academia:

C.S. Andrews, managing director, Bord na Móna; Colm Barnes, joint proprietor, C. & R. Barnes; A.W. Bain, chairman, Irish Life Assurance Co. Ltd.; R.F. Browne, chairman, ESB; Professor John Busteed, University College, Cork; T.C. Courtney, chairman, CIE; Vincent Crowley, partner, Kennedy Crowley & Co; A.C. Crichton, distiller, Bow Street Distillery; J.F. Dempsey, general manager, Aer Lingus Teoranta; Dr Dillon Digby, managing director, Pye (Ireland) Ltd.; George Duncan, professor of political economy, University of Dublin, Trinity College; Martin Gleeson, chief executive officer, City of Dublin Vocational Education Committee; Desmond M. Goodbody, director, J. & L.F. Goodbody Ltd.; Sir Basil Goulding, chairman, Gouldings Fertilizers; Joseph Griffin, managing director, Irish Glass Bottle Co. Ltd.; Percy Higgins, company director; P.J. Kavanagh, managing director, P. Kavanagh and Sons, manufacturers of K. & S. Food Products; P. Lenihan, managing director, General Textiles; A.H. Masser, managing director, Waterford Iron Founders

Ltd.; A.E. McIvor, general manager, John Player and Sons,
branch of the Imperial Tobacco Company Ltd.; George
O'Brien, professor of national economics, University College Dublin; Senator Liam O Buachalla, professor, University College Galway; T. O'Mahony, Dowdall O'Mahony;
Michael Rigby-Jones, managing director, Irish Ropes Ltd.;
Professor T.A. Smiddy, economist and director of Arklow
Pottery Ltd.

The three business organisations represented on the platform —
FIM, NAIDA and the chambers of commerce — would add their
nominees later.[3] The Lord Mayor seconded the proposal, which
was carried with enthusiasm by the 600.

Sir Charles wished members of the new council well, thanked
the Tánaiste and the other guests and congratulated the audience
on turning out in such numbers for what would "prove, in time, to
have been a very auspicious beginning of the new Institute". Later,
he may have allowed himself a moment of satisfying reflection on
the process which had, at last, brought a complex process to fruition. Michael MacCormac believes that, without him, the project
would not have succeeded:

> He had a marvellous style. I learned more about chairmanship from him than from anybody else. During the
> formation period he ran the meetings like the general he
> was. We would meet in Jim Beddy's office in the IDA on
> Mondays at 2.30 *sharp*. Meetings never lasted more than
> an hour. You wouldn't dare not turn up: if he was there, you
> should be there. Otherwise, at the next meeting: "Well
> now, Mr X, you weren't with us last Monday when we were
> dealing with a most important topic . . ."

> If there was a difficult exchange between members of the
> committee, he would let it go on for a few minutes and
> then: "Well now, gentlemen, we'll come back to that next
> week." We all knew the form: during the week the
> antagonists would be asked to lunch at St James's Gate. At
> the next meeting, he would open proceedings with "There

---

[3] These were: D.D. Frame (FIM), P. Moylett (NAIDA), and T.F. Laurie (Chambers of Commerce).

is a point we didn't deal fully with last week; here is the solution . . .".

Another survivor of the founding group, Michael Dargan, who worked closely with him over that period, wrote in *Management* this appreciation of Sir Charles on his death in 1969:

> His personal qualities were uniquely high. So high that they allowed him, an Englishman of short residence in Ireland and with comparatively short business experience following his army career, to make his great contribution in holding together the diverse and sometimes competing elements which fused in the institute. And he went on, as chairman of the young institute, holding these elements in genial but tight clasp until the fusion process was complete.
>
> His stature as a senior director of Guinness and the full support and encouragement of that great firm undoubtedly underpinned his efforts. But the sincerity of character and warmth of feeling towards the dignity of each human being, which illuminated his personality, helped even more. He added to these attributes and to his never failing courtesy and gentleness a firmness and decisiveness. This combination was irresistible at those moments of tedium or division in committee. His "come on now and let's get on with it" always brought ready response. This simple, sincere and able man left his stamp on the institute.

Sir Charles did, indeed, contribute profoundly to shaping an innovative and enduring institution. He is commemorated in the Sir Charles Harvey Awards,[4] conferred annually by the IMI on the leading graduates of MBA programmes in Irish universities.

---

[4] When Sir Charles Harvey retired from Guinness in 1961, the IMI opened a fund to mark his special contribution to the Institute. Sir Charles asked that the money raised from the members be used to further the work of the Institute. An award in his name was established to encourage management education at university level, a particular interest of his. He retired to a royal "grace and favour" residence in Hampton Court and died there in 1969.

CHAPTER FIVE

"TWO ROOMS, CLOSE CARPETED"

News of the birth of the Institute had been carried in the British papers, where it was referred to for the first time as the IMI. This brought a quick response from the Institute of the Motor Industry in London. The president, Stanley Dawes, wrote to Sir Charles, wishing the new organisation well but pointing out that his institute, which had a branch in Ireland, already used the abbreviation "IMI". He suggested that, to avoid confusion, the Irish management body should change its name to the "Irish Institute of Management", a proposition not favourably received by the executive committee. Instead, they asked Dawes for sight of the motoring body's logo so that a similarity in design might be avoided. This provoked a formal protest from Dawes that, in turn, brought a pithy closure from Sir Charles. The executive committee reported the correspondence to the first meeting of the council. Todd Andrews saw an opportunity of promoting his Irish version of the Institute's name — Foras Bainistíochta na hÉireann — to pole position, thus avoiding any possible clash. However, the chairman ruled, carefully, that "the necessity for prominence to the Irish form of the name will continue to receive attention".

The council's first meeting took place in the boardroom of UCD, Earlsfort Terrace, on the afternoon of 16 February 1953. Thirty-three of the 41 members were in attendance. The election of chairman of the council was quickly dealt with. Sir Cornelius Gregg proposed Sir Charles Harvey; R.F. Browne — again the chosen voice from the floor — seconded; the vote was unanimous. So, Sir Charles embarked on a three-year stint as the founding chairman of the IMI. He told the meeting that the executive committee had already begun a search to fill the position of secretary of the Institute.[1] An office secretary, Stephanie Power, had been appointed at an annual salary of £350.

The other urgent issue was membership. To streamline recruitment, T.P. Hogan suggested that the executive committee, which met more frequently than the council, should have authority to approve membership applications. The council agreed, but reserved to itself decisions on rejection. The programme and planning committee got on with a modest schedule of events. The first, a symposium titled *The Role of Management in Industry*, took place on Monday evening, 2 March 1953, in the Rupert Guinness Hall, Watling Street. The main speaker was to have been John Ryan, vice-chairman of the Metal Box Co. Ltd., a council member of the BIM. Local speakers included A.L. Downes of Thompsons of Cork, P. Lenihan, managing director of General Textiles of Athlone, and A.H. Masser, founder of Waterford Iron Founders and A.H. Masser Ltd.

The landmark occasion was, however, robbed of its star: heavy fog in London prevented Ryan's plane from taking off. Technology came to the aid of the organisers: his speech was teleprinted from London, and read to the audience by the honorary secretary, Michael Dargan. The local speakers performed well and a lively discussion left the attendance, pioneer participants at an IMI event, well satisfied.

Professor Busteed of UCC, getting in an early blow on behalf of "country people" said that, while he accepted the necessity for organising meetings in Dublin in the early days, similar functions should be organised in the provinces in due course.

The executive committee, busy with administrative affairs, told council in February that temporary offices had been found at 81 Grafton Street and that 200 applications had been received for the position of secretary of the Institute. Four short-listed applicants were seen by the committee and the job was offered to Paul Quigley, an engineer, at a salary of £1,200 per annum. Quigley, an ex-Army captain, was a senior executive at Irish Ropes, a progressive

---

[1] It was common for the term "secretary" to be applied to the senior salaried position in professional and voluntary organisations, implying more an administrative rather than a proactive, executive role. The title was later changed to "director of organisation and secretary".

firm that pioneered the application of productivity-enhancing systems. Michael Rigby-Jones, son of the company's founder, was an IMI enthusiast. He later became chairman of the Institute but, tragically, died in the Staines air disaster in 1972, in which many Irish business leaders perished.[2] Rigby-Jones agreed to an early release. So, within three months of the inaugural meeting, the Institute was equipped with premises, two full-time staff and an outline programme for some months ahead.

Broader issues of policy now began to engage the executive — how was the Institute to relate to other organisations? The Dublin Trades Union Council had written to the executive committee early in February 1953 conveying its concern at any incursion by the Institute into the industrial relations arena on the side of the employers. The Institute was sensitive to the issues involved: it did not want to be seen as a bosses' organisation, but as a neutral resource considerate also of the workers' point of view. It is understandable that trade unionists — not just DTUC — would have seen it as a somewhat sinister addition to the employers' armoury, introducing management systems detrimental to the interests of workers. The Institute decided to look for meetings with the governing bodies of the movement, then organised in two national congresses — the Congress of Irish Unions (CIU) and the Irish Trade Union Congress (ITUC).[3] The council discussed strategy for the meetings, including offering the unions some form of affiliation, even representation on the council. But it quickly backed off when someone suggested that potential members might be put off by a formal link with the trade unions. If the example of the British Institute of Management was raised — where unions were represented on an advisory panel — the IMI delegation were to point out that this was at the request of the British government which had helped establish and finance the BIM.

In fact, the question of representation did not arise at either meeting. At the ITUC, Jim Larkin, TD, its leading light, and the general secretary, Ruairi Roberts, wanted to know what precise role the

---

[2] See Chapter Sixteen.

[3] Not long afterwards, both congresses began lengthy unification discussions under the chairmanship of Professor John Busteed. These led in 1956 to the setting up of the Provisional United Trade Union Organisation which, in 1959, evolved into the Irish Congress of Trade Unions.

Institute intended to play. Would it behave like management consultants — introducing new procedures without consultation, resulting in uncertainty, stress and even loss of jobs? Sir Charles replied that the Institute would certainly promote efficiency; that was its role. But it was not an employers' organisation; it was independent. It would not allow itself to be used in disputes between individual firms and the unions. He added that there was widespread acceptance of the need for increased efficiency and pointed out that the British and American unions had a positive attitude to productivity.

Larkin said that the unions welcomed any organisation that would reduce "the present level of chaos in industry". But he took issue with the Institute's claim that it was "free and independent", warning that if it took the employers' side only, it would soon be in conflict with the unions. If it provided an independent forum where both sides could be heard, the IMI would be filling "a new and useful function".

At both meetings, Sir Charles asked for the unions' goodwill. Senator W. McMullen, president of the CIU, said there was nothing incompatible in the objectives of the Institute and those of his group of unions: the question of increased production "touched the basic considerations of the economy". According to the secretary, Leo Crawford, the question in the minds of trade unionists was: what would labour's reward be for increased production? He suggested that the danger for the Institute was that it would be confused with the FUE — the employers' industrial relations arm — which, he said, had refused even to meet the CIU to discuss the issue of redundant workers.

Both were positive meetings. McMullen of the CIU and Larkin of the ITUC offered their good wishes, although Larkin was more circumspect. They were, as he put it, shy of committing themselves but the Institute could take it that "the terms are not unfriendly". Four years later, Sir Charles, in an uncharacteristic flight of rhetoric, put the Institute's assurance to the unions on the record as he welcomed their leaders to the launch of the first extended management course:

> It is to be hoped that any suspicion which may have existed
> as to the purpose and motives of the Institute will have
> completely disappeared. I would like again to assure the

trade unions that the Institute is concerned with better management because it is our complete conviction that better management must truly be to the advantage of all members of the community. Better management, however, in its entirety, cannot be achieved by the manager alone . . . [It] can only be achieved in a good industrial climate . . .

It is important in the best national interest that we move together harmoniously and so utilise on the highest plane the country's resources and the skill of our people for the economic good of the nation as a whole.

Reporting back to the council, the Institute's team recommended a follow-up meeting with the FUE to ensure its acceptance of the Institute's neutrality in the often bitter warfare which characterised Irish industrial relations at the time. Harvey, Dargan and Quigley met John O'Brien and a group from the FUE later that summer. They told the FUE of their contacts with the unions and the undertaking given that the IMI would not become involved at the industrial relations coalface. The FUE had no difficulty with that and praised the Institute for what it was doing to raise the standard of management and promote training within industry. O'Brien offered to seek funds from the International Labour Office in Geneva to help the Institute provide special training in industrial relations. It was a cordial meeting. The FUE view was that it was best that it not be formally associated with the IMI; nonetheless the Institute could count on its support.

There were territorial rumblings in other directions. Trinity's Professor Duncan, although a council member of the Institute, was worried about the Institute's intentions in relation to the universities and asked for a meeting. The chairman told him that they had not yet got around to discussing the relationship with the universities but that it was likely that a special sub-committee would be set up to look at the issues.

The Institute's attitude was that it would be sensible to work, where possible, with existing institutions. Nevertheless, some of the professional associations were nervous about the new body. Michael Dargan was asked to prepare a list of relevant organisations and to be "careful in selecting those which would be most useful". Ten were invited to discussions: the four accountancy bodies — the Institute of

Chartered Accountants, the Institute of Cost and Works Accountants, the Society of Incorporated Accountants in Ireland and the Association of Certified and Corporate Accountants; two secretarial organisations — the Chartered Institute of Secretaries and the Irish Institute of Secretaries; as well as the Institute of Personnel Managers, the Incorporated Sales Managers' Association, the Textile Institute and the Institute for Industrial Research and Standards.

The meeting was in the Ballast Office, the elegant headquarters of the Dublin Port and Docks Board in Westmoreland Street, its fine clock marking a place of tryst for generations of Dubliners. Denis Hegarty, general manager of the port board, made the boardroom available for the meeting, which was friendly, all of the associations promising full support to the IMI.

Ruairi Roberts's remark about management consultants at the meeting with ITUC reflected a view, not confined to trade unions, on this new breed of experts. Established international firms operated according to careful ethical guidelines. Others, not so burdened, promised quick fixes and, not infrequently, left behind a trail of disruption and worse. The relatively unsophisticated Irish business community was easy prey to the charlatans of the profession. The council acted in May 1953 to try to protect members from the worst of the predators: the Institute would maintain a list of approved consultants to which companies would be advised to refer before committing themselves. There was a reluctance to set up a formal register with rigorous entry standards because it would have to exclude indigenous consultants, who were unlikely to satisfy the probable criteria. This would effectively result in a register of UK firms only. In the absence of an official register, members were advised to discuss any plans to employ consultants with the Institute in confidence. If they were leaning towards firms with "form", they would be counselled to think again.

For a while, the Institute kept its distance from all consultants. When the P&P (programme and planning) committee reported difficulty in getting speakers for the first IMI conference, Sir Charles ruled that industrial consultants should not be used as speakers "unless it is unavoidable". Gradually the Institute developed a good relationship with "the big four" — Urwick Orr and Partners (UOP), Associated Industrial Consultants (AIC), Personnel Administration (PA) and Industrial Engineering (IE). Their extensive knowledge of management practices was grist to the IMI's more advanced courses. The Institute continued to keep its guard up against those firms that lured clients with promises of unprecedented growth. One notorious American firm, in particular, bled some unfortunate, long-established Irish businesses dry.

The executive committee put the finishing touches to Paul Quigley's letter of appointment in March 1953 and he was in situ before the end of the month. Now that the administrative reins were in sure hands, Michael Dargan, with some relief, resigned the post of honorary secretary. The executive committee and council paid deserved tribute to him "for the tremendous energy and ability he has shown in forwarding the affairs of the Institute".

The Institute took possession of the Grafton Street offices (see sketch on the next page) on 1 April — "two reasonably large rooms, close carpeted with built-in furniture and good toilet accommodation". Described by the executive committee as "a modest letting", it was at the corner of Grafton Street and Johnson Court, up four flights of stairs above Bacon Shops Ltd., one of a chain of five beloved by Dubliners.[4] The rent was £300 per year. The staff was Paul Quigley, secretary, his assistant, Stephanie Power, and a temporary shorthand typist. Business hours were ten to four on Mondays, Wednesdays, and Fridays, ten to seven on Tuesdays and Thursdays. Quigley was authorised to purchase "major equipment" — a duplicator, typewriter and filing cabinets. Space was tight, so committee meetings were held elsewhere — the council in the UCD boardroom, and the executive committee, courtesy of Jim Beddy, at the IDA offices in St. Stephen's Green.

Money was slow to come in. Membership was sluggish: after four months there were only 120 corporate members and 125 individuals. Impatient at the pace of recruitment, the executive committee delivered a reprimand to the people in charge, the FMO committee (finance, management and organisation). The minute is stiff:

> It was generally felt that more energy should be put into this question of recruitment and the matter was referred

---

[4] Now occupied by Ernest Jones, Jewellers, and Herman's Klipjoint, Unisex Hairstylists.

for the further attention of the FMO committee, from whom
it was hoped to get rapid and impressive results.

*The IMI's first headquarters, 81 Grafton Street, from a sketch by Jack
Cudworth, commissioned for the Institute's Silver Jubilee in 1977*

The council asked Quigley to clear the decks of other work and
concentrate on recruitment; committees were asked to do their
own administration. Everyone was pressed into service to compile
lists of potential members for Quigley to pursue. All expenses
were scrutinised in the struggle to balance the books. At times,
this drove the Institute to unashamed parsimony. Invited to give a
lecture to members, an industrial psychologist from Glasgow University asked if he could stay in the Gresham. The chairman of the

programme and planning (P&P) committee was instructed to point out to him that the Institute was barely getting on its feet; he was offered, instead, accommodation in the Guinness staff house.

Promotion of corporate membership remained an uphill battle. Subscriptions were modest enough but, to sweeten the pill, the Institute looked for tax exemption for companies. Michael MacCormac, in his role as honorary treasurer, went to see the Revenue Commissioners with two requests — tax exemption for members on their subscriptions and tax exemption for the Institute on any retained surpluses. The commissioners were amenable and he got most of what he sought. From August 1953, subscriptions of corporate members were tax-allowable. Individual members could not claim tax relief on their subscriptions, but the Institute could exclude these in calculating any annual taxable surplus. Corporate donations to the Institute were treated as grants, neither deductible by the donors nor taxable in the hands of the Institute.

The first regional committee was set up in Cork. This was at Busteed's initiative and he put his university fully behind it. The local FIM, the Cork Chamber of Commerce and prominent local firms like Dunlop, Dowdall O'Mahony and the City of Cork Steam Packet Company became involved. The Cork regional committee was followed soon by Waterford and, later, by Galway and Limerick. Having a regional committee in Limerick was not enough for a columnist in the *Limerick Chronicle* who, in 1958, had a bone to pick with the IMI:

> It [the IMI] is a highly desirable organisation and we have nothing against it except the stark fact that not a single Limerick man has been elected on the Council. Are we jumping too much to a conclusion in thinking that this omission is because Limerick has now no industry of any consequence? In any event there is not a leading figure in the commercial life of Limerick — the third city of the Republic — amongst the 50-member Council. Judging from the names of those elected, a person need not necessarily be an industrialist to make the grade in the Council — there are quite a number of dons from the universities and heads of vocational schools, as well as executives from semi-State industries such as the ESB and CIE. We must confess ignorance as to how the Council is elected, but whatever the process it is quite clear that the Limerick

members, and there are quite a few, have only a very
small voice since they are, apparently, quite incapable of
electing one of their number.

This hint at a latter-day Siege of Limerick was noted at headquarters: W.H. O'Donnell FCA, chairman of the Limerick regional
committee since its foundation, was co-opted to the council at its
next meeting. Other committees were added in time, based on
Dublin and the main provincial centres of business. There are now
seven such regional groupings.

For the first few years, the programme and planning committee
chose and organised the Institute's programme of events. There
was a lecture at least every month, most speakers coming from the
UK. Where possible, the Institute piggy-backed the universities or
professional associations, adding an IMI lecture to their visiting
experts' schedules, thereby broadening the range of issues and
keeping costs down. The Institute also began visits to leading companies to see how they were organised. Members would tour a
plant, hear an exposition by senior management about the industry, the company's goals and, importantly, the management techniques and controls in use.

The big event in the first year was the national conference on
training held in September in Cork — a tribute to the energy of the
new regional committee. The format — Thursday evening to Saturday morning — endured for many years. Professor Busteed offered
UCC's dairy science building for the sessions. Sir Charles Harvey
hosted — and paid for — a sherry reception. The budget was meagre. Name badges, then a novelty, cost 3d each; delegates were
asked to leave them in a box on the way out for re-use. The attendance was a creditable 131. With the exception of the chairman of
the Institute, who addressed the dinner in the Imperial Hotel, and
T.P. Byrne of Aer Lingus, who spoke about supervisory training, the
speakers were from Britain and Northern Ireland. The last session
was chaired by Kevin McCourt, the father of marketing in Ireland.
McCourt enjoyed a long and distinguished career in industry in
Ireland and abroad. He was associated with the Carroll tobacco
company and Irish Distillers and was the first Irish director-general
of RTE.

The first year's programme covered many detailed aspects of management — cost control, work-study, personnel selection, the sourcing of capital — and macro topics such as free enterprise in the Irish economy, and management principles and practice. The usual format was a talk by an expert, often a senior manager from a large company, followed by discussion. Management films, novel at that time, were loaned by the European productivity movement.

Apart from attending these events, senior managers were encouraged to work together on management topics of practical interest. Where possible, experts would sit in to help. The reports of these study groups would form the nucleus of special conferences, sharing the teams' work with a wider audience. The first groups were set up in mid-1953. Issues studied included the effect of price changes on the maintenance of capital, office organisation and the implications of Ireland joining the European Free Trade Area (EFTA), then a probability. The latter led to the publication in 1956 of the Institute's first submission on government policy, *Ireland in the European Free Trade Area*, written by Gerry Quinn, lecturer in economics at UCD. The study groups continued for a few years. Some of their output was published but they gradually faded away.

John Leydon stayed in close touch with the Institute, keeping it informed on relevant international developments. MacCormac says that, in those early years, Leydon had a strong influence on the way the Institute developed:

> He was a very influential member of the executive committee. He had an unusual but effective style: he would remain silent until something cropped up on which he had a view. He never spoke from the top of his head. When others had had their say, Leydon would produce a paper in tiny handwriting, and just read it out. For him, that was that. You didn't argue. Harvey normally accepted Leydon's intervention as definitive, so his influence on policy was considerable.

Leydon regularly briefed the council on the work of the OEEC (Organisation for European Economic Co-operation),[5] urging the Institute to use the resources of this international agency, which

---

[5] Later OECD (Organisation for Economic Co-operation and Development).

ran courses for both managers and teachers of management and promoted management training methods in general. The term "executive development" was invented at an OEEC conference in England in September 1953. An interesting nugget from that meeting is a list of the 11 most popular devices US companies employed in the early 1950s to develop their managers:[6]

> Merit/performance reviews; visits to other companies; attendance at conferences; distribution of reading lists and management bulletins; group meetings; job rotation; advanced management courses at Harvard and elsewhere; use of consultants; committee assignments; executive inventories.

The OECD decided to use this checklist to benchmark the state of management development in its member countries. The results of this exercise formed the basis of an international conference of experts in management in the Administrative Staff College in Henley-on-Thames in September 1953. The IMI could not afford to send a delegate but Dr Basil Chubb, registrar of the schools of commerce and public administration at Trinity College, gave the IMI an account of it. There was a follow-up four-week multinational management course in France in 1954, for 40 potential chief executives at a cost of £200 each. As Ireland was "poor, financially and in experience" it stood to gain more than other countries, said Chubb. He urged Irish companies to go. There is no evidence that any of them did.

Its hands full planning the programme of events, the programme and planning committee was unable to deal with its other roles — setting up services for members and considering the institute's educational role. An education and information committee (E&I) was added, chaired by Sir Cornelius Gregg. His brief was to get a library and information service established, to inaugurate a bulletin for members and to consult with the principal educational bodies on the design of longer management courses. Early in its working life, the committee talked to the universities and vocational schools about including management education in their curricula. The High School of Commerce, Rathmines, was quickest to

---

[6] *Source*: National Conference Board of America.

respond. The CEO of the Dublin VEC, Martin Gleeson, a member of the IMI council, said they would send a teacher from the Rathmines school to the Polytechnic in Kensington for training in management teaching. The Institute warmly supported Gleeson's initiative and told him that it would encourage industry to avail of his courses. The college was soon offering a range of courses in management, gradually building a reputation as a centre for sound, practical, business studies. Sean O'Ceallaigh, principal of the High School of Commerce, was co-opted to the executive committee.

The IMI leadership, prompted by council member Jack Eason, was keen to push ahead with a periodical as the primary medium of communication with its growing membership, signalling to other business organisations, the Government and the media that the young institute was there to stay. The E&I committee examined proposals from five printing and publishing houses and, in August 1953, recommended the proposal of Mercier Press, Cork, to publish a bimonthly 48-page journal, *Irish Management*. The IMI would supply 75 per cent of editorial matter, Mercier sourcing the remainder internationally. Mercier would supply the Institute with a thousand copies of every issue, free of charge; the Institute would be responsible for postage. Editorial policy would be under the IMI's sole control. Sir Cornelius Gregg was given the go-ahead to complete the contract.

Mercier got the publication out with commendable dispatch. Vol. 1, No.1, appeared in January 1954 with L. Sierick as editor. It was a healthy issue of 52 pages including a promising number of advertisements. There was a foreword by the Tánaiste, Sean Lemass, and an "editorial" by Sir Charles Harvey. The featured article was by the Capuchin monk, Dr Peter Dempsey, from University College, Cork, professor of psychology, enthusiast for management education and a contributor to the IMI over a long, distinguished career. He offered readers a critical analysis of the writings of some of the early management theorists, principally F.W. Taylor[7] and Henri Fayol.[8] There were book reviews, abstracts, and practical contributions on

---

[7] Author of *Principles of Scientific Management* (1911).

[8] A French mining engineer, a contemporary of Taylor's, who wrote extensively about management, although not widely published outside France until long after his death in 1925.

industrial production, current legislation, industrial relations and a report, with picture, of the Institute's first conference held in Cork the previous autumn. Completing the issue were a company profile and three pages covering the Institute's activities and services. The price in the bookshops was one shilling.

Irish Management was welcomed by the executive committee and the council as "a very good production". However, the demands of feeding it with articles, even bi-monthly, proved burdensome on the education and information committee. Sir Cornelius Gregg suggested a separate editorial sub-committee of people with experience in writing and publishing. Michael MacCormac was asked to chair it. Among those who served on the committee over its lifetime were Garret FitzGerald, then writing a weekly economic comment column in *The Irish Times*; Michael Gorman, founding editor of the acclaimed Bord Fáilte magazine *Ireland of the Welcomes*; an economist, Pat Loughrey of Batchelors; and the solicitor and entrepreneur Felim Meade.

The magazine's presentation was attractive. Managers looked forward to its arrival with its mixture of news and articles on their arcane profession. But even the specialist part-time committee soon felt the strain of filling it with interesting copy. Cracks began to appear in the relationship with Mercier Press; they were too far removed from what the Institute was doing to continue to source articles that were relevant to the Institute's evolving agenda. After three years, it was decided not to renew the Mercier contract but to move *Irish Management* in-house. A full-time editor/information officer, Paddy Dillon Malone, was appointed in 1958. The printing contract went to Mount Salus Press, closer to home in Sandymount. The Institute was now responsible for both editorial and advertising although, as part of the contract, Mount Salus agreed to "chase" the advertising copy and printing blocks, bothersome and time-consuming tasks. Two years later it was decided to switch to monthly publication. The "*Irish*" part of the title did not survive the transition: it was dropped as unnecessary and, indeed, odd, implying as it did that there was such a thing as peculiarly *Irish* management! In January 1960, the journal appeared for the first time as a monthly, sporting its new masthead, *Management*.

To get back to the beginning: at the inaugural meeting, a commitment had been given that all members of the council and executive committee then elected would resign at the first AGM, but would be eligible for re-election. There would also be a new constitution for approval by the members. The first AGM was held in December 1953, close to the anniversary of the inaugural meeting and in the same location. The first part of the meeting was open to the public. Lemass was there to hear the Institute's progress report. Sir Charles Harvey spoke of the difficulty the IMI had in "obtaining public and professional support for the idea around which the Institute was built — the raising of the standard of management in Ireland". Active support for the organisation had been forthcoming on a heartening scale but the volume of membership was not yet sufficient to enable it pay its way. The excess of expenditure over income was £370. The accounts showed that there were 164 corporate members contributing £1,100, with 260 individual members and 41 associates.

Complimenting the Institute, Sean Lemass linked it to national policy and to his current campaign to drive up exports:

> All plans and hopes for raising the standard of living, for ending unemployment and checking emigration, for reducing the weight of the tax burden and for improving social conditions, depend on our success in this export drive. That is the reason why we must support it continuously and tirelessly. It is why the work of the Institute is being watched with such deep interest, and why the report of the Institute's council with its record of impressive achievement can be hailed as an encouraging and heartening document.

Lemass stayed on for a talk by British management expert, E.F.L. Brech[9] on *The Principles and Practice of Management*. This was followed by a vote to approve the new constitution and, then, the council elections. Of the outgoing council, eight did not go

---

[9] Co-author with Lyndall Fownes Urwick of *The Making of Scientific Management*.

forward.[10] The chairman thanked them for their service to the Institute. The rest were re-elected along with four new members: N.M. Bruce of W.D. & H.O. Wills; the legendary Lieutenant-General M.J. Costello, general manager of Comhlucht Siúicre Éireann; William Dresser, Arthur Guinness Son & Co. Ltd.; and Kevin McCourt.

The new council met a week later in Newman House on the Green. Sir Charles Harvey was re-elected for what he said would be "the limit of my chairmanship". He believed that the chair should not be kept too long by one person. The executive committee was unchanged except for Colm Barnes and A.H. Masser, who filled the vacancies left by the departure of Eason and O'Brien. Sean O'Ceallaigh, principal of the High School of Commerce, was added later.

The Institute was in a poor financial state. The annual loss was now running in the region of £1,000, a substantial sum. The executive committee strengthened the FMO committee and asked it to redouble its efforts on membership. The committee mounted an intensive drive, including a direct mail campaign at managers in the bigger firms. Stephanie Power was sent to Limerick, her native city, to sell membership in the aftermath of an IMI function there. Paul Quigley addressed the Cork Rotary Club and spent a few days recruiting. In a special promotion, the new journal was dispatched free to a sample of non-members. Stephanie Power's efforts in Limerick were a fine success and she was warmly praised by the chairman for signing up 11 corporate members.

Retailers were under-represented in the Institute, so Sir Cornelius Gregg persuaded S.H. Leake, chairman of Selfridges, a heavyweight in retailing, to speak in Dublin. He invited P.H. Smith of C.B. Coombs of Clarendon Street, president of the drapers' chamber, to preside. The meeting had an unexpected consequence. After returning to London, Leake wrote to Sir Charles Harvey offering to sponsor a young Irish retailer on a three-month training assignment in Lewis's of Manchester or Selfridges in London. They would even pay him £7 a week. The council accepted Leake's offer.

By July 1954, the financial position had improved. But the council decided that the sources of revenue needed to be broadened. For

---

[10] Louis O'Brien, James Davy, Davy Frame, A.W. Bain, Vincent Crowley, A.E. McIvor, T. O'Mahony, and Jack Eason.

the first time, the Institute made a charge for lectures. By the mid-point of its second year, a pattern of activities had been established. There was at least one lecture in Dublin every month, usually in the Rupert Guinness Hall, courtesy of Guinness. Regional centres also saw an increase in local activities. The central event in the 1954 calendar was the annual conference, held in Galway. There were 140 participants and it turned in a handsome profit of £200. This was a hands-on, how-to-do-it conference on work-study. Because of the link with productivity, the executive committee decided, belatedly, that there should be some trade union involvement. Two weeks before the event, the two congresses were invited to send two observers each. They would be guests of the Institute for the sessions and for meals, but not for accommodation!

Earlier, council member Tom Laurie, who was the head of Esso in Ireland, offered to organise a course on "conference leadership", in reality a training course for trainers by Esso's management training staff. The universities were invited to participate but only UCC accepted. Although Esso picked up all the costs involved, the budget-conscious executive committee imposed a registration charge, which contributed £100 to the bottom line. The course was highly rated by the 12 participants, mainly senior personnel managers who learned to design and run short in-company courses. The council noted, for the benefit of the non-participating colleges, that the UCC participant found it particularly relevant!

The executive committee's careful husbandry of resources was again evident when the lease for Grafton Street came up for renewal in 1954. The lack of space was biting and the four-floor climb did not help. The committee decided that "more suitable offices should be obtainable at no greater cost". A number of premises were looked at and space was taken at 79 Merrion Square (see sketch on the next page) — three offices, including a large room with built-in shelving — at £300, including rates, very little more than the Grafton Street rent. The cost of renovation was estimated at £314 but the committee was able to reduce this because A.H. Masser agreed to supply free paint and Eric Rigby-Jones, Irish Ropes' founder, carpeted the place for nothing. The Institute transferred to Merrion Square in January 1955. A new recruit to the staff, Inagh Duff, was given the task of assembling a library for the members in the shelved room, which doubled as a boardroom.

The IMI's second home, 79 Merrion Square (Sketch by Jack Cudworth)

Now that a grander address had been achieved, the executive committee, prompted by Kevin McCourt, then contributing to IMI courses on the novel concept of public relations, decided to acquire a logo, or "crest" as it was called. A.H. Masser suggested:

> It might be worthwhile approaching Mr Louis le Brocquy in this connection; his usual fees are rather high but he might be agreeable to reducing these in the case of the institute.

T.P. Hogan undertook "to sound the position through a brother of Mr le Brocquy with whom I am acquainted". The record is silent on the outcome of the suggestion, but the Institute was crest-less until 1958. Then, as part of the strategy to mark *Irish Management*'s change to direct publication by the Institute, Thurloe Connolly of the Design Research Unit of Ireland was commissioned to redesign the magazine. A logo came as part of the design package — a handsome blind-embossed treatment of the initials IMI on the cover. The refit was referred to rather ponderously in the first editorial of the new-style journal:

> The object of the journal remains that of the institute: to raise the standard of management, by showing what it is and what it should be. It is our earnest hope that the journal's new clothes, like those of the emperor, will serve to reveal rather than to cloak the anatomy of management in Ireland.

As is the fashion in these matters, the logo underwent periodic redesigns in the decades ahead. Masser, always with a keen eye to the externals, suggested to the executive committee some time later that "the president or chairman of the Institute, when appearing at public functions, should be provided with an appropriate Collar of Honour". Weirs of Grafton Street designed "a badge in silver gilt with green silk collarette", with added silver bars for the names of holders of the office. Weirs quoted an all-in price of £32 10.0d or £50 for a 9ct gold version. The Institute settled for the silver gilt.[11]

Merrion Square contained the Institute comfortably enough from 1954 to 1956. But, with the publication of a report in that year recommending the setting up of a Management Development Unit (MDU),[12] it was clear that larger premises would be needed to accommodate extended courses run by the unit. Sir Charles Harvey

---

[11] The chain of office went missing over a quarter-century later. The chairman of the day, adamant that he had given it to a member of the IMI staff for safekeeping after a function, caused a ransacking of every press and nook in the Institute for what was then an item of valued heritage. Nothing was found and eventually a replacement was commissioned. A year later, when his term was over, the then ex-chairman's secretary, clearing out his "IMI desk" asked him what the heavy metal bundle was in the large brown envelope . . . !

[12] The Joint Committee on Education and Training for Management (see next chapter).

suggested to the executive committee in September 1956 that, "as property prices are at present low" the committee might consider buying rather than renting. He, Michael Dargan, Denis Hegarty and Michael MacCormac settled on a fine residence in leafy Leeson Park, two stories over basement at a cost of £2,985. There were 11 rooms in all, the two main reception rooms generously proportioned and suitable for conversion to a library and seminar room. A dining room, dubbed the Hunting Pink Room by the previous owners, provided a second lecture room in the basement. At the first function in the new headquarters in the autumn of 1957, Sir Charles Harvey paid special tribute to Michael Rigby-Jones and Irish Ropes for their "public-spirited generosity" in carpeting the entire premises in their popular and hard-wearing *Tintawn* product.

The Institute, with spacious, well-endowed premises, was now equipped to get down to even more serious work.

The IMI's third home, 12 Leeson Park (Sketch by Jack Cudworth)

CHAPTER SIX

DANGEROUS AND ELUSIVE WORDS

In its first years, the Institute's programme, although innovative, lacked coherence and was often based on what or who was available rather than any formal analysis of needs. In mid-1954, it was decided to attempt to measure the national need for management education and training. Michael Dargan persuaded the council to invite the participation of the universities and the vocational colleges in the study. A Joint Committee on Education and Training for Management was formed consisting of representatives from industry, the five university colleges, the vocational education authority and the Institute, 13 in total — all at senior level — with Dargan in the chair.

The committee adopted a challenging agenda:

- Break into their main elements the knowledge, skill and experience required in the successful practice of management and identify those which could be improved through education and training, within the firm or otherwise;

- Examine the suitability of present education courses in Ireland in so far as they were relevant to management;

- Survey education and training for management in other countries;

- Recommend what additional facilities, if any, should be provided in Ireland and how, where and by whom such facilities might in the ideal be provided;

- Examine any difficulties likely to be encountered in their provision and suggest possible means of overcoming them.

Michael MacCormac, a member of the committee, says that the choice of Dargan as chairman was crucial:

> Dargan's style drew the best from people on this and later committees. He wasn't a graduate — possibly just as well: it enabled him to create a kind of coalition between industry, the universities and the vocational sector.

This committee put the Institute on a course that was to change it from a private association of managers running occasional lectures to a national authority on the education and development of managers, exerting a substantial influence on the evolution of national policy on the subject. Its ability to build a coalition with the education system was central to that achievement.

The Joint Committee's report, *Education and Training for Management*, was published in April 1956, Sir Charles Harvey welcoming it as "a masterpiece". It was a credit to the committee who had produced, in a short time with limited resources, a wide-ranging set of proposals. A sample of 20 firms had been chosen for close study to see what management training went on and to measure current attitudes to management development. All showed interest and said that they did some training but most admitted that more needed to be done. A few smug souls declared that their current procedures could not be bettered.

The committee concentrated its efforts on two areas: fostering in-company management development procedures and improving the supply of courses at third-level colleges and at the IMI itself. As a starting point, they adopted E.F.L. Brech's definition of management:

> A social process entailing a responsibility for the effective planning and regulation of the operation of an enterprise, in fulfilment of a given purpose or task, such responsibility involving:
>
> * the installation and maintenance of proper procedures to ensure adherence to plans;
>
> * the guidance, integration and the provision of the personnel composing the enterprise, and carrying out its operations.

At an early stage, the committee sought to define the ideal manager:

> We are all agreed that, unless a man has the requisite moral fibre, no amount of knowledge, education and training will enable him to become and remain a successful leader. It is, we think, necessary that we should state this right at the commencement of our report.

The paragraph went on — mysteriously:

> Physical qualities are also important, but not in the context of our report. Both they and the moral qualities are matters to be borne in mind in selection rather than in training.

Intuition was recognised as playing a role. The report described it as "a mental activity which does not follow the ordinary course of reasoning":

> It is an immediate and direct type of knowledge which cannot be explained: the mind is in action, but also a contribution seems to be made by instinctive tendencies, dispositions, emotion, experience, desire and judgement. It should be used as a guide to action rather than to thought — the good manager will act on intuition only when his reasoning also tells him that the suggested action is the best suited to the circumstances. He will keep his intuition under strict control.

A then widely held view — that experience could be the only teacher — lay behind the cynicism that often greeted the emerging IMI. It had hindered the Institute's expansion, its membership recruitment and fund-raising. The report faced it, four-square:

> Experience is, perhaps, hardly separable from knowledge and skill, because both knowledge and skill may be considered to be in part the outcome of experience. It is not a requirement of the successful practice of management except in so far as it contributes to knowledge and skill. In itself, experience is worthless; intelligently used, it is indispensable to good management. At the same time the

separate term "experience" is particularly useful in determining the stages at which training may be given and for that reason, if no other, we were satisfied that it should be maintained as a separate element.

It is, of course, essential that special emphasis should be placed on experience in successful management practice. Skill in management cannot be taught by theoretical study alone: in fact, the development of the potential leader is a continuing process which begins in the individual's whole training and formal education and is supplemented by his experience in his business and social environments.

The committee analysed the elements of knowledge and skill required in management. The emphasis was more on direction and control rather than on consultation and motivation — a sign of the times — although knowledge of the psychology of groups and the ability to communicate were included in the characteristics of the successful manager.

Before discussing the supply side, the report listed methods that firms could use to develop their managers — delegation of responsibility, job rotation, selected reading, membership of associations and institutes, internal management and supervisory courses. Senior managers were left in no doubt that they were primarily responsible for training their subordinates; every company had to commit itself to the development of its people.

The bulk of the report was about the responsibility of the third-level system to provide quality management education. Universities were advised to stay close to industry to ensure their relevance to the world of business. But they had a wider role than to train "men for management":

A successful university education not only gives a man knowledge in some branch of learning, it also trains him to pursue the truth; to collect and assess data systematically, exhaustively and objectively; to formulate hypotheses, to test them, and to reject them if found wanting; to organise his own work and to discover his own abilities and resources.

The report singled out for analysis disciplines directly relevant to management — economics, commerce, public administration — analysing the content of courses and recommending ways of deepening and adding to them. The vocational education committees were praised for their quick action in Dublin and encouraged to extend their courses throughout the national vocational education network. They were advised to strengthen their links with local businesses and to use business people as lecturers.

The report noted the lack of short, full-time residential management development courses in Ireland. A survey of management education and training in Europe, Britain and the US had shown that these broadened the vision of future top managers, easing their transition from specialist roles to general management. The committee wanted more of these courses in Ireland aimed at middle management in big firms and top management in small firms, with the emphasis on leadership training. The residential aspect was important because it facilitated informal exchanges between participants — a valuable bonus.

The report recommended that the IMI should be a major supplier of management training, pointing out that, unless the IMI had an educational arm to provide full-time education and training, it would not achieve its central aim:

> The long-term survival of the institute, supported entirely on the contributions of its business members, may depend to a large extent on the direct service which can be given to them in the educational and training sphere.

The committee went on to recommend that the Institute set up this "educational arm" — a management development unit (MDU) under a full-time director of studies — commenting, ruefully, "if the Institute does not undertake this responsibility it is unlikely that any other agency will do so". Policy for the MDU would be determined, not solely by the Institute, but by a governing body — similar in constitution to the Joint Committee. The report observed that the proposed body would be "in an advantageous position to stimulate and encourage research work into business problems related to management". The committee, noting that lack of funds was "an obstacle to the universities and to the vocational education committees", asked the Institute to support them in their applications for funds for research.

The IMI council promptly agreed — even before publication of the report — to set up the recommended management development unit. Thereby, it determined the future thrust of the Institute.

Government, the education authorities and the media welcomed the report. In an interesting dissertation on management in *The Irish Times*,[1] Dr Basil Chubb[2] referred to a recent call by Sean Lemass for "efficient management":

> These are dangerous and elusive words: dangerous because they can so easily become a meaningless slogan to be uttered by those who believe that their job is done with the uttering, and because there is more to our salvation than management, of however high an order; elusive because of the difficulties of definition and measurement . . .
>
> The success of managers, Mr Lemass's "efficient management", is seen in smooth running operations, in contented and enthusiastic staff, in high productivity, and in low costs. . . . We must have on top of that a good deal of *systematic knowledge*. . . . There is, in fact, a fairly distinct body of knowledge and skills to be acquired, for management is fast becoming a true profession.

He reminded readers that the Institute was ploughing a difficult furrow, operating in a country that was "small and poor; overshadowed economically by its neighbour and without a long tradition of industry". It had two main tasks:

> First, it has to stimulate interest and to sell the idea that better management practices are possible, are desirable and that they pay. In many ways, this is the task of establishing the need for its own existence, not least to attract the financial support of industry on which (it is worth noting, in these days of government subsidy for so many things) it wholly relies for its funds.

---

[1] Chubb, Basil (1956), "Management in Ireland: The Task of the Institute", *The Irish Times*, 10 April, p. 5.

[2] He represented Trinity College on the Joint Committee.

The Institute's second task, he said, was to adapt the increasing body of knowledge and skills available from overseas to Irish circumstances. This would be "long and laborious", as the job of persuading industry and commerce of the value of this work had scarcely begun.

Between the completion of the Joint Committee's report and its publication in April 1956, the Institute tried to sound out the possibility of State financial support. Its very first application for funds went to the Department of Industry and Commerce in February 1956, accompanied by a copy of the Joint Committee's report. The nub of the case was that the level of Irish industrial productivity was directly related to the quality of its managers. A book,[3] based on studies by 61 British industrial teams of US productivity systems, was quoted in support:

> There is no peculiarly American "secret" of high industrial productivity; the principles and practices behind it are familiar; they can be carried out just as productively in any other country with good management, good human work [*sic*] and good equipment . . . and the only real problem of productivity is that of securing the degree of "goodness" of management, human work and equipment.

The proposed MDU would, in the Institute's submission, be "a practical step (and the best step in present circumstances) towards the solution of the problem". It would be up to the business community to pay a "substantial share" of the cost but, because this was largely an educational issue, the submission argued that the state had a duty to assist. The application was considered at an internal conference in the department in March, drawing from the industries division an interesting observation on a point that was to be raised often in the 40 years following:

> It might well be asked why the institute could not find the full cost of these courses from industry and business throughout the country instead of asking the State to defray a substantial part of the cost. This attitude is not sur-

---

[3] Hutton, Graham (1955), *We Too Can Prosper,* British Productivity Council, London.

prising, however, as it appears to be the case that business firms generally adopt a parsimonious attitude towards the financial needs of the various associations to which they belong. Trade unions on the other hand build up their financial strength through contributions from their members which must involve an appreciable sacrifice to the individual member.

The writer concluded that it would be difficult to justify a grant to the Institute's educational project unless a similar amount was given to an educational project "for the benefit of employees, e.g. the Catholic Workers College". Finding that the college had recently applied for funds to the Minister for Education, General Richard Mulcahy, the author of the memorandum advised his departmental colleagues that their minister, William Norton,[4] was "of opinion that the report and the application which is based on it, relating as they do to educational matters, are proper for consideration by the Minister for Education".

General Mulcahy did not agree and returned the file to Industry and Commerce. The possibility was then raised of the state recouping the money from the US-sponsored European Co-operation Agency (ECA) then considering a provision of £350,000 for a programme that included "management projects". The IMI had been working on the ECA angle with the American ambassador, William H. Taft III. He had advised that an application for ECA funds would have to be made to the US authorities by the Government, who would receive any grant on behalf of the Institute. The ambassador arranged for an official of the US office in Paris, a Mr McPhail, to visit the IMI and study the Joint Committee's report. Later he brought McPhail to meet Minister Norton. McPhail reported favourably on the IMI: he had been impressed by the people he met and by "their realistic attitude to the problems confronting them".

The issue was raised publicly at the launch of the Joint Committee's report by Minister Norton in the Gresham Hotel on 10 April 1956. Seizing the opportunity provided by the presence of two min-

---

[4] Tánaiste and Minister for Industry & Commerce in the second Costello Government.

isters[5] to put the Institute's role into a national context, Sir Charles Harvey said that production of good leaders in all spheres of Irish activity was of the highest national importance. The establishment of a management development unit as an educational project was as important to the nation as any other form of higher education. The Joint Committee had calculated that an initial capital grant of £7,000 would be needed for the MDU to cover accommodation, library and equipment. An annual subsidy of £4,000 would be required for five years "over and above fees received from students" to meet the MDU's net operating costs, including the salaries of a director of studies, a deputy and other staff. If the Government put up the capital amount, perhaps with the help of an ECA grant, the Institute was confident it could raise the annual subsidy element from industry. Harvey told the ministers that his council regarded the MDU as essential and urged government to support it. If they failed, he said, they would be leaving the future of Irish industry to chance; they would be failing to make provision for the development of future leadership. The alternative was for Irish industry to rely on imported managers:

> Ireland exports so many skills that it would be a pity indeed if it had to import this one, managerial ability, on which the future economic health of the country so largely depends.

The chairman of the Joint Committee, Michael Dargan, threw his weight behind Sir Charles's plea:

> The more one studies problems associated with management the more one realises that the management function is the variable factor which usually determines success or failure of a business. The capacity of a country's business leaders determines substantially how it fares in world trade as compared with other communities. Unless steps are taken immediately towards implementing the recommendations of the Joint Committee or taking appropriate alternative measures towards raising the standard of management, the effect on the standard of living of our people will be serious.

---

[5] The Minister for Education, General Richard Mulcahy, was also there.

Norton responded positively: he pledged that, subject to the co-operation of Finance, government support would indeed be forthcoming.

The Tánaiste left the Gresham confused by the figures mentioned in respect of the grant. His department had put the figure at £27,000. Sir Charles Harvey had quoted £7,000. The minister's confusion arose from an initial approach to the department a month or two earlier when the MDU costs were given as £27,000 — £7,000 start-up expenses and an annual £4,000 subsidy over five years, now to be financed through an appeal to members. Norton latched onto the lower figure and in a private moment they indulged in a little gentlemanly negotiation: he had asked Harvey, "What would you think of £5,000?" Harvey replied, "We would be very pleased indeed if this could be made £6,000." When Norton got back to his Dáil office he called a senior official and asked him to look at the figures again in the light of Sir Charles's remarks and to "put a case at once to the Department of Finance to settle for a grant for £6,000 to start them off".

CHAPTER SEVEN

A FORK IN THE ROAD

The Joint Committee's report brought the IMI to a fork in the road. It had the choice to remain a representational body, prodding the state and other institutions to meet managers' needs for training or, infinitely more difficult, it could, by accepting the Joint Committee's recommendation, become, itself, a centre for management training. It opted for a dual role: adding to its membership structure and functions a substantial in-house management training capability.

A consultative board[1] was set up in April 1957, under the aegis of the Institute, with a membership similar to that of the Joint Committee. Its purpose was to ensure that the latter's recommendations were pursued — including those relating to the other participating bodies. It had seven members from the universities and technical colleges and seven from industry. Michael Dargan, who had earned the respect of all for his handling of the Joint Committee, was invited to chair the board. But, first, the IMI chairman, Tom Laurie, wrote to Dargan's Aer Lingus boss, Jerry Dempsey, for permission:

> I can conceive of nobody who would be better fitted for
> this important task. Apart from his keen interest in the
> work, and his leading position in Irish thought on the sub-
> ject, he gave a very clear demonstration of his ability to
> lead such a mixed group, from widely divergent back-
> grounds, in his brilliant chairmanship of the Joint Commit-
> tee on Education and Training for Management.

---

[1] The "joint governing body" called for in the report.

The time had now come to launch the MDU, the IMI's response to the Joint Committee's report. The appeal to industry was fruitful; over 100 firms subscribed a total of £22,000. The state had promptly applied, on the Institute's behalf, for an ECA grant of £6,000 for capital expenditure and had received unofficial approval. A condition of the grant was that it could not be applied to expenditure incurred before the date of formal approval. Part of the grant was for the purchase of premises, essential if the MDU was to proceed. The government's negotiations with the US dragged on and on. Over a year later, in July 1957 when the time was running out for the purchase of 12 Leeson Park, the grant had still not been formally approved. The Institute was in a quandary: closing the sale would put the purchase outside the terms of the grant. However, with the help of Ambassador Taft, the IMI was permitted to alter its grant application, substituting other later expenditure for the premises purchase. So the Institute was able to close the deal on Leeson Park and move from Merrion Square in August 1957.

With the finances taken care of, for the short term in any case, the Institute began an international search for a head of the new unit. Norman C. Rimmer (42) was head of studies of the executive development programme of the British Institute of Management. He accepted a one-year contract from the IMI and moved to Dublin. He had an impressive string of credentials — a distinguished academic record at Oxford; captain of his college and county rugby teams; a teaching career interrupted by service in World War II from which he emerged with an MBE and the Dutch decoration, Knight Officer of the Order of Orange Nassau with Swords. By the time he came to the IMI he had established an international reputation in management training, having worked with the European Productivity Agency in Paris where he had five American professors of business administration on his staff. He was an effective, if unorthodox, teacher. Paul Quigley describes him as a brilliant, if sometimes temperamental, teacher of management:

> Rimmer reported to me for pay and rations, as it were, but, for the content of what he did, he related to the consultative board and, specifically, to Michael Dargan. He would come into the big conference room in Leeson Park, talk to twenty or thirty senior people and really enthuse them. He had a

way of teaching that caught people's attention. Sometimes he would start with a topic apparently off the point.

Quidnunc of *The Irish Times* describes this technique in a report of one of Rimmer's courses held in the Royal Hibernian Hotel:

> Students of the course were offered, as a subject for discussion and ballot, a selection of six reproductions of paintings of ancient and modern masters. Leaning informally against the wall from mantelpiece and ledge, Oskar Kokoschka rubbed frames with Canaletto, Vlaminck, and Van Gogh, and a great, if somewhat unfashionable work by Constable chaperoned a dazzling Maurice Wilks slice of Donegal with the shine of a sun in it rarely seen within a thousand miles of these murky shores.

All 21 students were asked to give their preference, be prepared to defend it and estimate what the original might be worth. Quigley recalls that someone valued a Venetian canal scene at £50; it turned out to be the Canaletto, then worth £250,000. Rimmer's moral: "Never rely on your own taste to judge what the market will buy!"

Rimmer's first IMI appearance was in the Rupert Guinness Hall in May 1957. This was to introduce him and his ideas about management development to his new Irish constituency. A convivial dinner in Sir Charles Harvey's house in James's Street preceded the lecture. When Rimmer got to the rostrum he proceeded to attack some sacred Irish cows — like the cost of having everything, including street signs, translated into Irish. Did the Irish realise what equal status for the Irish language was costing the economy? How could we expect to run any sort of industry if we added to our cost base in this way?

However, he soon got down to work and began to plan, in close consultation with the consultative board, the shape and content of the MDU's first course, two weeks long, opening in mid-September 1957 in the Institute's new Leeson Park premises. It attracted 23 participants from manufacturing, banking, insurance and transport.

The council planned to mark the first such course in Ireland with a reception. Sean Lemass was invited but replied that he would be abroad on a short holiday. For the council, however, there could be no substitute, not even William Norton, minister in the recently ousted coalition government whose help with the grant had made the MDU possible. They switched the reception to the end of the course and Paul Quigley was asked to offer Lemass the new date:

> Please forgive me for troubling you again on this matter but you will appreciate our anxiety to have your approval for management training as widely known as possible.

The Tánaiste was accommodating and, on the occasion, stressed the importance of management training not only to the firm but to the economy:

> There never was a time when competent management was not necessary for a successful business, but in the conditions of modern industry the importance of management and, therefore, of training for management have increased very considerably.
>
> . . . The standards of training and efficiency prevailing in industrial management are matters of public concern. A trained efficient manager can no longer be regarded as a sort of "optional extra" which an industrial firm can take or leave at its discretion.

Evaluations of early MDU courses showed that the participating managers derived great benefit from what, for all of them, was a new experience. During the first year, the unit ran three two-week programmes as well as a number of shorter courses.

Rimmer, drawing heavily on his contacts in the European Productivity Agency, arranged a procession of visiting management consultants and practitioners to Dublin and the larger regions.

In April 1958, Rimmer returned to England where he was appointed director of studies at Ashridge College. To ensure continuity, Aer Lingus agreed to second its training supervisor, Hugh MacNeill, to head the MDU for two years. While lacking Rimmer's swagger, he brought to the role a deeper understanding of Irish managers and quickly established his credentials as a designer and leader of courses. His two years with the IMI was a period of consolidation and measured development of the Institute's new training activity. Around the time of MacNeill's secondment, because of the increased output, an executive was needed to take charge of accounts and administration. The Army was a useful re-cruiting ground at the time; many officers who joined during the Emergency were finding their way back to civilian life. A telephone call was made to the Chief of Staff, Gen P.A. Mulcahy. His adjutant, Captain J.D. (Des) O'Brien, who was in his office at the time, de-clared interest. He was appointed and remained with the Institute until his death in 1971.

The establishment of the MDU coincided with a fundamental change in the direction of Ireland's economic policy, the defining day of which was 12 December 1957 when Kenneth Whitaker, scarcely a year after taking office as Secretary of the Department of Finance, wrote a minute to his Minister, Jim Ryan, seeking authori-sation "to work out an integrated programme of national develop-ment for the next five or ten years". He followed this with a paper titled *Economic Development* which, with the support of his minis-ter and of Sean Lemass, Minister for Industry and Commerce, was submitted for government approval. Uniquely, for a proposal so fundamentally challenging of established policy, it moved, in a matter of months, from conception to adoption. The first Pro-gramme for Economic Expansion, published a mere 11 months af-ter his minute to the minister and based almost entirely on his paper, was a catalyst for change, unmatched, either before or since, for its positive impact on the national psyche.[2]

Whitaker has since described the depressing context that moti-vated his seminal work:

> During the fifties we felt that despair and disillusionment were overcoming us.[3]

> The years 1955–56 had plumbed the depths of hopeless-ness. The mood of despondency was palpable. Something had to be done or the achievement of national independ-ence would prove to have been a futility.[4]

---

[2] In 2000 the Institute struck a gold medal to honour Dr T.K. Whitaker, refer-ring to him as "a singular visionary who exerted enduring leadership in Irish affairs, at the highest level of public service", and describing his influence in the shaping of modern Ireland as "potent and prevailing".

[3] In interview with Ivor Kenny (1987), *In Good Company*, Gill & Macmillan.

[4] Whitaker, T.K. (1983), *Interests*, Institute of Public Administration.

The introductory observation in *Economic Development* challenged the basis on which the economy had hitherto been managed: "The greatest fault lies in pursuing a policy after it has proved to be unsuitable or ineffective." The essence of his proposition was clearly set out:

> It would be unrealistic, in the light of the probable emergence of a Free Trade Area, to rely on a policy of protection similar to that applied over the past twenty-five years. Bearing in mind that the only scope for substantial expansion lies in the production of goods for sale on export markets, it is clear that there will be no place for weak or inefficient industries. It will be the policy in future in the case of new industries to confine the grant of tariff protection to cases in which it is clear that the industry will, after a short initial period, be able to survive without protection.

Whitaker later described the main effects of his doctrine:

> It put grass before grain. On the industrial side, it put export-oriented expansion, even if under foreign ownership, before dependence on protected and inadequate domestic enterprise.

Businesses in general were slow to respond to the new economic doctrine and its implications for their survival. Established strategies had to be rethought and replaced by a new view of the future based on hard competitiveness. The quality of a company's management would be the key to this transition. Progressive companies noted that attendance at an IMI course challenged their managers, exposed them to new ways of looking at their jobs, equipped them better for their leadership role and gave them effective techniques to help them plan and achieve change. A significant "extra" was the novel experience for most of having to perform in the company of their peers from other businesses. When executives had participated in extended courses, in particular, their value to their companies was enhanced. Not universally, though. Some older managers felt decidedly uncomfortable and inadequate when alien concepts with strange terminology were proposed by subordinates freshly back from a management course. They were occasionally told to forget that "IMI gobblede-gook — you are now back in the real world".

In 1960, Hugh MacNeill's secondment was up. The position was advertised but the interview board could not agree on a replacement. They took another look internally. Ivor Kenny, the information officer, had been recruited only a few months earlier to replace the departing Dillon Malone. Prior to joining the IMI, he had been double-jobbing as a teacher in Blackrock College and an "announcer" in Radio Éireann. The IMI advertisement offered a £1,200 salary, a 25 per cent increase on what he had been earning in both roles. He had an MA in political science and had done a spell in the London School of Economics. To address a deficit in management experience, on joining the Institute he attended as many management courses as he could. Despite this cramming, he was astonished to hear, six months later, that he was being considered to succeed MacNeill as head of the MDU. Clearly, he needed urgent immersion in an industrial environment. Michael Dargan arranged a stint in the inferno of Pressed Steel in Cowley, followed by an intensive project in the maintenance department of Aer Lingus. He attended a demanding six-week residential management course with Urwick Orr & Partners, designed to train UOP's own consultants. Returning to Dublin as head of the MDU, he was immediately in at the deep end, planning the training programme for the rest of the year and leading some as trainer:

> I condensed a great set of notes from the Urwick Orr programme into a two-day seminar — "planning and leading" on the first day; "organising and controlling" on the second. I put that on around Ireland for immensely tolerant managers.

Years later, having a drink with a couple of his earliest alumni, he observed:

> "That management seminar you attended some years ago — that was my first."

> "We could tell!"

The scope of the training programme depended greatly on the availability of visiting experts, usually American, courtesy of the

European Productivity Agency. It would not have been difficult to keep ahead of the class because few managers at the time, apart from engineers, perhaps, had university qualifications. But for the consultative board it was not enough to keep a step ahead of the market. They were looking for ways of involving the universities in deepening the content of what the IMI was offering, in particular for senior managers. The first such collaboration was announced as the Irish Management Institute's First Residential University Summer School. Held in University College, Cork, in the summer of 1960, it was opened with a media flourish by the Minister for Industry and Commerce, Jack Lynch, on 27 June. The participants lived on campus for two weeks. The colleges rowed in strongly: lecturers, spanning several disciplines, came, not only from UCC, but from UCD, Trinity and the University of Michigan.

The economy had been showing the first signs of growth as the Whitaker inspired expansionist policy started to bear fruit. Exports were doing particularly well. Jack Lynch spoke of the importance of management in building on this success:

> This is particularly necessary in the context of the remarkable expansion of our exports to a world market where freer trade between countries makes for keener competition. This expansion has been a high contributing factor to the increase in the numbers engaged in industrial employment. While tax concessions on export profits have played a big part in bringing about this desirable trend, the replacing of outmoded methods of production by modern techniques and the increase of productivity have been important. Having regard to the spectacular expansion in exports it is obvious that Irish management is fully conscious of these precepts and I am confident that it will be ever on the lookout for extended and wider fields of industrial activity.

CHAPTER EIGHT

GROWING THE TIMBER

It was never Paul Quigley's intention to spend more than eight years with the Institute. In 1960, he left to become general services manager and, later, general manager of Shannon Free Airport Development Company. Michael Dargan has described Quigley's appointment as the Institute's first executive head as "a great stroke of good fortune":

> Quigley became not only secretary but director of organisation, convener of conferences, and writer of papers. Not least of his attributes was his ease of manner, which allowed him to get on so well with everybody. Sir Charles Harvey and Paul Quigley made a wonderful team.

He was succeeded by James de V. Mansfield. Mansfield had been secretary of the Retail Grocers, Distribution and Allied Traders Association (RGDATA). At his final interview, some members of the executive committee, unencumbered by political correctness and concerned to maintain the Institute's political neutrality, expressed unease about the "de V." (for de Valera). He agreed to drop the offending initials for the duration of his appointment, which, as it turned out, was not long.

Soon internal tensions became evident, largely because of the relative independence of the MDU. When it was set up, it had been grafted onto the original membership organisation but its policy was guided by the consultative board, not the Institute. To a large extent, it did its own thing with the head of the unit reporting, not to the director of the Institute but to the consultative board, in particular to its chairman Michael Dargan. Quigley, Mansfield's predecessor, was quite happy with that arrangement. It allowed him to concentrate on the membership/representational role and on building the Institute's national organisation. When Ivor Kenny took over from MacNeill as head of the unit, he continued to report to the consultative board. This created difficulties for Mansfield, who found that he had little influence over what was becoming an increasingly important aspect of the Institute's work. It was a strained situation. It ended in the spring of 1963 when Mansfield left to become a management consultant.

Meanwhile, the MDU was exceeding the expectations of the Joint Committee that had set it up. In 1960, it was decided that it was time to take another look at the evolving state of management education/training in the country, including the progress of the MDU. A "review committee" was appointed. By mid-1961 it had formed some preliminary views on the MDU's future. Dargan wanted them tested before publishing the final report. The United States offered the best context for that review. The unit's recently appointed head, Ivor Kenny, applied to the European Productivity Agency and the Scholarship Exchange Board for funds for a US study tour. As the EPA was to be wound up in 1962, this was a last chance to benefit from its coffers. Kenny submitted a proposal with twin objectives:

- to have tested by eminent authorities the preliminary suggestions on the growth of the educational activities of the Irish Management Institute;

- to establish personal contact with fellow management teachers in the US to ensure a continuing supply of American specialists to the Irish Management Institute.

His application was approved and he set off on a two-month mission covering 11 cities:

> I used the mission to validate what we were thinking, or to challenge it. I talked to the best and the brightest; my most valuable encounters were in Harvard, Chicago and Stanford. I had had some useful experiences in the UK but the US was much more supportive and open and there was a hard intellectual edge there. It was so much ahead

of the rest. What that visit did for me was to inject some of
the American "let's do it" spirit.

He reported to the review committee in November with precise
recommendations for the development of the MDU. These were
adopted and recommended to the council at its meeting in January
1962. The core proposal was that the Institute would "grow its own
timber" — recruit four full-time specialists with experience in marketing, finance, production and personnel. The committee also
proposed "an investigation in depth into Irish managerial resources at a cost of about £5,000" and the acquisition of "a large
house on some acres of ground" with the potential for residential
facilities. Clearly, these sweeping recommendations could not be
met without a fundamental expansion of the Institute's finances.
The committee asked council to "examine the question of further
assistance from business, grants from foundations abroad and
government support".

The decision to divisionalise the MDU into marketing, finance,
production and personnel was radical. It laid the foundation for
what in due course became the national management centre. It also
introduced into the IMI an enduring, and sometimes uneasy, dichotomy — an Institute of management within an Institute of managers.

Recruitment of the four — dubbed "the Four Horsemen" — began in the spring of 1962. The first search was for a deputy head of
the MDU — a specialist in one of the four disciplines with strong
leadership skills and marked ability to conceptualise. Given that
there would be an emphasis on course planning and teaching, evidence of those skills, also, would be a key criterion. At the time it
was the practice in some US circles to put final candidates through
a group interview where they would have to perform in front of one
another.

Ivor Kenny asked Hugh MacNeill to sit in on the process:

> Hugh and I sat in the conference room in Leeson Park. The
> short listed candidates were brought in together, asked to
> sit at the table and have a discussion. One of the group,
> Brian Whelan, an accountant and joint general manager of
> an industrial bank, clinched it in the first few minutes; he
> waited until everybody sat down and then sat at the head

of the table, virtually chaired the meeting and walked into the job.

Whelan had an impressive academic/professional record and was a high achiever in sport, an easy mixer and comfortable with top managers — an important trait also for the young recruits who followed him into the IMI. Although a financial expert, he soon left specialisation behind as he got to grips with the scope of the Institute's objective, to raise standards right across the spectrum of management. He and Kenny shared the planning of the MDU's expansion.

The next search was for a marketing specialist "who would study the training requirements in marketing of the Institute's members and organise and conduct courses on marketing and selling for senior management". Colm Geary, a market research expert, was appointed in September. His job was to integrate the marketing function and its related topics such as design, packaging and product development into the expanding range of IMI courses. He was succeeded a year later by Eamonn McDermott, the Dublin area manager of CIE.

In October 1963 a psychologist, Dermot Egan, was appointed organisation and personnel executive "to study the training requirements of Irish business in industrial organisation and in personnel polices and practices and to organise and conduct a programme of instruction to meet their requirements". Egan, a graduate of UCD and Columbia, New York, had been recruited to Aer Lingus by Michael Dargan and appointed head of marketing management training. He had lectured occasionally at the IMI and was offered this full-time appointment, subject only to the formality of an interview. He had not intended to tell his boss, Dargan, until the job was his. He walked into the IMI's interview room to find that the chairman of the interview panel was Michael Dargan!

Next on the shopping list was "a production specialist, with a science or engineering background, to research and develop a programme in production/operational management". Noel Mulcahy, manager of quality control and research and development with SPS International in Shannon, got the job. He had been part of the management team that set up the plant in Shannon, transferring the electronic component manufacturing function from the US. He had experience with Standard Telephones and Cables in London. He had also worked as an engineer in Radio Éireann, tramping the mountains and hills of Ireland in 1956 surveying sites for transmitters for the new television service. In SPS he was responsible for quality assurance, a novel concept as far as many Irish companies were concerned. He had also conducted an internal management course and helped with a PA Management Consultants finance course for the Limerick Junior Chamber. So when he arrived at the IMI he was already equipped with comprehensive teaching material and the experience to go straight into action. First, he mapped out a programme and a budget for the year. At the core of his programme were 60 teaching days. This set a benchmark for output and net financial contribution, which the new trainers — management specialists as they became known — were expected to deliver.

That appointment completed the team of specialists — finance, marketing, personnel and production. But, because of Ivor Kenny's elevation to the post of director,[1] Brian Whelan (finance) succeeded him as head of the MDU and was no longer a full-time teacher. Martin Rafferty, a chartered accountant in the Irish Sugar Company Ltd., filled the finance vacancy. He, also, was a UCD graduate and had spent three years in the textiles industry before joining the Sugar Company. His boss, General Costello, had sent him on a Harvard course and was less that pleased when, soon after his return, the company lost him to the IMI. The general did not hold it against him — or the IMI — because during the 1960s, Costello was a frequent and popular speaker at IMI evening meetings throughout the regions. Rafferty arrived in the Institute with a rich fund of stories from his days with the general, dealing with the beet farmers of Ireland. This lore and hands-on experience in the family pub in Glenamaddy, County Galway, provided grist to Rafferty's teaching style.

His appointment completed the Four Horsemen — Dermot Egan, personnel; Eamonn McDermott, marketing; Noel Mulcahy, production; Martin Rafferty, finance. Their combined impact on Irish managers was considerable. Managers coming on courses

---

[1] See page 82.

were met by teachers who, having a full awareness of local industrial realities, could help them understand and apply the latest concepts and techniques across all the disciplines of management.

The "hottest" management topics were marketing and the behavioural sciences. McDermott, an extrovert, delighted in his role. His unorthodox approach to the teaching of marketing grabbed the attention of even his most conservative clients. The Institute was asked to provide a management course for a group known as "the major religious superiors", the heads of the large Catholic institutions. A marketing module was included. The priests and nuns were out of their depth — and quite terrified — in this lay environment with its strange jargon. In bounced McDermott: "OK guys, and what are *you* selling — happiness?"

Dermot Egan's arrival coincided with the emergence of a rich vein of research on the application to industry of the young discipline of behavioural science. Some managers welcomed this new perspective on the management of people — with its emphasis on resolving organisational issues in a collaborative rather than confrontational way; others were quite hostile — "mumbo-jumbo" was a typical put-down. Traditional managers, comfortable in their hierarchical command culture, saw industrial psychology as threatening. Trade unionists, also, brought up on adversarial industrial relations, had little time for the interactive, problem-solving approach advocated by behaviouralists. They saw it also as presenting management with powerful new techniques to manipulate the workforce.

Gradually, research emerging from studies in actual companies was to demonstrate that progressive policies could indeed benefit everyone concerned, management and the workforce. When, in the Glacier Metal Company in Wembley in the 1950s, a series of productivity studies carried out by a team of social psychologists appeared to show that personnel policies, which took account of the needs and preferences of workers, brought forth a dividend in increased productivity, line managers, whose concern had been solely with systems of production and top-down discipline, began to take notice and pay more attention to the human dimension. W.B.D. Brown, managing director of Glacier, told the IMI conference in 1959 that he believed that "management in every country in the world is as yet in a condition that I would regard as primitive" and without "real understanding of the social systems for which they are responsible".

Initially, courses on industrial psychology were targeted at personnel managers. Soon, however, behavioural science became a component in extended courses for all senior managers, who found that it gave them new insights into their own behaviour. Experimentation with this exciting new tool sometimes went beyond relevance. A writer to the letters column of the *Evening Press*[2] in 1962 complained about a grant being used to fund an IMI course on sensitivity training, describing the topic as "an exotic indulgence of doubtful value". Charles McCarthy, a trade unionist and academic, reflecting on the strife-ridden 1960s,[3] implied that the application to Irish workplaces (presumably through the IMI's aegis) of the teachings of some international proponents of behaviour science led managers to adopt pernicious and manipulative management techniques.

In a review of McCarthy's book, Noel Mulcahy pointed out that studies had validated the conclusions of reputable behavioural scientists:[4]

> I am sure that Charles McCarthy does not want us to . . . attribute to the data of other societies a degree of uselessness that would render the generalisations void. But there is a danger that we might become too insular and imagine that this little island of ours was specially selected for anthropology so distinct that it could not bear comparison with others.

With specialists in each of the four main functions of management, the IMI could offer business a balanced spread of courses. Using their links with professional associations, the staff put on joint seminars with bodies such as the Institute of Marketing and Sales Management, the Irish Work Study Institute, the Irish branch of the Institute of Personnel Management and various finance organisations. In November 1965, Liam Connellan, a production controller

---

[2] *Evening Press*, 12 December 1962.

[3] McCarthy, C. (1973), *The Decade of Upheaval*, The Institute of Public Administration.

[4] *Management*, January 1974.

with ACEC Ireland, joined the team of four. A UCD engineering graduate, he had accumulated valuable production experience, first with a Swedish steam turbine manufacturing company, STAL, and then with Associated Electrical Industries in the UK. While with ACEC he had been a member of the Waterford regional committee. He joined the team at a time when the ascending curve of IMI activity had become almost vertical.

Brian Whelan's early promotion to head of the MDU[5] happened because of the departure of the director James Mansfield. The incumbent, Ivor Kenny, put his hat in the ring for Mansfield's job, director of the Institute. Despite his lack of a business background, he was confident, having worked closely with the review committee, that he knew at least as much as any other possible candidate about the challenges facing the Institute. The report of his US tour comprised a major part of the committee's findings, which, he told the interview board, would form his agenda as director.

Clearly, it was a strong candidature. Nevertheless, the executive committee agonised about the experience issue. They decided on a compromise. The chairman, A.H. Masser, meeting Kenny on the steps of Leeson Park, took him aside and offered him the position of *acting* director. Kenny's heart sank. The "acting" tag would have weakened his mandate when what the Institute needed was strong, unequivocal direction. With spontaneous resolve, he told the chairman that an "acting" appointment would send out the wrong signals and that he would have to think about it. His courage was shaken when Michael Dargan later put a hand on his shoulder: "Ivor, you're taking a very dangerous course." But the job was his — without the "acting" tag. This was the start of 19 years at the IMI's helm.

The recruitment of the Four Horsemen and their support staff put strains on the Leeson Park accommodation. The chairman, Masser, was also distributor of a wide range of international products, including Portakabin, a smart new concept in temporary ac-

---

[5] As the Institute adopted management development as its core function, it no longer made sense to have a semi-autonomous Management Development Unit. In 1964, the MDU was subsumed into the main organisation, its head, Brian Whelan, being appointed to the new position of deputy director of the Institute.

commodation. A generous deal was done and four Portakabins were imported into the garden at Leeson Park, where they were stacked two-on-two with a neat external staircase. The total cost, including furniture, carpets and heaters, was £2,067.

The Institute's growing confidence and the strengthening of its membership base prompted an ambitious decision to run a charter flight to the triennial world congress of CIOS, the International Council for Scientific Management, in New York in October 1963. The five-day congress was addressed by over 200 speakers and attended by 4,000 "directors of the world's daily work", to quote a participant tired of the inadequacy of the word "manager". David Rockefeller called the congress "the largest and most significant management meeting in history". The IMI was not lost for hyperbole either, describing its 21 member delegation — a modest smattering among the throng who attended — as "the greatest proportional national representation by any country outside the United States". The Irish involvement, however, almost did not happen. The economics of the charter required passenger numbers of well ahead of the 21 members who had booked. The Institute placed a discreetly worded advertisement to drum up extra bookings at an attractive price. Breakeven was reached when young people of little means emigrating to the United States found that the IMI's return fare was at a considerable discount to the single fare quoted by the airline on its scheduled service. These bemused one-way travellers accounted for a majority of the group surrounding CIOS's "Welcome to New York" banner that greeted the plane at Idlewilde airport.

CHAPTER NINE

A HA'PORTH O' TAR

In 1958, the six founding countries signed the Treaty of Rome, establishing the Common Market. Sean Lemass, who succeeded de Valera as Taoiseach in 1959, was determined that Ireland's hard-won political independence would now be underpinned by a competitive economy so that it might take its place in this wider economic alliance — the only viable way forward. As Ken Whitaker put it:[1]

> If there was failure to achieve economic goals, this would set the political gains to nought. Furthermore, the growth in the economy was to be achieved by an outward-looking, competitive approach. There was to be no more hiding behind stultifying trade barriers; the industrial forest was to be cleared of dead wood and new growth created.

Lemass would have considered the IMI one of his new-era foresters. The Institute was an important collaborator in the national push to adapt and restructure Irish industry ahead of entry to the European Economic Community. Economic issues were climbing to the top of the national agenda as government forged a trilateral alliance with the trade unions and the private sector. Two partnership mechanisms, in particular, reflected this — the Committee on Industrial Organisation (CIO) (1961) and the National Industrial Economic Council (NIEC) (1963).

---

[1] Whitaker, T.K. (1983), *Interests*, IPA.

The outward-looking initiatives of the 1950s — in particular, the setting up of the IDA and the introduction of tax relief on export profits — had started to pay off. The economy picked up momentum as the government got serious about it. A pattern of sustained growth became established, following tentative incursions into export markets, albeit with much handholding by state agencies, particularly Córas Tráchtála (CTT).

The CIO sent mixed public/private sector teams to check the state of industry's readiness for free trade. They found the detritus of three decades of protection: small-scale units, little specialisation, short production runs, plant under-utilisation, poor design, scarcely any R&D and negligible marketing. The findings sparked a programme of grants to address the deficiencies, sector by sector. The grants helped companies to re-equip and upgrade plant. But the CIO studies also highlighted the need to re-equip entrepreneurs and managers with a more acute sense of the realities of change. The extent of the latter problem was far beyond the scope of the Institute, the only organisation with the relevant expertise. How could it possibly respond to the expected upsurge in demand? The Taoiseach, Sean Lemass, anticipated this in September 1962. When A.H. Masser presented him with the report of the review committee, Lemass conceded that the Institute's resources could not be expected to cope with what he described as "a national need for expanded training activity". He complimented the IMI on the "great strides" it had made to raise the efficiency of industry: "I regard the programme of the Institute as one of the most important weapons in the national armament at this time." And, in a phrase that resonated in the IMI for many years, he told the Institute that, when tackling the management deficit, it "should not spoil the ship for a ha'porth o' tar". He promised that the Government would "receive with consideration and sympathy suggestions regarding financial assistance", quickly adding: "This does not mean that the Government is prepared to pick up the cheque for the expansion of the Institute's programme."

Lemass had endorsed the review committee's recommendation that the IMI become the national centre for post-experience management training. Given that many businesses had yet to be convinced of the value of management training, there was no question of asking it to underwrite the full economic cost. So, Lemass's ha'porth o' tar speech gave considerable comfort to a worried executive committee. Even in more industrialised countries, IMI's counterparts relied on grants. The year before he left, James Mansfield toured the main management centres of Germany. None survived solely on revenue from courses; all had significant funding from state or federal sources and/or from large foundations — often a combination of all three.

The IMI had tried the foundation route but without success — it had failed to meet the criteria of the big US foundations. Without government commitment, the Institute's strategy was simply not viable. There were some within the council who were against government funding in any form. The Institute had up to then paid its way and they wanted to keep it independent. Indeed, Sean Lemass, after making his offer, privately advised Masser and the Institute's top brass: "Remember, as soon as you take government money, the character of your institution changes." He was right. But, if it was to play the national role now prescribed, there was no other way.

The CIO study groups continued to pour out their accounts of the generally sorry state of industry. The IMI, although not part of the CIO, worked closely with it. There was little sign that the majority of managers were heeding the CIO's warnings of doom. To help get the message across, the IMI decided to base the 1963 national management conference entirely on the CIO reports. Titled *Signposts to Progress*, it was held in Galway.[2]

The CIO chairman, J.C.B. McCarthy, had succeeded John Leydon in Industry and Commerce. He briefed the conference on the CIO's unique, nation-wide study of industry sectors. His speech made for bleak listening. Sixteen surveys had been completed, covering over 60,000 jobs. They had uncovered low productivity, substandard plant, and downright bad management practices. McCarthy reported astonishing apathy to the results:

> All the industries surveyed were urged seriously to consider engaging the services of experienced consultants, and were told that the Government was prepared to pay

---

[2] The conference had outgrown Killarney's facilities but the town would catch up later.

half the costs involved. None of the industries have acted
on that suggestion.

The conference met in the wake of a breakdown in Britain's negotiations to join the Common Market. Ireland's application being
contingent on UK entry, there was private relief in government at
the extra breathing space. But Lemass was not about to let industry
off the hook. He told the conference:

> Our first decision is that we should proceed as if the Brus-
> sels breakdown had never happened [so that] by 1970, as
> originally accepted, we would have to meet the impact of
> free trade conditions in our home market.

Stung by the *laissez faire* response of many firms to the CIO findings, Lemass warned that he would get tough with sectors that
failed to respond to the incentives package that was there to help
get them into shape. There would be no sympathy if they continued to depend on tariffs, which he warned were a rapidly dimin-
ishing commodity in Irish industrial affairs. His remarks to the
conference were trumpeted across the front page of the *Evening
Press* under a two-inch banner:

"GET CRACKING OR ELSE . . . !"

The heightened economic activity in the 1960s put a premium on
know-how and brought a surge in demand for managers. Forward-
looking businesses responded with vigour to the new climate of
opportunity. Much of the growth was export-led, with many Irish
managers getting their first taste of tough foreign competition.
They had to learn fast and looked increasingly to the IMI as the
source of best management practice.

The Institute got down to preparing a comprehensive submission for funds to the Department of Industry and Commerce. Ivor
Kenny, Brian Whelan and Des O'Brien, the head of administration,
mapped out a three-year programme with income and expenditure
implications, including recruitment, training and salary costs of
new specialist staff. Space and facilities in Leeson Park were tight,
so larger premises and more equipment had also to be factored in.

The search for premises was a priority. The council, without waiting for the outcome of the grant application, gave the go-ahead. In the autumn of 1963, the executive committee recommended the purchase of Errigal, a substantial early-nineteenth-century residence on four acres in Orwell Road, Rathgar. It was set well back from the road with a large area in the rear for expansion. The price was £24,000, with an estimated £14,000 for refurbishment and adaptation. The grant, which had meanwhile been approved, consisted of an initial amount towards the purchase of premises, and subvention, to be reviewed annually, of 50 per cent of expenditure.

The IMI's fourth home, Errigal (Sketch by Jack Cudworth)

It was a complicated package: the sale of 12 Leeson Park covered 25 per cent of the purchase of Errigal, the Government matching that amount. The remaining 50 per cent was to be funded by an ICC loan arranged by Jim Beddy. The council was faced with a hard decision — whether it could commit the Institute to heavy annual outgoings with no guarantees of subsidy beyond year one. The uncertainty was too much for some and the purchase decision was referred back to the executive committee. The members of the executive committee — Jerry Dempsey was chairman and Michael Rigby-Jones vice-chairman — were closer to the issues than the average council member. With Lemass's ha'porth o' tar assurance, albeit on a year-to-year basis, they gave the green light for the purchase.

Errigal, the IMI's elegant new headquarters, was opened with a flourish in glorious weather by Dr P.J. Hillery, Minister for Industry and Commerce, on 6 June 1965. However, the sunshine quickly gave way to a cloudburst during which an exuberant guest was seen weaving, jacket-less, across the lawn during the height of the deluge, a hand carefully sheltering his glass of champagne!

Through the 1960s, the body of knowledge on management was expanding as a result of international research and experimentation. The Institute had to ensure that it remained fully briefed on the developments in its field while also satisfying a torrent of demand from Irish companies. The acceleration of both product development and demand put strains on the structure that had evolved around the Four Horsemen. The needs of the market were now becoming more sophisticated and particular. Teaching material that was fine for big companies made little sense to small businesses. Adaptation councils that the Government had set up to modernise industry were calling for training geared to specific sectors, such as footwear or furniture. Large companies were also asking the Institute to look at their problems and provide courses shaped to their exact needs.

Early in 1966, the executive committee approved a new organisation structure that took shape over the following two years. A number of "programme groups" were formed, each with its own head. Noel Mulcahy took charge of executive development, i.e. extended courses; Martin Rafferty, distributive trades; Eamonn McDermott, management techniques — short courses in the traditional functions of management — plus a new subject, computers. Dermot Egan became head of in-company management development and Liam Connellan, small business.

The small business unit was intended to be home to the advisory service of the Irish National Productivity Council (INPC). Officially, the IMI and the INPC had "a close working relationship". In reality, it was tense and competitive.[3] The strains are apparent in a February 1968 IMI council minute about the proposed transfer of the INPC's advisory service to the IMI. Council member Jim Doolan of UCD, critical of the IMI's handling of the issue, suggested that "a solution might be reached more readily if the Institute did not take a rigid institutional position in future discussions". Two months later, it was settled that the service would come to the IMI, but in January 1969, the executive committee decided that "because of the pressing needs for accommodation for the Institute's own staff, accommodation for the INPC advisory service cannot be offered at this stage". The Institute proceeded without it.

Recruitment of support personnel was stepped up. The number of managers attending courses quadrupled to 2,600 in the five years to 1967. Staff numbers grew from ten to thirty.

The 1960s were particularly tough for retailers. The pace of change was so rapid throughout the distributive chain that the INPC published a monthly digest of articles on developments in the industry from over 120 European and US distribution journals. Martin Rafferty was solely responsible for distribution and finance. In the early 1960s, with the establishment in Ireland of the first of the supermarket chains, the 40,000 retailers began to take notice that the self-service revolution had arrived on their own turf. Suddenly, there was a surge in demand for information. Chambers of commerce and retail associations clamoured for Rafferty's time, but always with the proviso that he should avoid Tuesday nights when *The Fugitive* was on TV — the retail revolution could wait for Wednesday!

One winter, he travelled to every town in Ireland with a population of over 5,000 to warn retailers that their world was about to change. The reaction in the packed halls varied — mainly disbelief, but there could be anger too. One evening early in 1966, an American retailing guru, Walter Channing, accompanied him to a night meeting in a north Cork town. Channing told retailers that

---

[3] See Chapter Ten.

they would face competition like they never saw before, once the supermarkets hit the town. An elderly trader, stoked with militant fervour by that year's jubilee of the 1916 Rising, rose and told the bemused American:

> Fifty years ago, we drove the foreigners from these shores.
> If they think they can come back now and take over our shops — you can tell them we'll drive them out again!

Demand for courses surged as most retailers realised that, to survive, they had to change. In the spring of 1966, because of the numbers of retailers and their geographic spread, a special unit was formed to look after the sector. After a vain external search, Rafferty was persuaded to take it on himself. Two new specialists in retailing, Denis Murphy and Michael Kehoe, were added to the unit. Diarmuid Moore, an accountant, took over Rafferty's finance portfolio. Five years later, Michael Kehoe would follow the Rafferty trail to prepare surviving retailers for another change — this time for the D-Day of decimalisation, 15 February 1971, a date sensibly chosen by the authorities because it normally had the fewest number of cash transactions in the retailing year.

The IMI filled out its new structure in 1968 with more appointments. Frank Cunnane, an experienced management consultant, became senior specialist in production; Tony Moynihan, the IMI's first computer expert, was named senior specialist in data processing and operations research. Liam Gorman was the first to be appointed to a purely research role. He had worked in the Tavistock Institute of Human Relations in London, one of a handful of organisations specialising in the application of behavioural science solutions to problems of organisations. He had moved back to Dublin to work in an educational research centre attached to St Patrick's teacher training college in Dublin. While there, he designed a verbal reasoning test to help measure the ability level of students against national norms. Dermot Egan invited him to join the in-company team as a research psychologist. At a council meeting, the management consultant and academic, Dr Bill Murray, questioned the appointment of a psychologist. Was the Institute becoming academic? He was assured that Gorman's role would be entirely practical: to examine how organisations could be made more effective and to help the Institute develop training methods appropriate to that end.

The last of the new quartet, Phil Clarke, was also deployed to Egan's unit. As a graduate, Clarke became involved in the 1950s in active republicanism. He was arrested and imprisoned in Armagh. While there, he and a fellow republican prisoner were nominated as candidates in the North's 1956 Westminster elections. They were both elected but their admission was denied in the grounds that "a convicted felon serving over 12 months imprisonment is a disqualified person". After his release, Clarke cut his links with republicanism and taught in the College of Commerce in Rathmines until joining the IMI in 1968.

As the 1960s boom continued, demand for top executives became acute. State of the art as they were, the IMI's senior specialists were targets for attractive top management offers. But experienced management trainers were even scarcer than good managers. The Institute had a problem: it could not afford to match the salaries being offered by business to its key people. By and large, the specialists did not want to leave: they were experiencing immense job satisfaction as a team of pioneers, creating an organisation of some importance, involved in national policy development and acquiring privileged insights into a range of businesses across the industrial spectrum. Still, something had to be done to help address the widening remuneration gap with their peers in industry — without adding to costs. The executive committee agreed to permit the senior specialists to top-up their IMI earnings with consultancy assignments and/or directorships of limited term. The executive committee maintained a tight grip on this concession. But, despite such benefits, before the 1960s were over, two of the Four Horsemen had left: Martin Rafferty to build a career in banking, industry and pharmaceuticals, serving also on many state boards; Eamonn McDermott to become marketing adviser to multinational corporations until his untimely death in 1989 at the age of 57.

Throughout that period of change, the IMI maintained and expanded its international links. The benefits accrued in enhanced teaching material and methods and the creation of a coterie of visiting staff from business schools, universities and consultancies. There were also interesting collaborations in research.

From its foundation, the IMI had looked to the US schools as its model for the teaching of management. The content of the earliest courses owed much to Peter Drucker, whose *Practice of Management*[4] was, as a result, to be found on many managers' bookshelves. When, in February 1969, the IMI announced that it had invited the great Drucker to Dublin, the demand for tickets was overwhelming. This was the first of a series of IMI/Esso Foundation Lectures, funded by the company to mark the retirement from the Institute's presidency in 1967 of Tom Laurie, former head of Esso in Ireland.

The largest venue available for the Drucker lecture was the concert hall of the Royal Dublin Society. Even that could scarcely contain the crowd of 1,200 that turned up. Such was its success that the IMI acquired a training film, *The Effective Executive*, based on the lecture. This formed the basis for discussion at *Evening with Drucker* meetings in every region of Ireland for an entire year. Almost twenty years later, Drucker was invited back to be conferred with Life Fellowship of the Institute. He asked to be driven around the Wicklow hills. His guide, the IMI's then director-general, Brian Patterson, was rewarded with what he describes as an unforgettable day, the venerable Drucker bounding from the car to walk in the heather, marvelling at everything he saw, and, in between, freely philosophising on management and on life in general.

But back to research. Professionals in personal development have always been fascinated by why it is that some individuals perform well above the norm. An interesting profile of the successful Irish manager of the 1960s emerged through a collaboration in 1966 between the Institute and the University of California, Berkeley. For over ten years, Berkeley's Institute of Personality Assessment and Research had conducted studies into the characteristics of individuals who had made exceptional contributions in science, engineering, architecture and the arts. With the help of funding from the Human Sciences Committee of the INPC, Dermot Egan arranged with Frank Barron, a leading psychologist at Berkeley, to conduct, jointly with the IMI, a similar study into the characteristics of successful businessmen in Ireland.

Thirty-seven top managers, chosen for leadership capability, allowed themselves to be studied by American psychologists, as-

---

[4] Drucker, P. (1955), *Practice of Management*, Heinemann, London.

sisted by senior IMI people. They covered a range of sectors — air transport, shipping, banking, construction, manufacturing, large-scale merchandising, agribusiness, food, drink, tobacco and the public sector. All were male; average age, 44. Family backgrounds showed a pattern of "rather strict" mother to whom the boy felt closest and with whom he had little discord. The father was generally described as energetic, decisive, somewhat distant and commonly preoccupied with business or professional matters rather than with family activities. As a sign of the times, the most strongly tabooed activities in adolescence were "staying out late", "missing church on Sundays" and "fighting with brothers and sisters". Following a battery of tests and interviews, the authors of the study[5] concluded as follows:

> This group of Irish managers are impressively stable, intelligent and socially effective. They give the impression of being content with their lot, though open to innovation; however, as a group they would not like to be original at the expense of being controversial. The more original among them have much more of an edge to their personalities. They see themselves, and are seen by others, as daring, tough, cynical, assertive, power-oriented, and unconcerned about their "popularity" or their obedience to conventional demands. An impression verging on wilfulness and acerbity is created by them at times, though not in petty ways; they have a strong sense of destiny, independence of judgement, cognitive flexibility and inquiringness [sic]. There is an odd combination of masculinity and sense of the poetic about them. Their vision is of conquest, mastery, personal dominance, command.

Regrettably, it was not possible to compare the Irish group with their peers abroad because of a lack of similar studies elsewhere.

In its work, the Institute had to relate not only to leaders, but to the entire management spectrum across all disciplines and all levels of hierarchy. Supervisors, or frontline managers as they are more

---

[5] Egan, Dermot and Barron, Frank (1968), "Leaders and Innovators in Irish Management", *Journal of Management Studies*, UK, Vol. 5, No. 5.

usually termed today, have been described as the "clutch" of the industrial machine — the management layer that ensures that the sum of the company's combined managerial thrust is translated into optimum product on the shop floor or at the point of delivery. Effective businesses pay a lot of attention to the quality of the firstline team.

In the 1970s, following meetings with the Industrial Training Authority, AnCO[6] (An Chomairle Oiliúna), ambitious targets were set for supervisory training. Bert Walls, who transferred from in-company to lead the enhanced programme, pioneered many developments in supervisory training, including the *Bert Walls Supervisory Training Programme*, a programmed learning package designed to help training managers in industry conduct their own five-day basic supervisory training programme in-company. The package, complete with course notes and audio-visual aids, included a game module where teams from the group competed against each other in a quiz on the contents of the package. It also prompted trainers on how to link the course content with company goals. The British Institute of Management decided to sponsor the package in the UK, following positive reaction from member companies, such as that of the training manager of Shell/BP in London: "Many of the supervisors said it was the best and most relevant training they had undergone."

The general supervisory training programme mainly consisted of a range of three-day courses and a two-year certificate programme. Before 1972, the certificate course was run by the Irish Institute of Supervisory Management (IISM) under licence from the British institute. Part of it was not very relevant to Irish supervisors, based as it was on UK law and practices. At the request of the IISM, the IMI took it over and, for a while, ran the course "in association with the IISM". Formally, the IISM was the promoting body but it had little clout in marketing the course. Eventually, in 1972, its president, Tom Hand, and his colleagues, all of them supervisors in well-known companies, asked the IMI to take them over. The executive committee did so by resolution:

---

[6] See Chapter Fourteen.

> It was noted that the Irish Institute of Supervisory Management proposed to wind up and transfer their activities and assets to the Irish Management Institute. It was agreed to take over the assets and activities and to admit, on application, to individual membership of the institute the twelve members of the council of the IISM, ex officio.

The Certificate in Supervisory Management (CISM) needed a thorough redesign to meet the needs of Irish supervisors. An examination board reviewed the content, oversaw standards and supervised the conduct of the course. For many years, the board was chaired by Vincent Farrington, principal of the College of Commerce, Rathmines; it included former officers of the IISM, representatives of AnCO, the Department of Education and others nominated by the IMI. Board membership was no sinecure: a curriculum had to be devised, manuals had to be written. Among the contributors were two of the supervisors who helped found the IISM, Tom Hand of CIE and Patrick Smyth of Gateaux. AnCO seconded Martin Hickey and Joe McAuley to the project. Between them, they compiled seven manuals that formed the basic content of the two-year part-time course. The board also had the advice of Micheál Ó Súilleabháin, a senior inspector of the Department of Education.

Because of the geographic spread of applicants, the course was made available in approved centres throughout the country from Letterkenny to Tralee, in technical colleges (later RTCs) or local post-primary colleges. The IMI, guided by the examination board, provided syllabus and teaching material and marked papers, but did not itself teach the course. When Ray Leonard took charge of supervisory training in 1974, the certificate course had 85 students; 20 years later, when he handed it over to Paul Donovan, numbers had grown to over a thousand.

The CISM was the first "academic" course run by the IMI and its first incursion into distance, or open, learning. The certificate was well regarded by industry; it was an accolade of academic achievement valued by supervisors, not least those who, before the days when third-level education became more accessible, had to leave formal education in their mid-teens. The programme was strongly supported by business. Some, like Aer Lingus with large numbers of supervisors, set up their own training centres with qualified teachers; Irish Ropes ran the course in the evenings, in-house, staffed by teachers from nearby schools. The course, continually developed and upgraded, now under the direction of the IMI's Robert Galavan, is held in 30 centres. It is recognised as the prime qualification in supervisory management in Ireland.

CHAPTER TEN

TERRITORIAL IMPERATIVE

Distrust and suspicion tended to infect the relationship be-tween the IMI and some of its contemporary agents of change, especially if they appeared to encroach on what the IMI considered its territory. The Irish National Productivity Committee (later, Council) was a case in point. The INPC had a particularly difficult gestation. The European Productivity Agency (EPA), an adjunct of the OEEC, wanted to establish joint employer/labour productivity committees in all its member states. But a move to set up an Irish committee in 1957 had failed: the FUE, an essential con-stituent, would have nothing to do with it. The lack of a productivity centre in Ireland, "unlike the majority of OEEC countries", was noted in T.K. Whitaker's 1958 paper, *Economic Development*. Sean Lemass asked the IMI to intervene: if a productivity centre was not possible, would it look into the formation instead of a national committee "concerning human sciences and their application in industry"? It had to include unions and employers.

The IMI had several meetings with relevant organisations and, in 1958, produced a formula that met FUE objections about working with the unions. The joint body would confine itself to research into human problems arising from the introduction of new technology: it would look at labour/management relations, the attitude of workers to technological change and the placing of workers in jobs which fitted their personal capabilities. Lemass decided to go with the new committee.

The compromise was spotted by an *Irish Times* leader writer; an editorial criticised the minister for taking a soft option:

It is regrettable that the minister now seems to have defi-
nitely turned his face against the setting up of a productivity council, one of whose functions would include all the
work of the proposed committee. This newspaper recently
pointed out that a productivity council, such as those
which operate in every country in Western Europe except
Ireland and Iceland, would make a substantial contribution to the raising of productivity standards and the improvement of relations between employer and worker.
The trades unions, the Management Institute, several
semi-state bodies and the Federation of Manufacturers
went so far, nearly two years ago, as to draft a constitution
which was then sent to the minister. For reasons unstated,
the Federated Union of Employers did not sign the proposals and Mr Lemass is understood to have informed the
Provisional United Trade Union Organisation[1] that he does
not favour the establishment of a productivity council.
How, then, can he justify the formation of another useless
committee in the shape of his present proposal? . . . It is
difficult to understand what reasons the minister and the
FUE can have for delaying the formation of such a council;
and why, if they have sound cause, they have not shown it
to the public.

Nevertheless, a new body known as the National Joint Committee
for the Human Sciences and their Application in Industry was set
up in October 1958. It comprised FII, FUE, IMI, various unions and
educational bodies. The chairman was Fr E.F. O'Doherty, Professor of Logic and Psychology, UCD; the secretary was Noel McMahon of the Department of Industry and Commerce. As *The Irish
Times* predicted, it did not have the funds to do anything useful.
Soon, pressure resumed for the establishment of a national productivity committee. Again, Lemass asked the IMI to try to find a
consensus, this time successfully. At the first public session of the
new body in May 1959, Lemass acknowledged the Institute's role
in bringing it about.

Despite the part played by the IMI in the birth of the INPC, their
subsequent relationship was never easy. Initially, the IMI was glad

---

[1] Set up to facilitate the merger of the Irish Trade Union Congress and the
Congress of Irish Unions.

to use the INPC's links with the EPA to ensure a supply of expert lecturers in management.

Denis Hegarty, general manager of the Dublin Port and Docks Board and a founder member of the IMI, was an INPC enthusiast. It was probably he who had prompted Lemass to get the IMI to sort out the trouble with the FUE. Hegarty himself acted as go-between with the different interests — unions, employers and educationalists, negotiating their co-operation. He sought and got nomination to one of the two IMI places on the INPC council. The other place went to the director, Paul Quigley and subsequently to Ivor Kenny.

As the INPC developed muscle, the IMI saw dangers of overlap. When the INPC applied for an increase in its grant for courses and information services in October 1964, J.F. Dempsey wrote to the INPC chairman, trade unionist Ruairi Roberts, expressing concern that the proposed programme could infringe IMI territory, particularly its training business:

> The Institute is concerned that the INPC should consider providing out of state funds a service which in large measure would duplicate the Institute's service and which would make it increasingly difficult to secure the financial commitment of industry.

Dempsey also objected to the INPC's proposed information service: it would clash directly with the member-funded service of the IMI. He suggested a working group to look at the issue. Because the INPC's proposals were to be entirely financed from public funds, he copied the letter to the Department of Industry and Commerce.

Roberts refuted the Institute's charges:

> Only on rare occasions and where there is some good reason are any of our courses or seminars directed to management only or to labour only. Generally these activities are directed to joint management/labour audiences.

The INPC's move into courses and information services was, in Ivor Kenny's view, an indication of a strategy to manoeuvre the INPC closer to the IMI's core market. Jerry Dempsey and other senior members of the Institute agreed with this assessment. But Denis Hegarty did not at all share this view. He had involved himself deeply in the INPC, in its council and committees, frequently representing it at international productivity meetings in Paris and elsewhere. Aware of the tensions between the director and Hegarty, the executive committee decided that the more appropriate representation on the INPC council would be director and chairman, *ex officio*. Dempsey wrote to Hegarty to tell him of the decision. In a lengthy reply, Hegarty put the blame for the deteriorating relationship between the two bodies entirely at the door of the IMI and its director:

> The IMI in its early stages established a good relationship with other bodies and stimulated their activities to the great benefit of the country. It played a major role in the establishment of the INPC and had great prestige in that organisation. In recent years, however, it has given the impression of being defensive and touchy and interested in maintaining its position by limiting the work of other bodies, when it should, in fact, have no difficulty in doing so by the quality of its own work. I think this situation has arisen largely because of the misconception that the IMI can be run like a business undertaking. Whereas it is, in fact, an institute with the latter's much more complex relations with other bodies.
>
> I believe the [executive] committee has not been in sufficiently close touch with the matter and has allowed itself to be influenced by the exaggerated fears of the director and by the, perhaps, unconscious promotion of a "staff" policy, which is not in the best interest of the country, or indeed of the institute.
>
> I have experienced no conflict of loyalty as between these two bodies, though I have found some wry humour in being considered by the IMI as being too pro-INPC, and by the INPC as being too pro-IMI, when I was merely trying to be pro-country.

He concluded, with apparent resignation, that he would "be glad to be free from an embarrassing situation". However, by the time Dempsey advised council of the decision at its meeting in January 1965, Hegarty's mood had changed. The meeting turned into one of the most difficult in the Institute's history. Hegarty was furious.

He considered the INPC his "baby". He saw the change as cutting him off from an organisation he helped to establish and in which he had been intimately involved. He was supported by one of the IMI's founders, T.P. Hogan. Referring to the reasons put forward for the change in representation, Hogan wondered if the IMI considered itself such a superior body to the INPC "that it must have its chairman watching things". Was there a suggestion that the IMI was not properly represented on the INPC? If the director was on the INPC council, how could the Institute be "underprivileged in getting its views across?"

Dempsey, defending the decision, said that, next to the director, the chairman was most conversant with the business of the Institute. Hegarty was not having this. He accepted the right of the Institute to decide who should represent it, but questioned the motivation for the change. He told council that there was a strong feeling in the INPC that the Institute was being less than cooperative. In an unusual departure from the protocol of council meetings, he laid the blame for this squarely on his fellow representative, the director, Ivor Kenny. He had been "troubled by the policy and attitude the director adopted to the INPC" and he felt that it was his, Kenny's, "mistaken view" that had influenced the executive committee to make this change.

Jerry Dempsey intervened to say the director, as the Institute's chief executive officer, had the full support of the executive committee, to which he was accountable. There was a sharp exchange, with Hegarty telling Dempsey that his primary duty was to the council and Dempsey retorting: "I do not care to be reminded of my position."

The point at issue for Dempsey was whether the executive committee had acted within its power in deciding on the change:

> The executive committee have taken the decision to change the representation. We think we are performing our function properly.

By now, other members were anxious to defuse the situation. No one challenged the executive committee's right to decide but they wanted to ensure fair play for Hegarty. The previous chairman, A.H. Masser, assured Dempsey:

The actual representation is a matter for the executive
committee. In this case I do think that we should give Mr
Hegarty full freedom to talk on the matter of the change.

Hegarty referred to the operational changes being proposed by
the INPC and which the Institute found contentious. He said the
proposals that were before government were "in complete con-
formity with any plans the Institute may have" and that the INPC
had "adopted a principle that it would not undertake any work
which could be better done by a constituent body". He again
blamed the Institute for the unhealthy relationship which had developed and noted that the INPC differed from the IMI in one important respect: "In the INPC, the voluntary people are much more
in command of the situation."

When Hegarty complained that, though IMI personnel were
asked to address INPC functions, INPC officials had not been invited to "cross the IMI's threshold", Dempsey pointed out that the
joint working party formed to look into the differences between
the two bodies had met at the IMI. Masser latched on to that point,
proposing that the matter should rest until the working party had
reported.

The minute of that January meeting simply records that a working group was studying the Institute's relationship with the INPC
and that the council would consider its report at the next meeting.
It barely hints at the tension generated at the meeting:

> In the course of discussion reference was made to the ex-
> ecutive committee's decision in regard to nomination of a
> representative to the INPC and it was agreed that the
> executive committee had acted within its authority.

The working group referred to included Ivor Kenny and Brian
Whelan for the IMI with John Gannon, secretary, and Adrianus
Vermeulan,[2] consultant, for the INPC. It had met in November and
listed the issues for clarification. It met again the following month
and appeared to reach a measure of agreement. The INPC repre-

---

[2] Adrianus Vermeulan had been an economist with the European Productivity
Agency. When the OECD superseded the EPA he became a consultant to the
INPC and a major influence on its development.

sentatives undertook to draft a joint report. But that was before the IMI dropped Denis Hegarty. This and reports of the IMI council row in January incensed the INPC. When Gannon and Vermeulan's draft report arrived at the IMI on 19 January, it was rejected by return as representing "neither in tone nor in content the discussions of the working party". The Institute's "disappointment" with the "unacceptable" report was conveyed to Gannon, who told Kenny that he understood the IMI's disappointment, explaining disarmingly that this line had been taken because of a change of policy at the INPC since the last meeting. The working party went on to prepare a final paper that simply set out the issues between the two bodies, with an accompanying commentary from each organisation.

Both executive committees considered the paper in February. The new chairman of the INPC, J.C. Tonge, was, coincidentally, a council member of the IMI. He and his predecessor, Roberts, drafted a basis for an agreement between both organisations. Claude Tonge told the IMI council nine months later that the IMI and the INPC were "co-operating fruitfully" and the Institute's new chairman, Michael Rigby-Jones, informed council that the matter was now closed.

But relationships had been soured and for many years both bodies were, at best, wary of each other. There were exceptions. For example, in the mid-1960s, when Louden Ryan, chairman of NIEC, concluded that a lack of planning by small to medium-sized business was one of the causes of poor performance by the sector, he asked the IMI to produce a simple guide to planning. To make it more readable, it was decided to include a case study. Denis McGrane of the INPC's advisory service, which had accumulated a lot of data on how small businesses functioned, contributed a well-constructed case study to illustrate the planning approach.

The product of this model collaboration, a practical handbook, *Planning your Business*,[3] was distributed widely to smaller enterprises. It proved useful to its targeted market and its principles and examples have since been widely recycled. Incidentally, the book almost suffered a disaster — ironically, through a lapse in planning

---

[3] Irish Management Institute (1966), *Planning Your Business*, Stationery Office, Dublin.

by its editor! McGrane's case study was set in a fictional manufacturing company. The editor suggested that it would help if the company had a name. Of those names suggested, "Irish Pride Ltd." was considered the most fanciful — and, therefore, the safest. Final proofs had been checked and the production run was about to start when one of the authors was overtaken by a company van promoting a range of victuals and bearing the legend, *Irish Pride*. The copy was grabbed back from the rolling presses and the less imaginative "XYZ Ltd." substituted throughout.

In 1970, the INPC commissioned international consultants, Svein Dalen and Tony Hubert, to look at the organisation and report. They did so in June. The finding that most interested the IMI related to the advisory service.[4] The experts agreed with the IMI's long-held view that it should be taken out of the INPC because, in the words of the report, it was "too big for the totality" and would "hamper developments in other areas". Also, the confidential nature of its work made it inappropriate to have it report to a joint union/employer organisation. They did not rule on where the service should go, but suggested the IDA or the IMI as possible hosts. There followed months of inaction on the report. The Confederation of Irish Industry lost patience and withdrew from the body. The following April, the IMI's executive committee seemed to be headed in the same direction:

> Following a comprehensive discussion, during which the view was strongly expressed that it would be inappropriate for the Institute to be associated with an organisation which was becoming discredited and whose direction the Institute had no power to influence, it was decided that the director would report following the next meeting of the INPC.

In September, the INPC's executive bureau finally circulated its response to the report. It rejected the findings on the advisory service, incorporated some of the recommendations and proposed a restructuring of the organisation under the name "Irish Productivity Council" (IPC). Predictably, the IMI found the executive bureau's response unsatisfactory and told it so. By this time, a

---

[4] See page 91.

consensus was developing that, with the withdrawal of the CII and the disaffection of the IMI, the time had come to dismantle the multi-representational governing council in favour of a committee drawn solely from the Irish Congress of Trade Unions and the Federated Union of Employers. That proposal was carried by the centre's committee of management in September 1971, ending the IMI's unsatisfactory involvement in the governance of an organisation it had done so much to found.

With the advisory service issue finally out of the way, relations improved between the organisations, leading to sustained, fruitful co-operation between the advisory service and the IMI, in particular in support of the Institute's Business Development Programme. Subsequently, all IPC divisions were amalgamated into a broad management consultancy service. In the late 1990s, government funds were gradually withdrawn as the organisation became self-sufficient. It continues, under the joint mandate of IBEC and ICTU, to offer a service to Irish business.

And what of the original compromise organisation, the National Joint Committee for the Human Sciences and their Application in Industry? Although deprived of its *raison d'être* by the eventual arrival of the INPC, it tried to maintain a separate existence but it was without funds. In June 1960, after 18 frustrating months, Professor O'Doherty asked Noel McMahon to arrange for him to meet the new Minister for Industry and Commerce, Jack Lynch, to discuss funding. Although only a junior executive officer in the department, McMahon knew the prospect of funds was hopeless. But, dutifully, on the committee's behalf, he composed a pithy memo to the minister: how the committee had been set up by his predecessor, Sean Lemass, but how, because of lack of resources, it had had to limit its output to propaganda work; that it was without funds, personnel or facilities and, while there was "a considerable measure of understanding of the benefits to be derived from a study of the human problems of work", it "was not constituted or equipped . . . to make any progress towards achieving its ends".

McMahon copied the memo to his chairman, O'Doherty. The version that went to the minister, however, had an additional sentence from the young official:

On one or two previous occasions, when a similar proposal was made, I succeeded in diverting the committee
from seeking an interview with the minister on matters
which were, in my opinion, rather trivial; in this instance I
felt that I would not be justified in objecting to the course
proposed and I agreed to transmit their request.

Professor O'Doherty got his meeting with the minister. But that was
as far as it went. The resources were not forthcoming and the National Joint Committee for the Human Sciences and their Application in Industry was, not long thereafter, taken under the wing of
the INPC and continued to do research under the development
division of that body until the end of the 1970s, when it was dis-
solved.

CHAPTER ELEVEN

UISCE FÉ THALAMH

The Hegarty/INPC affair triggered a collateral incident that brought further turmoil to the normally serene council meetings. The chairmanship of council is the Institute's highest-ranking office — member-in-chief, as it were. It — and the vice-chairmanship — are decided by vote of the council. The term is two years. The move from vice-chairman to chairman is, in effect, automatic, so the main interest every two years is in the nomination for vice-chairman. Although the latter office is not specified in the articles of association, the Institute has had a vice-chairman since 1955. Every two years, the executive committee would propose to the council a vice-chairman who would succeed the chairman, without a vote, at the council meeting following the end of the incumbent's term.

From the end of Sir Charles Harvey's term to the mid-1960s, an informal pattern had developed, with the chairmanship alternating between private enterprise and semi-state bodies. An astute member, noticing this, also observed a coincidental alternation between Protestant private sector businessmen and Catholic semi-staters! That, indeed, was the case: T.F. Laurie (private/Protestant), D.A. Hegarty (public/Catholic), A.H. Masser (private/Protestant), J.F. Dempsey (public/Catholic), M. Rigby-Jones (private/Protestant).

In July 1965, Jerry Dempsey would be succeeded by his vice-chairman, Michael Rigby-Jones. The previous November, the executive committee, in choosing a successor to Rigby-Jones, reviewed a list of chief executives of member companies. Although the construction industry played a big role in the economy, it was only thinly represented in the IMI. The committee believed that a high Institute profile for a figure from that sector would help bring the industry more into the IMI's orbit and decided on Gunnar Larsen, chairman of Cement Ltd. Larsen, a member of a prominent Danish family in the shipbuilding, cement and air transport industries, had served as Minister for Public Works and Transport in the Danish cabinet during the war. Later, he came to Ireland as managing director of Cement Ltd.

He accepted the nomination. The rule said that he had to be a member of council before he could be appointed, so he was co-opted to the executive committee, which gave him *ex-officio* membership of council. He was now eligible for formal ratification at the July council meeting.

Unknown to Jerry Dempsey, a rump of disaffection had developed around Hegarty because of what supporters saw as his shabby treatment by the "establishment" during the INPC rumpus. They decided to challenge the executive committee's nomination in July with a nominee of their own.[1] But who? Hegarty was out of the question: he was currently vice-president, having been chairman in 1959–61. T.P. Hogan agreed to stand. He was an impressive choice: after all, he and Sir Charles Harvey, as chairmen of the groups that merged in 1952, had been co-founders of the Institute.

The bombshell burst on 24 April. A letter arrived addressed to the chairman, signed by the vice-president, Denis Hegarty:

> Dear Jerry,
>
> On behalf of the signatories, I enclose a statement of intention to put forward the name of T.P. Hogan for the office of Vice-Chairman at the forthcoming elections. We thought it best to advise you of this at the earliest possible time. He was one of the first, if not the first, as you know, to propose the establishment of the Irish Management Institute and he has himself an outstanding record in the field of management. We are convinced that the nomination will commend itself to the members of the Committee.

---

[1] It was later claimed that they were unaware of the executive committee's decision to nominate Larsen. This could well be so; because of the practice of keeping the nominee's name under wraps until the day of his appointment, the decision had not been noted in the minutes of the executive committee circulated to the council.

The statement was signed by 13 members of the council, about one-third of its elected strength. Apart from Hegarty, it included Trinity academics, G.A. Duncan and Amory Pakenham-Walsh, Claude Tonge, chairman of the INPC, Sean O'Ceallaigh, principal of the College of Commerce, and Frank Lemass, general manager of CIE, of which Hogan was a director and future chairman. Professor Liam O Buachalla of UCG was also on the list but later, when he realised that the nomination was controversial, he sent a contrite note to Dempsey:

> I am indeed very upset that I should have, in any way, infringed the traditional or established practice concerning the election of the chairman and vice-chairman of the Institute. Should I have done so, I will have done it unwittingly and express my regret. I should like, if possible, to cancel my signature to the document which seems to be the cause of the difficulty.

It was too late for that, however. Tommy Hogan had written to all members of council, including Gunnar Larsen — a taciturn, private man, who must have wondered what on earth he had let himself in for. Larsen copied the letter to Dempsey:

> Dear Mr Larsen,
>
> I have allowed my name to go forward for election to the position of Vice-Chairman of the IMI, at the request of a large group of council members, who have already proposed me in writing.
>
> I may say I did not seek this honour, but naturally I should be embarrassed if the proposals were unsuccessful and therefore I am asking you to vote "early and often" for me.

Now that Hogan had appealed directly to members of the council, there was consternation at the heart of the Institute's establishment. The chairman, J.F. Dempsey, wrote at once to all council members:

> In view of a recent development which is at variance with established practice concerning the election of Chairman and Vice-Chairman of the Institute, I feel obliged to convene a meeting of Council prior to the annual general

meeting in order that you may be fully informed in the matter.

The meeting will be held in 12 Leeson Park on Monday 17 May 1965 at 4.30 p.m.

I am anxious to have the fullest possible attendance at this very important meeting and I do hope you will find it possible to attend.

Hogan replied politely but said that, as he had already appointments in England on this date, it would be impossible for him to attend. His CIE colleague and co-signatory of the nomination, Frank Lemass, also apologised for inability to attend. But Todd Andrews, sensing a fight, said in a brief note to the chairman: "Of course I will be along. Am I right in assuming that there is '*uisce fé talamh*' [sic] flowing?" The *uisce fé thalamh*[2] was, in fact, in full spate. The president, Tom Laurie, told Dempsey that, when asking for his support, Hogan used the term "agreed to run for office".

> In reply I have expressed surprise at his choice of words which would seem to presuppose an election and I have pointed out that the rule is for the Executive Committee to propose its Honorary Officers which is invariably accepted and adopted by the Council. Therefore if he happens to be the selection of the Executive Committee there is no need to appeal for support. . . . In other words if the procedure is in accordance with established custom he is "home and dry".
>
> I trust that T.P.H. will be able to understand and appreciate the purpose of my writing!!

Early in May, Dempsey set up a meeting with Hogan to discuss the situation that had arisen and to see if a dogfight over the vice-chairmanship could be avoided. No note survives of Dempsey's version of what transpired, but it appears that there was no progress. Subsequently, Hogan wrote at length to Dempsey:

---

[2] Intrigue; literally, "underground water".

Monkstown Castle,
Monkstown, Co. Dublin.

14th May 1965

Dear Jerry,

Recently you were good enough to invite me to meet you at your office in connection with my nomination by a number of members of the Council for the office of Vice-Chairman of the Institute. You explained that, as you considered that my nomination constituted a departure from previous procedure for this appointment, you had decided to call a meeting of the Council on the 17th inst. to ask them to consider the matter. I then indicated that unfortunately I was already irrevocably committed to fulfil a vital business engagement in London on that date and would be unable to attend the meeting.

The Memorandum and Articles of Association of the Institute were drawn up most carefully to ensure that it would be widely representative and that democratic processes would operate in its control and policies. One of the first responsibilities of the Council must be to safeguard the spirit as well as the letter of that Constitution. The very fact, therefore, that a procedure which is not provided for in the Constitution seems to be regarded by some as now established by practice in itself calls for Council intervention to make the actual position clear beyond the possibility of future doubt. From this point of view alone a direct nomination for Vice-Chairman by Council members is highly desirable.

I think it proper, however, that I should set out for the information of the Council the position as I see it, and I should be glad if you would have this letter read to them at that meeting.

The Institute, as you know, was formed as a result of the initiative of two groups — one, a group of managers of which I was Chairman, and the other a group in association with the Department of Industry & Commerce. The two groups had the good sense to amalgamate and Sir Charles Harvey was appointed Chairman and I was appointed Vice-Chairman of the provisional committee established to set up the Institute. This somewhat formidable task was successfully accomplished and with the establishment of the Institute I became a member of the Council and I have continued as such ever since.

I have never, at any time, then or now, sought the office of Chairman of the Institute, but when I was informed recently that a representative group of Council members desired to put my name forward for the office of Vice-Chairman with a view to my subsequent appointment as Chairman, I consented, with full knowledge of the position in regard to procedure and after the most careful consideration of the matter.

My proposers and I were fully aware that the very much larger and more representative Executive Committee of previous years had been permitted to suggest to the Council a name for Vice-Chairman. The Committee had adopted this procedure to ensure that a carefully considered nomination would be put before the new Council. At all times, however, it remained possible for any Council member or group of Council members to put forward names additional to that proposed by the outgoing Committee and they, and their nominee, had to accept this risk, as the decision as to who should be appointed remained with the Council as a whole.

My proposers, numbering one-third of the Council, decided to advise you of my nomination as early as possible, (in fact in April, more then two months before the election due to be held in July) so that the Executive Committee would be aware that no further nomination was required from them unless, of course, they wished to put forward a candidate in opposition to me at the Council meeting following the A.G.M. My proposers regarded this latter event as unlikely, as they confidently hoped that the members of the Committee would also recommend my nomination.

They were supported in this by the fact that no indication had appeared in the Committee's Minutes of any action taken by the Committee in the matter of a nomination.

If, however, the Committee subsequently decided to put forward another name I was personally quite satisfied that any nomination should go before the Council for their election. If they thought fit that I should fill the office, I would do so to the best of my ability. If they decided otherwise I would accept the Council's judgment without question and continue to serve the Institute in whatever capacity might be open to me.

The position, as you have put it to me, however, raises a much more serious question for consideration by the Council on the 17th instant. It is no longer a question as to whether I, or any other person, should be elected to office for the next few years. The issue, which you have raised, is a constitutional one of fundamental importance to the whole future of the Institute; it is this — does the fact that the Council has permitted the much larger and more representative [Executive] Committee of previous years to recommend a person for election to office preclude the Council from considering any other nomination at any time if they decide that the circumstances warrant it? If that is so, it means that the Council has abandoned the only effective authority it possesses, i.e. the right to elect its executive, and Council members will indeed become, as some members suggested at a recent meeting, "rubber stamps". It would moreover mean that in practice small groups, and particularly the one or two influential individuals to be found on most committees, would in effect have the right to select the Chairman and Vice-Chairman and so perpetuate their control and their policies.

However good the intention may be, nothing could be more calculated to deny to the Institute the inspiration, renewal and refreshment so necessary to its growth. And nothing could do more to undermine its claim to be widely and effectively representative of Irish management.

Every person on the Council, without any exception, is a member because he holds high and responsible office in his own organisation. It is, in fact, doubtful if there is in Ireland a body with comparable membership. It should be open to any member of the Council to aspire to office and to achieve it if he has the support of his fellows and it is healthy that such a choice should be made openly and not secretly and that justice should not only be done, but should be seen to be done.

I have little sympathy with the view, which I understand has been expressed, that such competition would split the Institute. The Institute is now well established and should be able to proceed by the ordinary democratic process. We would certainly be unworthy to call ourselves managers if we had not the maturity to operate such a process, accept the consequences and still continue to serve the Institute loyally.

Looking back on our conversation I feel that there may be an impression that I allowed myself to be unduly influenced in this matter. It if exists, such an impression would be very far from the truth. In agreeing to let my name go forward I acted with deliberation and with full knowledge of the facts. The constitutional question which you now raise makes my decision irrevocable, irrespective of any personal inconvenience or disadvantage it may involve for me, in that I am convinced that the good of the Institute demands of the Council active participation in matters of policy and not merely nominal support.

I propose, therefore, to allow my name to go forward on the 5th July 1965, for election. I will accept loyally on that day the decision of the Council whatever it may be and will continue to serve the Institute in whatever capacity may then be open to me.

The fact that I may differ from the Executive Committee in my view of its role in this matter does not diminish in any way my admiration for the good work they have done for the Institute in so many other directions.

Yours sincerely,

T.P. Hogan.

Hogan copied the letter to the signatories on the document of support. But he also sent a copy to Basil Booth, managing director of APV-Desco, the prominent stainless steel fabricators, with a handwritten note, which belied the measured objectivity of the letter: "This long document is meant to baffle the brains of the Establishment boys!" Booth told Dempsey about the note but not until after the council meeting.

Hogan referred in his letter to "the larger and more representative executive committee of previous years". The large committee of 18 members had become ineffective and attendance levels had fallen. This led to the emergence of an "officer board" that took most of the decisions, although it had no constitutional basis. To address the problem, the executive committee was reduced to eight members. The smaller committee was welcomed by the council and approved at an AGM. At the time of the controversy, the committee which had chosen Larsen consisted of the chairman, Dempsey, the vice-chairman, Rigby-Jones, John H. Donovan of Esso, John Leydon, then chairman of the Insurance Corporation of Ireland, Michael MacCormac, Ian McCallum of the Irish Refining Company, W.F. Roe of the ESB and J.S. Turpin of Guinness.

There is no evidence to support Hogan's contention that "one or two influential individuals" had "in effect the right to select the Chairman and Vice-Chairman and so perpetuate their control and their policies". Nevertheless, a less coy approach to the drafting of executive committee minutes — which were circulated to the council — would have helped the cause of openness and would have dampened suspicions of cronyism harboured by Hogan and at least some of his supporters.

The council room was packed for the special meeting in May. Thirty-seven of the 43 members attended. The minutes are brief and, unlike the record of other meetings which usually were quite discursive, they are silent on the to and fro of the exchanges. They consist of four cold paragraphs:

> The chairman referred to the circumstances in which he felt obliged to call this special meeting of council.
>
> A letter from Mr T.P. Hogan (council member) dated 14 May 1965 was read by the chairman and circulated to members present. A letter from Mr W. Dresser (council member) was also read.[3]

---

[3] Dresser, a retired Guinness engineer, wanted the meeting to know that he wished to add his support to Hogan's nomination.

The action of the executive in selecting a candidate to be recommended to council for the position of vice-chairman was held to be in accordance with established procedure and was duly endorsed.

In view of the situation arising from the action of a number of council members in proposing a candidate for the office of vice-chairman the executive was requested to give consideration to making a recommendation to appoint a second vice-chairman.

The chairman, Dempsey, personally drafted the minute. Writing to Desmond Goodbody after the meeting, his anger with Hogan was still showing:

I, and I know I am speaking also for the members of the executive committee, very much regret the recent development and we feel, and believe this feeling is shared by the majority of members of the council, that the situation which caused me to convene the special meeting of council was not brought about by any action of the executive committee.

Basil Booth, in his letter to Jerry Dempsey about Hogan's "baffle the brains of the establishment" note, said:

What troubles me is that when Mr Hogan telephoned me first it was to say that he had been nominated for the position of vice-chairman, and in my innocence I assumed that this nomination was from the Executive. On this understanding I assured him of my support.

I understand that the council has empowered the executive to decide to recommend the appointment of a single vice-chairman or two. It is my view that, if the executive were to adopt the second alternative under the circumstances, it would be weakening its authority to select and would prove once and for all that string-pulling behind the scenes could be successful.

Jerry Dempsey's reply to Booth was frank. It pulls no punches about the whole matter and who was behind it:

I must say Tommy Hogan's note to you . . . gave me quite a jolt. To me it is quite incomprehensible why he should be taking up such an attitude.

Your intervention at the recent meeting was both timely and helpful, particularly to the "chair". I need hardly tell you that I found my position as chairman both difficult and embarrassing.

I am satisfied that Mr. Hegarty in particular knew the procedure better than anyone else, and it is quite clear from the correspondence that he was the co-ordinator of the group — if not in fact the instigator — who were called on to support the candidature of Tommy Hogan. What particularly shocked me was that he who knew the procedure so well should have chosen to avoid coming to see me in the first instance to tell me that a number of people had a man in mind and ask the Executive to consider him. However, he — Denis Hegarty — chose to do it differently and after he sent his letter to me he and Tommy Hogan then set about a canvassing and lobbying campaign which had many disgusting features. All in all, it was a deplorable performance.

When I meet the Executive Committee next Monday I will certainly bear in mind what you say in regard to the question of the appointment of a second vice-chairman.

All of this happened when Jerry Dempsey was coming to the end of what had been a fruitful and satisfying two-year term, a period of rapid expansion in the work of the Institute. Training activity had greatly increased; the Institute had, for the first time, secured government subvention; it had also acquired new premises. He had addressed the world conference of the International Council for Scientific Management, in New York, of which the *Sunday Independent* said:

Important names in the commercial aviation world packed the session addressed by Mr Dempsey to hear at first hand how Irish International Airlines took on the giants of the Atlantic run and achieved the highest load factor in this keenly competitive area.

He had also presented a paper to the International Academy of Management of which he had been elected a Fellow.

The outpouring of his frustration in that letter to Basil Booth was quite out of character and shows how wounded he was by the events of those few weeks. It has to be said, of course, that Hegarty must have felt equally hurt by the lack of consultation by the executive committee — under Jerry Dempsey's chairmanship — before deposing him from the council of the INPC.

Tommy Hogan, normally happy to take a back seat in these affairs, was another victim of this uncharacteristically acrimonious chapter in the Institute's young life. Given his key role in founding the IMI, it is surprising that he had not been offered the chair much earlier. As suggested at the council meeting, the executive committee duly proposed him to the council for appointment as a second vice-chairman. That compromise meant that Rigby-Jones would be succeeded as chairman by Gunnar Larsen, in 1965. Hogan was to succeed Larsen in 1967.

This was to be ratified at the July council meeting, following the annual elections and the AGM. More problems intervened, however. T.P. Hogan, probably because of what was seen by some as his divisive role in the succession controversy, failed to get re-elected to council. That made him ineligible for appointment as a vice-chairman. But this did not help the healing process that most council members wished to see. Once again, the short cut to council membership was taken; Hogan was co-opted to the executive committee. But the trauma of the previous months had left a sour taste. Hogan was never comfortable on the executive committee and when a few months later he was appointed executive chairman of CIE, he told Dempsey's successor, Michael Rigby-Jones, that he was resigning his vice-chairmanship and, with it, membership of executive committee and council.

So, one of the founders drifted away from the Institute in unhappy circumstances. However, later in life he was a familiar figure at important IMI occasions and he appreciated its enhanced position in Irish economic life. Denis Hegarty was at the time of the controversy a vice-president of the Institute. He succeeded to the presidency, which is a position of honour without formal powers, in 1967. In turn, he was succeeded two years later by A.H. Masser and from then on his involvement with the Institute declined.

CHAPTER TWELVE

LIFTING THE LID

It was the fiftieth meeting of the council, November 1965. For Michael Rigby-Jones, it was his first as chairman. One of the youngest council members, boyish in appearance with a deceptively diffident manner, he faced some formidable campaigners who had been involved with the Institute for much longer than he. Some of them had been in the trenches during recent "troubles" arising from the dispute about the Institute's representation on the Irish National Productivity Committee and the unprecedented challenge to the system of selecting office holders in the Institute. There were still pockets of resentment about the balance of power between the council and the executive committee, some believing that it had tilted too much in favour of the latter. The director, Ivor Kenny, had provided the new chairman with a cautionary brief for the conduct of the first council meeting since the bother:

> The primary objective will be to act as chairman of council in an objective fashion, to get the emotional temperature down so that the issues are clarified, if necessary by summarising the main points that have been put by members. The impression must not be given that the chairman is acting as chairman of the executive committee vis-à-vis council or is partisan to any one faction in council.

Rigby-Jones was, in any case, anxious to get the controversies consigned to history and to get the council — and the Institute — refocused on its core mission — raising the standard of management in Ireland. He reminded members of council that, prior to recent distractions, the Institute had made remarkable progress.

Since the publication of the review committee's report three years earlier, the number of courses annually had multiplied from 34 to 125, participants from 648 to 2,600. Revenue had grown from £26,000 to £122,000 and staff from 10 to 30.

But even in the short period since that report, things had changed. A new urgency was driving the Government's economic policy. Though it was still unclear when Ireland and Britain would enter the EEC, Lemass was determined to keep the heat on industry; tariffs were being steadily reduced and the Anglo-Irish Free Trade Area Agreement was in place as a trial run for EEC membership.

The clamour for better management was coming from many quarters — principally from the CIO reports and the Second Programme for Economic Expansion, covering the period 1964 to 1970, which stated that well-trained managers were vital to the achievement of its targets. The new National Industrial Economic Council (NIEC), had recommended an enhanced role for the IMI. All were part of a complex process of adaptation to bring about fundamental change in the structure and efficiency of industry and distribution.

Rigby-Jones put it to the council that the IMI must participate prominently in this process. It was evident, from official concern about the management skills deficit and the substantial public funds coming to the Institute, that the Government saw the IMI as a key resource in its modernisation policy for industry. The Institute faced hard decisions. The review committee's vision of the Institute's future had been based on a consensus of the participating institutions, rather than objective scrutiny. It needed to be supported by rigorous research.

That research had already begun in the hands of Breffni Tomlin, a UCD economics graduate, who joined the Institute in 1962. His brief was to carry out a definitive study of the IMI's market: to establish the number of managers working in Ireland; to assess the current standard of their management and, thus, establish their training needs. This had never been attempted in relation to management anywhere so there was no model to turn to. From a study of American management literature, Tomlin compiled a list of management practices used routinely by effective US companies. This provided a basis for judging where Irish companies stood — what today would be called "best practice benchmarking". Clearly, the work could not cover all business. Instead, a statistically valid sample of about 150 firms in the transportable goods industry, each employing a minimum of 20 people, was chosen for intensive study. Distribution and services were excluded, which is why the resulting book was called *The Management of Irish Industry*.

All the firms in the sample were visited. Tomlin sought the following information from the chief executives:

- The number of managers in the firm and a profile of each in relation to function and level in the company, age, education, nationality and exposure to management training;

- The firm's likely recruitment needs arising from expansion and wastage;

- The interviewee's assessment of the company's training needs;

- The use by the firm of specific techniques of management;

- The interviewee's opinion on the facilities for management training, current or planned (e.g. the IMI, universities, VEC colleges, etc.), preferences and likely use of them.

The findings of the research were sobering. As expected, large companies were *au fait*, if not with best practice, at least with good practice. Small companies were, also predictably, more informal and seat-of-the-pants. But the chilling finding was the state of the middle-range companies — between 50 and 500 employees. These were few enough in number but they employed many people. Given their patchy management practices, it was clear to Tomlin that competition would put many of them out of business. They were neither small enough to hide nor big enough to ride out the storm. Some were long-established family firms, running to seed, relying on the business acumen of the incumbent generation, who often accepted the helm as a matter of family duty.

The CIO teams in their reports recorded a similar scene and reached equally dark conclusions that were, regrettably, largely borne out in time. Those that survived — like Smurfit and AET (now represented by Glen Dimplex) — did so because of the vision and energy of young mould-breaking entrepreneurs. Tomlin:

> Smurfit was good at what it did but nobody could envisage
> its transformation to a *Fortune 100* company, the biggest

packaging corporation in the world. When I visited AET in Dunleer in 1963 it was basically a manufacturing agent for General Electric. Over 500 people worked there. It was well managed, with sound practices in place. But without protection, it could not survive. When the moment came, Martin Naughton, who ran a production line, took his line and grew it into Glen Dimplex. Both successes demonstrate the capacity of entrepreneurs such as Michael Smurfit and Martin Naughton to defy constraints and to achieve extraordinary goals.

But for many companies, there were no such saviours and, sadly, in the new competitive age, the bulk of indigenous manufacturing firms found themselves with no future, except to turn out the lights.

On a brighter note, it is clear from the study that the semi-state companies were, by far, the most expertly run organisations, in terms of the number of professionals they employed, their structures and procedures. It could be argued that it was easier for them, as most were in the sheltered sector, often with monopoly status. Some would be considered closer to the bureaucratic model — and the world has long experience of running bureaucracies.

Nevertheless, they provided a good training ground for young managers. Some were process or extraction industries, in which engineering was the predominant discipline — and Ireland has always produced good engineers. One or two had strong international connections through which valuable know-how was imported: the ESB had enjoyed a close, formative relationship with the German giant, Siemens Schuckert. The international air transport industry was an early user of the most sophisticated management practices. Aer Lingus led the field here in that regard.

The universities and professional bodies provided some preparation for business management. Opportunities for such graduates were mainly in the public sector and in agribusiness and that was where they mainly went. The dairy industry — creameries and agri-factories — had a ready supply of young professionals from UCC's four-year degree course in dairy science, who brought with them a methodical, engineering mindset. Tomlin's research showed that Bord na Móna was staffed by engineers and by graduates of the much-maligned B.Comm,[1] which had begun as early as 1908; Aer Lingus by engineers and chartered accountants. The ESB was much the same. As the ability of general business to absorb such people was limited, the rest emigrated.

The research confirmed what the CIO had concluded: in industry after industry in Ireland in the 1960s, there were far too many small companies, few of them particularly good and, certainly, a mere handful with the potential to become internationally competitive. As for the IMI, says Tomlin: "In some cases, we were teaching entities that were not viable how to be better at being not viable."

Tomlin's other task was to compile a list of all the institutional facilities in Ireland for education and training for management. A questionnaire listed all management-related degree and non-degree courses and professional qualifications. Chief executives were asked what use the firms made of these facilities and what they thought of them. Not surprisingly, in light of the other results, most were unfamiliar with degrees and did not offer a comment, except to say that they would be unlikely to be in the market for graduates. Where graduates were employed, companies commented favourably on the quality of engineers and scientists, but would have liked a greater emphasis on management in the courses. IMI and other post-experience management courses were rated well. The four-year research brought further confirmation of structural disequilibrium in the indigenous manufacturing sector, and of a serious skills deficit in its managers.

The findings were compiled in a 420-page book, *The Management of Irish Industry*, published by the Institute on Thursday, 20 October 1966. The book was presented to George Colley TD, the Minister for Industry and Commerce, by the chairman, Michael Rigby-Jones, in the Shelbourne Hotel, in front of an impressive audience of leaders of the public service, universities, educational and professional institutions, business and the trade unions. Rigby-Jones, having made the point that "the initiative of managers is the engine which drives the economy", described the book as "a searching, factual look by managers at their jobs, their background and training and their standards of practice . . . the first undertaken anywhere in the world on a national scale". Colley called the re-

[1] See pages 9–10.

port timely. He said that the Government had been concerned about the management gap and would circulate a draft national programme on management education based on the findings of the report. He asked institutions concerned with the education and training of managers to send him their comments.

The book was launched shortly before Sean Lemass retired from public life. Two days before he left office in November 1966, he received a small group from the Institute. Michael Rigby-Jones presented him with a specially bound copy. He was clearly pleased that the Institute which he had helped to launch 14 years earlier had come so far and was helping to change the economic landscape. In February 1971, he came to Orwell Road one evening and chatted with the staff about his lifetime in politics, and his part in the evolution of Irish industrial policy. A few months later, on the 11 May 1971, Sean Lemass, the "shadow founder" of the IMI, died.

The consultative board had been reconstituted in late 1963. Colm Barnes took over as chairman from Michael Dargan. Barnes broadened the membership to include Queen's University and the Northern Ireland branch of the British Institute of Management. He also added David Marples from Cambridge, a frequent visitor and advisor to the Institute. The new board was quite large and met only when there was real business to be done. It went more or less into abeyance pending the completion of the Tomlin study. When Colley asked the Institute to submit proposals for a national policy on management, the task fell to the board.

When Colm Barnes took over, all the participating bodies had territory to defend. In the case of earlier boards, none, other than the IMI, was doing much management development. But by 1966 that had changed: every institution represented on the board had some vested interest. UCD and Trinity had produced their first MBA and MSA graduates. Sean O'Ceallaigh had a range of interesting options available in the Rathmines College of Commerce. Management-related studies were available in UCC and UCG. Tom Barrington had a range of programmes on public administration in the IPA. Nevertheless, the meetings were remarkably free of territorial manoeuvring. Breffni Tomlin, rapporteur to the board:

I must say there was no overt, or covert, fighting of corners. Everyone went in there intending to do the best they could. Nevertheless, it was just more complicated by then and it was much more difficult for the IMI to play the role of referee when it was the major player in the game.

The board finished its work in 1970. Along the way, it had refined its role. Although set up to advise the IMI on its education and research policy, when the report was published in April 1971, there was scarcely a word about the IMI. It addressed only the issue of expanding management education in the universities and the vocational education system. The main reason for the change of focus was that the IMI was forging ahead at its own rapid pace, alternatively creating and responding to ever-growing demand for training courses and in-company work. Unlike the universities and the vocational colleges, the Institute was not constrained by internal bureaucracy. It dealt directly with the Department of Industry and Commerce, with which it had established a sound relationship, successfully making a case for quite substantially increased State funding. In the four years during which the consultative board was deliberating, the number of managers attending the Institute grew from 2,100 to 5,750 per annum.

The universities and the vocational system saw in the board a mechanism for establishing a desirable consensus on how management education should develop at third level. This was broadly achieved: the universities would provide primary degrees as well as general and specialised postgraduate degrees and doctoral programmes; the vocational system would concentrate on certificate and diploma courses. For the universities, the most compelling proposal was that all management courses, undergraduate and graduate, as well as research should take place at a single university facility in Dublin. The recommendation was unequivocal:

> We believe that there is room at the present time in Ireland for only one facility which will offer a full range of specialised subjects for masters' and doctorate degrees and that this facility should be in Dublin, because a single postgraduate facility in Dublin is the only one with the potential enrolment to justify economically an activity of the necessary scale. The establishment of this facility will involve the

unification of both undergraduate and postgraduate work now carried out separately by TCD and UCD, because it seems that the only acceptable way to secure a single postgraduate facility is to join the undergraduate facilities.

The wording implied unanimity by the universities on this key point. After all, the group that proposed it included senior academics from the main universities: Professors J. Meenan and Michael MacCormac from UCD; Professor Peter Dempsey of UCC, Professor Labhrás Ó Nualláin, UCG and Amory Pakenham-Walsh, head of Trinity's Department of Business Studies. However, some time after the meeting that agreed the final draft, Pakenham-Walsh wrote to the chairman dissenting from the above recommendation. He "accepted with other members of the board, that Ireland could afford one facility only for the full range of advanced studies at an international standard of excellence". But he claimed that the board's deliberations had taken place in the context of a 1967 government proposal to merge the two Dublin colleges into a University of Dublin.[2] He said that, in the light of the 1970 decision of the NUI and Dublin University to go their separate ways, the board should have reconsidered its finding that the departments at TCD and UCD should be merged.

The board had more success with its recommendations on the vocational system, which had consistently demonstrated great flexibility in responding to need. The report traced a path that was indeed largely followed:

> In the vocational system, we should start to develop our facilities by aiming initially to have degrees in technological colleges only, a full range of diplomas and certificates in some regional colleges, with a more restricted range in the others, and certificates in vocational schools in towns outside commuting distance from a regional college but large enough to support a viable activity. This will allow us to provide facilities throughout the country on an economic basis and to expand them where demand justifies it.

The board stressed, in a rather convoluted way, the importance of the university and vocational systems proceeding together:

---

[2] See Chapter Thirteen.

> We recommend that we cater for the small groups of gifted people who can master the body of knowledge at its highest level and who will be needed for the most advanced level of practice and for the greater number of people who are required to function at a less advanced level. It would be futile on the one hand to produce only a small élite who had not got the well-trained support which would allow them to make their unique contribution, and damaging on the other hand to our most complex organisations, and consequently to all, not to provide for this small number a formation on the highest level.

> We hope it will not come to a choice between catering for a higher level and lower-level studies. If it should not prove possible to provide all the activities as widely as we suggest, we recommend that all should be provided on a more restricted basis rather than that some should be widely available and others not at all.

Looking to the future, the biggest lack the board perceived was the scarcity of teaching staff of the level of quality required. A proposal for staff development was worked out in great detail. The board considered this to be their most important proposal and "the first priority in the whole field of education for management, so much so that it is pointless to attempt an ordering of time-priorities until it is accepted".

While primarily concerned with future managers, the board also looked at ways of providing courses for current managers. It made suggestions as to how the qualification systems of management-associated professions could be related to the proposed national policy for management education. The report examined in some detail the nature and character of degrees and went some way towards defining the discrete, but complementary, roles of the universities and the colleges of commerce. It also suggested ways of facilitating transfer of staff from one to the other.

Apart from Pakenham-Walsh's caveat, which appeared as a footnote to the report, the consultative board's findings were unanimous. There was an overwhelming consensus that the institutions concerned needed to lift their game as far as management education was concerned.

CHAPTER THIRTEEN

MANAGEMENT EDUCATION AND THE UNIVERSITIES

Despite their early involvement in the Institute and hosting the occasional summer school, college heads in the 1950s — in particular professors of key departments, such as economics — showed little enthusiasm for management education. Participation by the eminent academics, George O'Brien (UCD) and George Duncan (TCD), in the founding group was due more to the "come-hither" of Sir Charles Harvey than to any enthusiasm on their part for management education. O'Brien was a director of Guinness which put him in Sir Charles's sphere of influence. Once O'Brien was on board, Duncan had little choice.

George O'Brien was one of the best-known academics of his generation. Michael MacCormac refers to him as "an economist of great quality, a most charming companion, a marvellous lecturer". He was on a number of government commissions. At the early meetings of Harvey's committee, whenever the discussion turned to universities, it was O'Brien who made the running. Duncan took a back seat and his attendance was patchy. MacCormac rates Duncan, too, a sound economist, but of rather rigid views who did not at all relate to business studies. O'Brien was supportive of the idea of a management institute but, like Duncan, he saw no role for the universities in training managers. It was not until MacCormac replaced him on the steering group that things changed in that regard at UCD.

Unlike his seniors in Earlsfort Terrace, MacCormac brought to the founding committee a real enthusiasm for management development. At the London School of Economics, he had participated in Britain's first diploma in business administration. It was, for him, an eye opener on what could be done at third level. He was later invited to lecture on UCD's B.Comm course. Although a graduate of the course in 1947, he did not hold it in high regard.

In the early 1950s, the B.Comm was the focus of much internal UCD politics. Nobody had time for it. Michael Tierney, when he became president at the end of the 1940s, aware of the poor reputation of the B.Comm among business people, wanted to abolish it altogether. In any case, he did not think that training people for commerce was the university's function. Following the retirement of the head of the department, Professor Barney Shields, in 1950, the chair was left vacant. When, as was referred to earlier, the degree was realigned towards economics, the commerce aspect in fact diminished.

MacCormac was keen to get his hands on the abandoned commerce element, reinstate it, and, based on his LSE experience, steer it in the direction of business studies. He had an uphill battle against the prejudice and indifference of successive deans. The faculty consisted of George O'Brien (professor and dean) and three statutory lecturers: John O'Donovan, James Meenan and Patrick Lynch, recently recruited from the Civil Service. MacCormac says:

> George O'Brien was at best passive on the issue. After George, Jim Meenan was dean of the faculty of commerce for 12 years, during which he did not want to know anything about the B.Comm. He would say, "You do what you like, don't bother me." Gerry O'Brien, a part-time professor of accountancy, had no use for business studies at all; didn't believe in it, one whit. Paddy Lynch on the other hand was supportive.

In the mid-1950s something occurred that changed MacCormac's status and gave him more arguing power. William Norton, Minister for Industry and Commerce in the coalition government, phoned him out of the blue — prompted, perhaps, by John Leydon — and offered him a four-month tour of US university business schools and departments, financed by the European Productivity Agency.

The visit impressed MacCormac. He compiled the subsequent report on behalf of all 18 European participants in the tour. It included recommendations on what European universities needed to do in business studies. Ironically, the report had its least effect on his own authorities back in Earlsfort Terrace. Nevertheless, things were never quite the same thereafter. The US experience had convinced him that the case for graduate studies in management was overwhelming. He was certain that, with a solid push from business, the UCD authorities would bend. He saw the IMI as essential to that process: it would help him persuade his fellow academics that business looked to the universities to provide management education. At every opportunity, he circulated IMI material to the president and members of the faculty — a relentless wearing-down strategy. The opposition was not confined to UCD itself: changes in courses in constituent colleges required the approval of the National University of Ireland (NUI).

> Although John Busteed had been involved in the inaugural council of the IMI and on the Cork regional committee, University College Cork remained my greatest opponent within the NUI. The president, Donal McCarthy, in particular, was against anything happening in management studies. Galway didn't give a damn, they weren't going to get involved so they didn't mind, but Cork was very anti.

Following the US trip, MacCormac set out to strengthen the B.Comm. He had by then been appointed college lecturer in economics and business administration. He was finally in a position to include "business administration" (not "management") in the course. His next aim was to try for a postgraduate degree:

> If I could establish postgraduate business studies I would be able to recruit specialist staff in subjects like marketing and management accounting. They could also teach the undergraduates, further enhancing the B.Comm. And that, more or less, is what happened. The standard of the B.Comm gradually rose: people who took the degree during the 1950s are not at all as dismissive of it as those who did it earlier.

He even got additional lecturers; the first, Frank Drechsler, almost by stealth. Drechsler, an engineer and full-time member of the department of chemical engineering, applied for the chemical engineering chair but was unsuccessful. A believer in business studies and now disillusioned with his own department, he gradually moved closer to MacCormac's students, taking on an increasing number of lecturing modules in the B.Comm.

In 1955, MacCormac was able to offer a master's degree, basically by adding an extra year to the B.Comm. He set his sights on an MBA. Here, the publication in 1962 of the report of the Review Committee on Education and Training for Management was particularly helpful to MacCormac. So were UCD engineering graduates who had attended IMI courses and fed back to their former professors the importance of including management in the engineering course. The climate within the college was gradually changing. At last, approval was received for the appointment of two more staff, Tony Cunningham and Jim Doolan. The latter had a Harvard degree and had also worked with the World Bank. Tony Cunningham had a PhD in marketing from Cornell, making him a rare commodity in Ireland. With this injection of management expertise, new modules on business finance and marketing were introduced into the M.Econ.Sc towards the end of the1950s.

It was rare for businessmen to be publicly critical of academia. One of the more forthright figures in industry at the time was Joseph Griffin, joint managing director of the substantial Irish Glass Bottle Company Ltd. The IMI asked him to address a meeting in November 1958 on the theme "education and industry". He began a remarkable speech with some perceptive remarks, noting a shift in the national temper in the aftermath of the publication a short time earlier of T.K. Whitaker's paper *Economic Development*, and observing that Ireland was "beginning — only beginning — to throw off the pall of gloom that had been darkening our days, confusing our minds and our policies and distracting our intelligence and our energies". He said of the new spirit:

> I sense it in many walks of life — in the social and economic spheres, in the towns and the country, in business and agriculture, in legislature and in government and in

the public services and it has even infected our financial institutions.

The universities — the object of Griffin's address — were notably excluded from his list. He praised the national (primary) schools, which had "served industry and the nation extremely well" and the vocational system, particularly in Dublin where "many have been astonished at the rate of growth in scope, in facilities and in the standards of training and proficiency". He reserved a broadside for the universities:

> I am conscious of the even greater service which our universities could give and the greater influence which they could, and should exert, not only in the field of industry, but in the life of the country as a whole. It is my considered view that, in those subjects and sciences such as engineering, economics, chemistry, which bear on industry, our universities have not even begun to give to Irish industry the service, the skills and encouragement and the inspiration which industry and the country in general have the right to expect.

When they complained of lack of resources, it was because they had failed to take public opinion with them. If a clear case had been stated, Griffin did not believe that any government would withhold support:

> Is there some superior reason for this failure — something in the spirit of learning which could not condescend to such a task? I believe that when a university fails to live near, and bring its students closer to the people of its own country and its fortunes, when it tends to isolate students — to place them beyond and above the people and when the minds of too many graduates are outwardly directed to bigger and richer nations of the world, then the university is failing in one of the fundamental purposes of its existence . . .

> The doctrine of our poverty in material resources continues to plague and debilitate our people like a dark and brooding superstition. Our educational system has not done enough to dispel it. It is not merely among workers or small farmers or the little people of the country that

this doctrine survives, but among the educated in business and commerce, in industry and agriculture, in public administration and, alas, in our educational institutions ...

Replying to Griffin's polemic, T.E. Nevin, professor of physics at UCD, quoted research showing that the traditional criticism of the theoretical nature of university training was dying out. On the contrary, industry "in the new fields of development calling for original ideas" appreciated a wider and more fundamental education in the sciences.

The Review Committee on Education and Training for Management, which began its work in December 1960 — and included representatives of industry as well as senior representatives of the universities, the vocational education bodies and the Institute of Public Administration — was agreed on what needed to be done at every level of the system to address the management education gap. It acknowledged that the universities were indeed behind in meeting the needs of business and recommended substantial restructuring of commerce courses, the inclusion of management studies in engineering and certain science courses, and the establishment of postgraduate studies in management.

The committee's report, presented to the Taoiseach in September 1962, was acclaimed for its objectivity. It helped to dislodge, within the universities' power structures, earlier prejudices against management education. Michael MacCormac claims that it was crucial in clearing the way in UCD for the MBA. Reflecting on the barriers that had to be overcome to establish business studies in a hostile internal environment, MacCormac gives credit to the IMI:

> The Joint Committee on Education and Training for Management and its successor, the Review Committee, helped me enormously. I would always be grateful for their reports, even if the people I was trying to influence didn't read them! But they established a new awareness, helped by newspaper comment, that the Institute was proceeding, that business was now interested in education for management and that the universities needed to do something about it.

UCD launched an MBA in 1964, a two-year part-time course, from 4.30 to 8.00, Mondays to Thursdays. It was aimed at graduates with at least three years' experience. MacCormac's IMI contacts paid off again: when he advertised for candidates, he got a good response from the bigger firms whose CEOs were involved in the IMI. The first 14 MBAs graduated in 1966. MacCormac then embarked on other projects, including a number of summer courses with professors from Harvard and Wharton. They succeeded in convincing the college that here were professors from departments of business studies in good universities well recognised and at the top of their profession. However, NUI prejudice did not entirely go away: it continued to put every paragraph of every proposed change in business-related courses under the microscope.

In Trinity College, the School of Commerce had been founded in 1926. The "academic" subjects (e.g. economics) were taught by full-time staff, and the "practical" ones (such as accounting, insurance, transport, business organisation and money and credit) by part-time staff who were mainly retired practitioners. In 1957, Trinity's B.Comm was extended from three to four years. In 1962, the course was further developed to lead to the Bachelor of Business (BBS) degree, the B.Comm degree being discontinued. The IMI certainly played a role in these changes; for example, in 1957, Paul Quigley, the secretary of the Institute, became a member of the college's School Committee, which was responsible for initiating course changes. In 1959, Amory A. Pakenham-Walsh (Paky to all) was appointed lecturer in management (he had been a part-time lecturer in money and credit for ten years), resigning from Guinness where he had been deputy chief accountant. Lured by an attractive salary but more important by a status denied him at UCD, Frank Drechsler joined Trinity in 1964 as lecturer in administration, followed by Geoffrey McKechnie in 1968.

Trinity introduced a graduate business course in 1964. Whereas UCD had opted for a two-year part-time formula, Trinity decided on a one-year full-time degree course, which it named Master of Science in Administration (MSA). It defined its market widely. Writing in the journal *Management*,[1] Pakenham-Walsh, acting head of business studies, said that the course was for:

---

[1] June 1964, "Management by Degrees".

those embarking on a career in business or administration: that is, for recent graduates . . . and for employees of business undertakings, of central and local government, of trade unions, of institutions and of associations who are qualified to benefit from the course.

He offered the following explanation of the choice of "administration" rather than "management" in the degree's title:

There is a common body of knowledge and set of skills available to help those responsible for work whether they fill these roles in privately, or publicly owned, undertakings, in central or local authorities or in hospitals, trade unions or universities.

There would have been many within the IMI and the IPA who would have given him an argument on the latter assertion because it lay at the heart of the separate development of both bodies. Pakenham-Walsh cast aside the traditional subdivision of management into its four principal functions of production, personnel, marketing and finance:

In recent times, the marketing evangelists had a deserved success in convincing both businessman and teacher of the superiority of the marketing approach. . . . In short, the original functional divisions have been made obsolete by the marketing thesis.

Michael MacCormac, in the same issue, defined a more precise objective for his MBA: "to develop future business leaders". For him, the days of the four primary functions of management were still not over:

Attention is given to the traditional functional [areas] only in the first year . . . knowledge of these functions promotes better understanding of the fundamentals of enterprise, operation and control.

Explaining the decision to go part-time:

We took the decision to make the course a part-time one because, taking account of the size of the average Irish business, it would not be possible to release the experienced graduate from his management position to come full-time.

The inauguration in 1964 of these two masters' programmes was warmly welcomed by the IMI. It was the culmination of years of effort to gain a significant place for management education on the agenda of the third-level system. To mark this milestone, the Institute created the Sir Charles Harvey Award to be presented to those who excelled in the MBA or MSA. The MSA, being a one-year course, meant that the first award went in 1965 to a Trinity graduate, Patrick J. Murphy, who went on, not only to have an outstanding career in industry; he also achieved eminence in the arts, becoming chairman of the Arts Council, president of the Contemporary Irish Art Society and a member of the International Council of the Museum of Modern Art, New York. UCD's two-year course ended a year later. Tom Toner, later a successful entrepreneur, company chairman and contributor to industrial policy formation, emerged the close winner. The Sir Charles Harvey Award remains a coveted prize for leading graduates of master's degree programmes in management, which have since proliferated throughout an expanded university network, North and South.

The consultative board's call[2] for a unified business school had been made in the context of an earlier move to amalgamate UCD and Trinity. At the 1967 National Management Conference, the Taoiseach, Jack Lynch, told the audience, which included academics as well as business leaders:

> If additional resources for education and training for management are to be used to the maximum effect and with the maximum efficiency, our aim should be to concentrate and rationalise our efforts rather than to disperse them.

Later, Education Minister Donogh O'Malley went further. Rejecting the advice of the Commission on Higher Education, he startled the academic world by proposing the merger of University College and Trinity College into a new University of Dublin. The Govern-

---

[2] See page 127.

ment asked George Colley and Donogh O'Malley to see if any interim rationalisation could be achieved. Colley asked the IMI to:

> Enquire into the possibilities for co-operation at graduate
> level in business education and into the possibility of a
> close formal relationship between the proposed new Uni-
> versity of Dublin and the Irish Management Institute.

Colley asked Dr J.F. Dempsey to chair a Working Group on Co-
operation in Business Education. It was compact enough: professors Basil Chubb and W.J.L. Ryan[3] from Trinity; professors P. Leahy
and Michael MacCormac from UCD; and, from the IMI, Ivor Kenny
and Brian Whelan who, with Breffni Tomlin, shared the role of secretary. The group reported that the business departments of both
universities were "too small in terms of breadth and depth of disciplines to provide the range of teaching needed at graduate
level", one of the reasons being the difficulty of attracting staff of
the right calibre

> partly because such staff are absolutely scarce, and partly
> because there are difficulties in assimilating them into the
> staff and salary structure of the universities.

Lack of space, technology and information services were also cited
in support of the group's single and unanimous finding that "the
graduate schools in business administration in the two universities
should be merged and a single Graduate Business School formed".

A single campus comprising both university schools and the IMI
would, said the report, bring a number of benefits apart from the
likely economies:

> The daily interaction between the institutions can help ob-
> viate the dangers to which such institutions are prone in
> isolation: a university of becoming too remote from the
> day-to-day practice of management, a post-experience
> centre [the IMI] of becoming too involved with day-to-day
> practice.

---

[3] Louden Ryan, Professor of Industrial Economy and head of Trinity's School of
Commerce, was appointed Professor of Political Economy in 1968 following
the retirement of G.A. Duncan.

> The interchange of information, ideas and experience, the coming together of informal groups to pursue matters of mutual interest, must lead to an increase in creativity and the growth of a spirit of support.

The group left open the possibility of a later association with the IPA on the same basis as the IMI. The preferred location was 10–15 acres on UCD's Belfield campus. This suggestion was coolly received in those quarters. Michael MacCormac had copied the working group's draft report to the president of UCD, J.J. Hogan, a few days before it was to be formally adopted. He got a stinging reply by return:

> Dear Professor MacCormac,
>
> I think there is a great deal of unreality in the revised Report of the Working Group on Co-operation in Business Education which you sent me on April 2 and which is to be signed on Friday . . .

There follows detailed objections to the wording of the report:

> The expression is so strange as almost to baffle any interpretation by me, as for example in the reference to "the continuing health of our cadre of managers". I am puzzled by the reference to the "development" of "those thousands now actually managing business enterprises" and to the transformation needed "in the standard of practice of many thousands of existing managers". Is there some idea of bringing these multitudes into the graduate courses of our Faculty of Commerce, whether or not they hold degrees?

Referring to the section on location of the proposed graduate school, the tone is icy: "I think you ought to consult me directly before entering into any negotiations or speculations on such a matter." The letter concludes:

> On the whole, it seems to me that this draft Report is less acceptable even than the earlier one, the objections to which I discussed in detail with you.

If you sign this Report you must do so in a purely personal capacity and not as in any way representing the College, the Faculty of Commerce, or of course the Governing Body and Academic Council.

MacCormac's reply hints at the gulf in understanding that had long characterised the approach of the college establishment to matters of management education:

Dear President,

I regret to hear that you think that the Report of the Working Group on Co-operation in Business Education lacks reality. In this I think there are two points of view and I believe that the existing graduate work is not sufficient for the needs of the country and that it does, in fact, need substantial expansion. It is in this framework that the report is written and the Working Group is unanimous in regarding the present graduate work and its facilities as inadequate ...

I am sorry to note in your last paragraph that you would find this Report completely unacceptable. I think that the developments that are suggested are only in line with what has happened in other countries and I do sincerely hope that Irish universities will not fall behind in meeting the pressing needs of the country for graduate business education.

The working group adopted the report with a few minor alterations to the draft. To address MacCormac's difficulty with his president, there was a preamble to the signatures:

The recommendations in this report were agreed unanimously by the members of the Group in a personal capacity and not necessarily as representing the views of their organisations.

The working group despatched the report to the minister with that sense of optimism shared by authors of similar studies before and since. But it achieved the fate of many — death in a drawer.

Donogh O'Malley said his proposal to merge the two great universities would end "a most insidious form of partition".[4] His sudden death in March 1968 at the age of 47 robbed the project of its main protagonist. Little more was heard of it beyond a brief mention in the Third Programme for Economic and Social Expansion, in March 1969:

> The Government are referring to the Higher Education Authority for consideration the question of establishing a new post–graduate business school in the new University of Dublin. The details of the proposal have not yet been fully elaborated but a close relationship is envisaged between the new school and the Irish Management Institute.

In due course, the inter-university merger proposal was voted out by both UCD and TCD. The joint business campus championed by the consultative board was then effectively a dead letter.

Although the IMI's relationships with members of the university staff remained good, that between the university authorities and the Institute cooled for a time. The Institute could be thin-skinned about this, as can be seen from an exchange at the national management conference in Killarney in 1973. Following Ivor Kenny's keynote paper, Dr Bill Murray, assistant managing director of CRH, a former IMI council member and a Trinity lecturer, challenged him from the floor. The exchange is interesting in that it provokes an uncharacteristically blunt expression of the IMI's then assessment of a hoped-for strategic partner:

> *Murray*: I sense a certain nervousness in people about the IMI. I think this may be due to the organisational skill that it has and to the highly competent staff. People may be afraid of the possible acquisitiveness of the IMI.[5] And yet it has not done enough in relation to the universities. I think the IMI could have done a lot more in relation to the government and the universities.

---

[4] Quoted in *Ireland: The Past Twenty Years* (1986) (ed. Jim O'Donnell), Institute of Public Administration.

[5] This was after a recent failed merger attempt with CII (see Chapter Sixteen).

Kenny: What we did about the universities was to publish a report, prepared with the full participation of the universities, and present it to the Taoiseach. From then on there was little enough the IMI could do to influence the situation. My own belief is that the university structure is an atmosphere which is hostile to business studies. This is borne out by experience in Britain and the United States. The university is a fairly closed community. It sets its own standards and measures its own effectiveness in attaining these standards.

You will be told quickly in a university that it is not the handmaid of industry. There is also a myth that the university is the only proper place for management education. There is an element here of crude credentialism. Credentialism is not what the IMI is about. It is about continuous learning. It *is* the handmaid of industry. Bill Murray may remember that we asked if we might build our training centre on the UCD campus and we were politely rejected.

He was referring to the cooling of the relationship between the Institute and UCD around the end of the 1960s. There are different perspectives on what this was all about. Michael MacCormac says that he was looking to set up some form of collaboration with the IMI but that he met resistance within the Institute:

During that period I spoke to the IMI about collaboration but it foundered within IMI rather than with me. Ultimately, when the Institute decided to go ahead with the management centre at Sandyford in the early 1970s, that was the end of it as far as UCD was concerned. It was a physical statement that the IMI didn't need UCD.

The IMI paints it differently. Before the executive committee finally decided on Sandyford it looked at a number of options. In 1969, the institute wrote to the UCD president, J.J. Hogan, exploring the possibility of a site at Belfield. The letter referred to the report of the Working Group on Co-operation in Business Education, and to its conclusion that "there would be positive advantages if the school and the IMI were to be physically contiguous on the university campus".

Michael Dargan (standing) and Peter Owens give a press conference
in 1952 to give advance details of the IMI's inauguration

Sean Lemass addresses the inaugural meeting of the IMI in the
Gresham Hotel on 9 December 1952; from left: Michael Dargan,
honorary secretary, Professor G.A. Duncan, TCD, J. O'Keeffe
(Association of Chambers of Commerce), P. Moylett (NAIDA), T.P.
Hogan (vice-chairman), the Tánaiste, Sean Lemass, Sir Charles Harvey,
chairman, F.C. Hooper, representing the BIM, and Davy Frame. The
Lord Mayor, Alderman Andrew Clarkin, is hidden by Lemass

Sir Charles Harvey addresses the inaugural meeting

A section of the audience at
the inaugural meeting

T.P. Hogan,
a founder of the IMI

Sir Charles Harvey presents Minister for Industry & Commerce, William Norton, with a copy of the report of the joint committee, April 1956. T.F. Laurie on left and General Richard Mulcahy, right

Managing through People was the theme that attracted this audience to the IMI's 1959 conference

Hugh MacNeill with a group of managers, c. 1959

Participants at an MDU course in Leeson Park in 1960; Paul Quigley, director, and Ivor Kenny, head of MDU, are second and fourth from right

Sir Charles Harvey says farewell to the IMI in 1963 as he retires to England; also pictured are A.H. Masser and Sean Lemass

Donogh O'Malley, then Junior Minister at the Department of Finance, addressing an IMI lunch in Greystones in 1964

Arriving in the rain at the opening of the IMI's new headquarters in
Orwell Road, June 1965; from left: Ivor Kenny, Director,
Dr P.J. Hillery, Minister for Industry and Commerce,
Dr J.F. Dempsey, Chairman, and T.F. Laurie, President

Denis Hegarty (standing) with others involved in the 1965
controversy; from left, Jerry Dempsey, "John" Masser, Gunnar Larsen

Sean Lemass in jovial form two days before he retired as Taoiseach in November 1966; from Lemass's left: Michael Rigby-Jones, who had presented him with a copy of *The Management of Irish Industry*, Gunnar Larsen, Colm Barnes, Breffni Tomlin and Ivor Kenny

Garrett FitzGerald lectures on a course in the mid-1960s

July 1967: the IMI's first eight-month course, the Business
Management Programme, including, front row, from third left, Paddy
Moriarty, ESB, Noel Mulcahy, course leader, and Brian Whelan

Chairmen and honorary secretaries of IMI regional committees with
IMI executives during a visit to Orwell Road in the late 1960s

Taoiseach Jack Lynch and Frank Lemass enjoy a Tony O'Reilly quip during his address at the 1970 IMI conference

At the 1972 Killarney conference: Tadhg O Cearbhaill, secretary of the Department of Labour (right), with Melville Miller, vice-president of the FUE, who died shortly afterwards in the Staines air crash.

A press conference in the Shelbourne Hotel following failed merger talks between the IMI and the CII, 10 October 1972; from left: Ivor Kenny, director IMI, Ronald Nesbitt, chairman IMI, Peter Keehan, president CII, and Liam Connellan, director-general CII

At the first meeting of the Doctoral Fellowship Programme, December 1973, from left, Prof. Michael MacCormac, one of the IMI's founders, with Ian Morrison, Prof. Louden Ryan and Roger Talpaert, secretary-general, European Institute for Advanced Studies in Management

Dr John Leydon, pioneering secretary of the Department of Industry and Commerce, and his successor J.C.B. McCarthy, in 1974

Herman Kahn, Futurologist, speaking at the 1973 conference

A 1970s National Management Conference with the Eidophor image projector in action

Attending the spouses programme at the 1977 conference

Michael Smurfit (left) with legendary *Evening Press* columnist,
Terry O'Sullivan at the 1979 conference on the theme *Performance*

At a Southern Region dinner: Michael Lovett, chairman of the region, Dr Peter Dempsey, UCC, and Jim Byrne, secretary, IMI

President Julius Nyerere of Tanzania on his visit to the IMI in 1979, where he met members of the Institute's faculty

The class of '96 receive their BAs in Management;
seated, centre, Chairman Jerry Liston

Graduates and faculty of the IMI/TCD MScOB course, 1997

Guests at the 1998 Council Dinner being introduced by Chairman,
Norman Kilroy, to the guest of honour, President Mary McAleese

Recipients of the Guinness/IMI Sir Charles Harvey Awards 2001 with
(front, from left), Barry Kenny, Chief Executive, IMI, Kevin Kelly,
Chairman, IMI, and Pat Barry, Director of Corporate Affairs, Guinness

Council Dinner 2002: Chief Executive, Barry Kenny, Chairman of
Council, Kevin Kelly, and guest of honour, Peter Sutherland

The library at the National Management Centre

Clearly, the IMI's request was not helped by the bother between the president and MacCormac about that same report. Hogan's reply was coldly polite:

> The developing needs of our university work make it impossible to recommend the leasing or transfer of land on the college site to any other institution.

He suggested the IMI "secure a site as near as possible to the college lands", concluding: "We greatly value co-operation between our Faculty of Commerce and the Irish Management Institute."

Ironically, as the universities moved farther in the direction the IMI had wanted them to go, competitive tensions increased between them and it. By the late 1960s, the Institute decided it would raise its game, working deeper and longer with the top echelon of managers and those heading for the top. There were good strategic and pedagogical reasons for the decision: IMI teachers were finding that they could not fully meet the development needs of senior managers unless they could work with them over extended periods. The specialists met to tackle this issue and to work out a way of extending the time they could work with senior managers in particular. Until then, the average course was two days; it was clear that this was too short an exposure to new ideas and the effect was easily dissipated back in the workplace. Dermot Egan suggested a formula for a modular programme: it would be aimed at top managers, who would be asked to commit themselves to the IMI for two days a month for about eight months, with "homework" to be done in between modules.

A programme, called the Extended Management Practice[6] training course, was created and tried out in Waterford over five months with 12 senior managers from the region. It covered the main disciplines and was taught by IMI staff and leading practitioners from industry. The course, highly rated by the participating managers, was then enhanced, extended to eight months and launched nationally as a central feature of the IMI prospectus for 1966/67.

It was quickly apparent that the extended courses were, indeed, much more effective in inducing real change in managers. This was

---

[6] Later, the Business Management Programme (BMP).

confirmed by the findings of Professor Reg Revans, a research fellow with the European Association of Management Training Centres (EAMTC) in Brussels, who had developed considerable data on how people learn, supported by other leading international management theorists with whom Egan and Mulcahy had forged ties and who were frequent visitors to the IMI. They, particularly Revans, strongly influenced the Institute's teaching philosophy at the time. Revans was working on his "action learning" idea — a concept that hinged on relating teaching to the actual job of the participant; in his words "subjects learn with and from each other by supporting each other during their attacks on common or related real problems". The IMI's modular programmes provided the ideal framework to put those theories into practice and helped put action learning on the map. Charles Handy of the London Business School was another who made an impact on the shape of IMI management training in that era:

> Surprisingly, the executive student is often very unpractised in communicating his concepts and hypotheses to others; surprisingly, until one realises that it has been technical information, not judgements and the force of arguments, that was often the key factor in the kinds of decisions and debates he was used to. However, as an individual rises higher in the hierarchy of decisions, the role of technical information tends to diminish and that of reasoned debate to increase.[7]

The modular courses put great store on the communications skills of the individual. The application of these and other contemporary concepts brought a fundamental change in the way the IMI worked with its key clients. Managers were asked to bring case material from their own firms, obviating the necessity for staff to find — or invent — case studies that would have relevance to small-scale Irish companies, never an easy task. Charles Handy commends the IMI for adopting the modular design rather than the full-time immersion favoured by other management centres. The pioneering emphasis on relating the learning directly to the job and the prob-

---

[7] From a paper published in the IMED Journal (Institute of Management Education and Development).

lem-solving to the manager's work was in his view crucial. He used a similar model when writing the first course for the Open University's business school.

IMI course leaders, driven by the need to stay ahead of the game, were avid researchers and consumers of what was, in the 1960s, a very rapidly expanding body of knowledge in management. There was a rich flow of research coming from the major business schools and universities. Managers attending longer courses were exposed to the thinking of top international theorists and practitioners because of the personal relationships established by the staff with some of the key innovators: Igor Ansoff, professor of American business, Vanderbilt University, Professors Vroom of Carnegie-Mellon, Hawrylyshen of Centre d'Études Industrielles and the Club of Rome, Tabatoni of Paris University, Taboulet of Jouy en Josas and Revans of EAMTC. These leaders made themselves available to the Institute, sharing their expertise with it. The fact that it was attracting this level of attention opened the door for other major contacts. Professors Argyris of Yale, McClelland, Dooley and McKinney of Harvard, became regular visitors to the Institute, David McClelland's Theory of Achievement Motivation providing the foundation for a series of courses on small business entrepreneurship run by Liam Connellan. They were exciting, stimulating days.

Extended courses were expensive to operate because of the intensity of the relationship between teacher and participant. They could not have been contemplated without considerable subsidy. This came in two ways: state funding of the IMI and training grants to participating firms under a grant/levy system operated by AnCO, the Industrial Training Authority.

In the early 1970s the IMI decided to explore the possibility of elevating its business management programme (BMP) to university degree status. Initially, this may have had as much to do with the desire of IMI staff for more intellectually exacting involvement, than from a strong demand from business. Certainly, the consultative board did not anticipate this development in its 1971 report. Without being explicit, it assumed a demarcation, with degree courses in the realm of the third-level institutions, and the IMI doing the rest.

There was little optimism that either of the universities would grant degrees to graduates of an external management programme. But the emergence in 1972 of a new degree-awarding body, independent of the universities, the National Council for Education Awards (NCEA),[8] of which UCD's MacCormac was a member, changed the picture. It had been set up to promote higher education outside the universities and had the power to grant degrees. Noel Mulcahy and Noel Donnellan, for the IMI, successfully made a case to the NCEA for a postgraduate, post-experience master's degree based on the BMP.

No sooner had this happened, however, than Michael MacCormac suggested a new liaison between UCD and the Institute, including a two-year joint master's programme in management practice. A joint academic research board comprised of both bodies would oversee the degree. The preference within IMI was for a university-validated degree; an NCEA degree was still a novel proposition and had not gained universal recognition. Of the universities, UCD was preferred. So the Institute welcomed MacCormac's approach but, according to Mulcahy, MacCormac tried to drive too hard a bargain, wanting the IMI to cede some of its programmes to UCD in return:

> MacCormac was willing to give us the master's but only on condition that UCD ran the cream of the executive development programmes (EDPs), our main moneymaking product. We could not agree to that. In any case, he would have had to clear everything through the NUI, where he anticipated that UCC would create problems. So the whole thing was getting messy.
>
> Shortly afterwards, at an Irish Congress of Trade Unions lecture, I was sitting beside Louden Ryan, Professor of Political Economy at Trinity. Leaning across conspiratorially, he said, "I hear you're considering a master's degree and you're having difficulty with MacCormac. Why don't you try Trinity?"

At Ryan's suggestion, an IMI team met Professor Martin O'Donoghue, dean of the faculty. Within weeks, O'Donoghue set out the basis of a joint programme, which he then steered through the relevant college committees — a remarkable achievement.

---

[8] Now, Higher Education and Training Awards Council (HETAC).

MacCormac, although at the time surprised by the IMI move, nevertheless understands the decision:

> I think everybody within IMI, and mainly Ivor Kenny, thought that UCD was too difficult to deal with and he was probably right. In the case of Trinity, decisions were easier: Louden Ryan could see that a deal was delivered.

The link with Trinity flourished. With the support of Professor O'Donoghue, the Institute and the college were able to announce in 1973 the first degree programme in management practice, MSc (Mgmt). The course began in 1975, teaching workshops were held at the IMI, with inputs both from Trinity and IMI staff. Personal tutors advised students on reading, research, study and choice of thesis subject. The MSc (Mgmt) had the distinction of being the first management degree in the world to be based on action learning, a methodology since incorporated in many management programmes in Europe and North America.

Theses were submitted for decision to Trinity's examination board where they had to meet the standard laid down for any master's level programme. Understandably, there were difficulties initially in harmonising the academic standard for this off-campus course with that of Trinity's established degree programmes; the extern examiner, Professor Ray Thomas of Bath University, was frequently called on to adjudicate. Soon the programme found its rhythm and a fruitful working relationship developed between the two organisations, driven particularly by Liam Gorman for the IMI and by Geoffrey MacKechnie for TCD. An MSc in Organisational Behaviour was added in 1977, with Gorman and McKechnie as joint programme directors. Later, Tony Dromgoole succeeded Liam Gorman as joint director of the MSc (Mgmt) course.

John Murray's appointment in 1988 as head of the business school at Trinity was the start of another period of intense innovation in the TCD/IMI partnership. Within a year, a companion course to the MSc (Mgmt) degree was added. This arose through an approach from a graduate of the MSc in Organisational Behaviour, Hugh Feely, head of human resources management in Allied Irish Banks Group, suggesting a master's in general management for senior managers in AIB. Murray, Gorman and McKechnie responded with the MSc Business Administration Programme (BAP). The first programme had 17 senior AIB executives and a leavening of ten managers from other large enterprises. The BAP is now a recognised preparation for managers — including many from the multinational sector — moving into strategic positions.

Another variation on the MSc (Mgmt) degree is the Strategic Management — Public Sector Programme (PSP) launched in 1993. This is exclusively for the public sector. In the early 1990s an alumnus of the original MSc (Mgmt), Paddy Teahon, then secretary-general of the Department of the Taoiseach, took charge of the Strategic Management Initiative (SMI), a master plan for the reform of the Civil Service. To help meet the human resources needs of the SMI, he suggested a master's for assistant departmental secretaries. Murray invited Gorman to help design the PSP. Like its associated programmes, the PSP has a sharp, practical focus. In the second year, students examine specific ways of improving the efficiency and effectiveness of the public service. This often involves scrutiny of radical public services initiatives abroad. The findings have already been beneficially applied to the Irish public service and an impressive number of the programme's graduates are now in the most senior positions in the public service.

The leadership of the programmes and the teaching input are jointly shared between the IMI and Trinity. Liam Gorman observes:

> The IMI as an influential organisation of managers brings to Trinity a critical mass of business experience and clients; Trinity provides academic rigour and, in marketing terms, an exceptional brand. As a model of university/ private sector partnership the relationship is unequalled.

The IMI can now offer managers prepared to undertake the demands of intensive study a broad range of degree courses. Over 700 graduates of the various MSc (Mgmt) programmes — firm believers in management education — now occupy leading positions in many business and public sector organisations.

The relationship with Trinity has also sparked a series of research initiatives undertaken jointly by IMI specialists and TCD counterparts led by Geoffrey MacKechnie of the School of Business Studies.

Latterly, associations have developed between the IMI and other universities. Under MacCormac, UCD went on to establish a top-notch business school. MacCormac had managed to assemble a core faculty of bright people, some of whom had been to the leading US business schools, others the product of his own MBA courses. By about 1975 the UCD Business School ranked high among European schools, in terms of the proportion of PhDs on its staff. In 1990, the Michael Smurfit Graduate School of Business was established, with Laurence Crowley as chairman; it is now Ireland's largest graduate business school with over a thousand students and a faculty well in excess of 100. J.V. Liston, a former IMI chairman, was appointed executive chairman of the school in 2000. Its executive MBA was rated twenty-fourth in the world in 2001.[9] The graduate school is largely complementary to the Institute's role, concentrating mainly on postgraduate management education, although it also offers some customised in-company management development for corporate clients.

There have been a number of links with the University of Limerick, including the co-funding of the IMI/UL chair of organisational behaviour, the holder of which, Patrick Flood, participated in an innovative strategic alliance on research with the Institute. This three-year alliance resulted in a co-authored book on strategy implementation, published in 2000.[10]

The most recent alliance has been a master's programme in information technology developed with NUI, Galway. This marks a significant milestone in the Institute's 40-year long relationship with IT, the defining industry of the age. Tony Moynihan, who joined the Institute in the late 1960s, led the IMI into information technology. The language then was about quantitative methods and operations research; the technology — the slide rule and the calculating machine. Moynihan was at point position, scanning computer developments for possible applications to the management role. At the time of the move to Sandyford, he ensured the inclusion of a room to house the IMI's first computer. This technological jewel, the

---

[9] *Financial Times EMBA 2001, The Top 50 executive MBA programmes* (FT, 22 October 2001).

[10] Patrick C. Flood, Tony Dromgoole, Stephen J. Carroll, Liam Gorman (eds.) (2000), *Managing Strategy Implementation*, UK and US: Blackwell Business.

PDP11, had to have its own atmosphere-controlled shrine and vibration-free flooring. Moynihan and Doug Notley, who subsequently co-founded the successful Notley Cahill company, developed computer familiarisation programmes — at first considered too avant-garde by all but a handful of large companies. Attitudes soon changed and in 1979, Moynihan[11] and Gus Liston felt that the market was ready for a diploma in management information systems.

Liston recalls the early days of the PC:

> We were quite excited by the arrival of the first personal computers. Most managers were still in awe of the technology. We ran a hands-on course to demonstrate the value of an early spreadsheet application, Visicalc. But the IMI could afford only a few machines. We borrowed PCs wherever we could — friends, anybody.

The equipment shortage was solved through a combination of unashamed mendicity on the part of the Institute and enlightened self-interest by suppliers — Digital, IBM, Nixdorf and Mentec.

To encourage small businesses to use computers, a comparative study was undertaken into their use in small businesses in Ireland, Greece and Denmark. It uncovered enough innovative applications to spark off conferences in Dublin, Athens and Copenhagen. The first computer applications in business were in finance and administration. Not all systems delivered what they promised. In the early 1980s, chairman of the IMI, David Kennedy, chief executive of Aer Lingus, sponsored research into office automation. The report of the two-year study, *Office Automation in Ireland*, published in 1983 provided a valuable cautionary service, pointing out the pitfalls as well as the benefits of the new systems.

Through the 1980s, computerisation pervaded business to the extent that the shape of organisations began to change. Managers could not be in control without, at least, a working knowledge of computer applications. To bridge the computer literacy gap, the IMI opened a dedicated IT centre in Sandyford where managers could go to get to know the PC. For over six years, Digital continually up-

---

[11] Tony Moynihan left in the early 1980s, becoming professor of computing in Dublin City University.

dated the equipment and, with Mentec, supplied software and supported the operating systems in the Institute. The timing was right: over 1,000 managers a year crowded to the IT centre.

Nowadays, all managers are expected to be familiar with computers and how to use them, so the IMI's IT centre is used less for teaching the computer basics; a visitor to the centre now is more likely to walk in on a group dynamics session, where members of the group are linked to a laptop network for quick interaction.

Recently, the IMI came to the view that, if IT specialists were to anticipate and manage the changes that the technology brought to their companies, they would need a profound understanding of how organisations worked. Liston discussed the proposition with Dr Gerry Lyons, a former senior executive in Digital, then director of a new information technology centre in NUI, Galway. The notion of a master's degree in information technology took shape. Both NUI, Galway, and the IMI approved the degree with admirable dispatch, enabling the first programme to commence in January 2000. Ireland's first Masters in Information Technology were conferred in spring 2002. They include not only IT specialists but also senior managers from other disciplines interested in acquiring a closer understanding of the business potential of new technology.

The notion of having a primary degree for managers has been around the IMI for quite a time. In the mid-1980s, Kevin Plunkett, a senior member of the IMI staff, decided to do something about it. He asked both Trinity and UCD, but neither would co-operate — primary degrees were considered their own core market. The NCEA, however, again provided the solution. The degree BA (Mgmt) was launched in 1986. It is taught entirely at the IMI. Entry demands at least seven years' experience, some of it in a management position. The average enrolment age is about 30. The BA (Mgmt) is a course for practitioners, unlike the traditional BA or BSc that are based on concepts of which the student has no practical experience. The accent is more on the behavioural sciences and on the management of people than would be the case in its closest counterparts, the B.Comm or the BBS. Unusually for a primary degree, a dissertation is included as part of the final examination. Students are encouraged to choose topics which have a currency in their organisations and are relevant to their career intentions. This helps a fusion of theory and practice, unique for a primary arts degree. The standard, monitored by the NCEA, is demanding and the BAs who go on to postgraduate degrees, either at the IMI or outside it, tend to perform strongly.

What motivates managers so relatively far into their careers to tackle a degree course? There is an element of the second chance about it, of unfinished business. But there is a more pressing consideration. At one time, a degree may have been a useful option but now it is virtually essential. Unless people are exceptionally gifted, if they are serious about progressing through the hierarchy of an organisation, a degree is a "must have". It also helps transferability; skills become much more tradable with a degree.

The Institute has a longer history in awarding other lesser "gongs", but which are valued nonetheless. Diplomas or certificates were added to the longer courses in a number of topics such as supervisory management, business studies, customer services, finance, manufacturing management, management information systems and strategy. In the mid-1990s, an agreement with the University of Ulster, Jordanstown, resulted in diplomas being awarded to participants in company-specific courses in Shorts of Belfast.[12]

So, the Institute today enjoys a wide network of alliances with universities and award-giving institutions, offering a broadening range of choice for managers wishing to acquire practical, post-experience academic qualifications as their careers unfold.

---

[12] See Chapter Twenty.

Chapter Fourteen

A Unique Partnership

As the 1960s progressed and the targets of the Second Programme grew more demanding, the need for bright managers was given a high priority. The Institute as the main driver of management development had become an instrument of national policy — an unusual partnership between the sectors.

Managers' performance had to be lifted even if industry was disinclined to pay the rate for the job. To help the IMI gear up, the government agreed in 1963 to fund the difference between direct costs and the revenue from courses. This was intended as a pump-primer only until the market was ready to pay the true cost. However, government funding remained a significant feature of the Institute's finances for the rest of the decade and beyond, averaging about 30 per cent of total annual revenue. The basis for the arrangement was never fully spelt out and was subject to tortuous annual negotiation. The Department of Finance refused a plea for fixed funding over a longer cycle, so plans could be made with some degree of certainty and reserves built against future capital needs.

Some council members worried that the high proportion of grant income would compromise the Institute's autonomy. People remembered Lemass's private advice after his "ha'porth of tar" speech, that the character of an institution changes with the acceptance of government money.

Jerry Dempsey spelled out the rationale for accepting State funds in his 1965 chairman's report to members:

> The interest and participation in our work of the Department of Industry and Commerce has been most fruitful.

The present scale of our activities would not be possible without government subvention. In any question of money, it is our policy to secure from business the maximum commitment. And we know that, when we put before our members a programme which they see is in line with their needs, [it] will attract from our members the necessary resources. In the context of national industrial reorganisation, however, growing demands are being made on us outside the services we offer our members. It is in this area and the area of basic development — the development of the quality of our work — that State investment is necessary, is most appropriate and is most effective.

The following year, Michael Rigby-Jones returned to the theme:

We are not a profit-making body. Any pressure to make us so is undesirable. Practically every management organisation in Europe, giving a service like ours, gets continuing state subvention. It is reasonable to expect continuing state subvention for this Institute. The Department of Industry and Commerce has stated that the Institute's work is regarded as a priority.

The issue resurfaced early in 1969 during a council debate on the need for new premises. Bill Murray implied that the IMI was on its way to becoming a state-sponsored body, and that this might be the last chance for the council to preserve the Institute's independence. He urged the executive to examine alternative methods of financing the work. He disliked in particular the *ad hoc* nature of the subsidy, which depended on annual bargaining; if adequate private funding was not available, then at least the public subsidy should be at arm's length from politics. He commended the way that Hong Kong subsidised management training by putting a levy on exports.

In fact, neither ministers nor officials ever sought to influence IMI policy or be represented on the council. The Institute got on well with the Department of Industry and Commerce. When responsibility for the IMI grant transferred in 1966 to the new Department of Labour, there was some anxiety that a more interfering relationship would ensue. This unease was not lessened by the news that the department would also be responsible for national manpower policy and that it would establish an agency to implement it. From the start the Institute kept a watchful eye on that agency, AnCO. It had a wide remit, including statutory responsibility "for training activities in all spheres of industry and commerce — except in the agricultural sector and the professions". This clearly covered management training.

The AnCO board included representatives of employers, unions and educational bodies. The chairman was the managing director of the Industrial Development Authority, Michael Killeen. Brian MacManus, a civil servant with experience of the Apprenticeship Board, a forerunner to AnCO, was appointed director. The IMI could have bid for one of the employer seats on the board but decided to keep its distance. It did, however, offer AnCO's chairman a seat on the council; Killeen declined "because of the possibility of conflicting interests between the two bodies in the future". The wariness was mutual.

Before long, there was talk of IMI's grant being routed through AnCO, rather than the Department. This is what the IMI dreaded most; it had no desire to have its funding supervised by a representative body. It moved smartly — and effectively — to head off the possibility. The argument used with the Department of Labour — and accepted by them — was carefully couched:

> The council of the Institute, having been elected by managers to represent their needs, would find serious difficulty in reporting to any other representative body. Any solution [to the routing of the Institute's funding] that would affect adversely the Institute's commitment from management — the commitment given its most visible expression in council — would be to nobody's advantage. The problem is to ensure that the Institute works in harmony with general training policy while at the same time retaining the initiative inherent in its independence.

That settled the matter — for the time being. Responsibility for funding moved from Industry and Commerce directly to the Department of Labour, rather than to AnCO. Despite its unease, the Institute had decided to work with AnCO; it was a formidable agency, increasingly influential in growing the Institute's market. To help the relationship along, the IMI suggested a staff liaison

committee that would meet monthly to deal with operational problems. To ease tensions further, a top AnCO team — including the
head of training, Dermot Whelan, and the head of research, Sea-
mus McDermott — was invited to an away-from-it-all meeting with
IMI counterparts in the Downshire Arms in Blessington. The AnCO
people outlined their training strategy, which was, in a nutshell,
that every manager — every supervisor, every executive in business — would undergo at least three days' training a year, increasing to four days by 1980.

Set against the then training output, this revealed an astronomi-
cal gap in the supply system. The push to the new target would be
driven by AnCO's stick/carrot series of measures, a levy/grant
scheme and industrial training committees (ITCs). The way the system worked was that every sector had its own ITC to analyse its
needs and identify the type of training required. In Blessington, the
IMI agreed to nominate education representatives to the ITCs: Noel
Mulcahy, head of management development, joined the textiles
committee, Dermot Egan, head of in-company programmes, the
footwear body, Liam Connellan, head of small business, furniture
and so on.

The ITCs looked at management positions at all levels and the
qualifications of the people in them. Where there was a skills gap it
would be bridged by training. IMI's Phil Clarke had his own term
for this process, "gapology". The "training needs analysis", as it
was more reverently termed, was done by the firms themselves
with help from the INPC advisory service. Each ITC presented the
company's findings to AnCO. If approved, a training plan was produced and the company was given funds from the levy pool. These
could be substantial, even to the extent of financing in-house training centres for bigger companies, complete with trainers.

The IMI people in Blessington questioned the realism of AnCO's
view of the future, particularly the "training for all" aspiration. They
reluctantly went along with the policy, at least reassured that the
Institute's evolving plan for new premises had not been overstated.
In time, the IMI became infected by AnCO's exuberance about the
market potential. When it was leaked that the technical grants
scheme was to be phased out, the Institute's representatives on the
liaison committee, fearful of the effect on demand, tabled data at
the next meeting showing that the average manager or supervisor

attended only 0.6 days' training per year against the ultimate AnCO target of four per manager. They added the titillating morsel that, in some of the high technology industries in the US, as much as a quarter of executive time was devoted to personal development! The point was won and the scheme extended for a further two years.

With this closer collaboration, the relationship with AnCO evolved from guerrilla status to something closer to strained co-existence. It was always wary, never warm. In the words of someone who worked in both organisations: "There was absolute equality in the relationship: we disliked them just as much as they disliked us!"

The issue of AnCO control over the IMI state grant was raised again in 1973 — for the first time at political level — when the newly appointed Minister for Labour, Michael O'Leary, questioned why control of IMI funding was not with AnCO. Ivor Kenny alerted Michael Dargan, his chairman, to this new "threat" and sent a confidential briefing to the secretary of the department, Tadhg O Cearbhaill, deploying the contra arguments. The Institute was a "democratic co-operative, founded by managers for managers". Responsibility for the Institute was "at the appropriate level — in the hands of those qualified to ensure that the Institute's work is both relevant and competent". The high respect for the IMI among its international peers[1] — the European Foundation for Management Development (EFMD) and the International Council for Scientific Management (CIOS) — was adduced for an institution which had been built up over 20 years "in a country which represents the EEC's starkest regional problem". As a measure of the confidence it had earned from Irish business, it was pointed out that the IMI had raised for its new national management centre "the largest sum given voluntarily by Irish business". The letter referred to the IMI's successful promotion of management education at the higher

---

[1] During the 1960s and 1970s, there was considerable interest among European management teachers in the pioneering work of the IMI. The Institute hosted a number of specialist conferences on management development in Dublin and involved itself in the various management development associations. In 1970, Brian Whelan, deputy director of the IMI, was elected president of the EFMD, subsequently becoming director-general.

levels of the educational system. It touched on its research record and the networks it had established over the years, through the advisory and consultative bodies, including its most recent creation, the business needs committee involving the IDA, the Institute for Industrial Research and Standards, Córas Tráchtála, the Confederation of Irish Industry and, indeed, AnCO. There was also the grand-sounding Irish Doctoral Fellowship Committee, which the Institute had set up under the chairmanship of T.K. Whitaker, comprising universities and national educational authorities to advise on the establishment of doctoral fellowships for Irish teachers of management.

The letter came to the core issue:

> We would like to see this relationship [with the Department of Labour] preserved and strengthened. If [the IMI] were to become accountable to AnCO for subvention, the co-operative relationship would be ended. We would then have a body, itself largely operational, in the position of partly controlling another operational body, a role designed to cause conflict. AnCO would be put in the position of both referee and player.

> We would also find it difficult to understand how IMI policy, fully debated and decided upon by the IMI council in consultation with all relevant bodies, could be contributed to by a further debate by a council consisting of employers' representative bodies and trade unions . . .

> The IMI's independence derives from its having the objective of raising the standard of management in Ireland. This is an educational objective, not based on the interests of a particular group. It is also clear and neutral. To have the Institute partly controlled by a body divided on traditional employer–union lines would cause a confusion of roles and diminish the Institute's present ability to represent authentically the educational needs of management . . .

> The State's most effective control over the IMI — in relation to its subvention — lies in two facts: the level of participation in our courses; and that, unlike any other educational institution in the State, we have succeeded over the years in maintaining a ratio of the order of 1:2,

State grant to our own income, both for capital and revenue, because we regard it as essential that State subvention, or control, should never be such as to take the edge
off the Institute's concern to maximise its revenue from, as
an indication of its relevance to, business.

Once more, the spectre of AnCO control was exorcised and the
relationship settled somewhat. But ten years on, in 1984, AnCO
published a paper, *Management Training and Development in Ireland*, that once more raised the temperature at the IMI. One council member described the paper as "self-serving and superficial".
Listing some of its conclusions, he wailed, "Have they heard *anything* we've said for years?" The IMI's then director-general, Brian
Patterson, who had already conveyed his annoyance to his opposite number in AnCO, Malachy Sherlock, at this pre-emptive
strike, was more restrained. He told the council that it raised a
number of serious issues with which the Institute agreed; its weakness was that its assertions lacked any research base. There had
been no consultation and it ignored the contribution to management training of the third-level colleges.

The report was seen within the Institute as a reassertion by
AnCO of a desire to become the superordinate body in management training. The executive committee, which had considered the
document earlier, decided there should be no direct response; to
do so would "implicitly accept AnCO's right to co-ordinate management training". Instead the IMI produced its own assessment of
what needed to be done. The result[2] was presented to the Minister
of Labour as the Institute's contribution to the 1984 White Paper on
manpower policy. The submission put less emphasis on training
than on development, by the way reasserting the Institute's special
strengths and long experience:

The process of management training has to be appropriate. Managers are developed more than trained — not by
what we might "do to them" but what we encourage them
to do for themselves. Simple knowledge inputs, through
lecturing or casework, are therefore less likely to produce
a better manager. To be effective, the process has to en-

---

[2] IMI (1984), *Strengthening Irish Management*.

courage, or even force, the manager to test new approaches against his/her experience and to apply these in risk-free situations or on the job itself. The process must then encourage reflection on the experience to consolidate new skills or attitudes.

These are the principles of action learning; in applying these principles, the IMI has been amongst the pioneers.

The paper ranged over many issues impinging on the performance of managers, including rewards and the role of personal taxation. Addressing the vexed issue of AnCO's quest for superordinate status, it pulled no punches:

> A desirable principle is that an authority or agency, to which the Government delegates responsibility for aspects of policy in the area of training provision, should not itself be a provider. No body can be both an effective player and referee.

The Institute proposed, with no little optimism, that the Government recognise it as the National Management Institute — the primary body for post-experience management training and development; that AnCO's operational role should be limited to what it was doing at present, and that the Minister for Labour should define the future roles of both organisations.

Later there were meetings with AnCO and the minister. Some progress was made and the relationship improved somewhat, helped by the fact that an IMI council member, Niall Greene, chief executive of the Youth Employment Agency, had been appointed chairman of AnCO. Nevertheless, Brian Patterson assured the council that he would continue to monitor the situation "tightly".

The technical assistance scheme ended in 1984. Even though it was replaced by a management training support scheme, from then on the transactions between the two bodies diminished and, with it, the spleen. In 1988, in one of those whirls of the merry-go-round that state agencies undergo from time-to-time, AnCO took a new shape as FÁS (Foras Áiseanna Saothair), the latter's focus being less on business than on the then key national concern, the unemployed.

CHAPTER FIFTEEN

CALL IT FIDO

> It should be borne in mind that there is nothing more dif-
> ficult to arrange, more doubtful of success and more
> dangerous to carry through than initiating changes.
> — *Machiavelli*

Tony O'Reilly, at the 1970 annual conference, on the theme *The Entrepreneur, a Force for Growth*, lamented the failure of business four years previously to establish a Nationwide Irish Business Organisation (NIBO). Present were many business leaders who still believed that a small country with a compact industrial base did not need a plethora of business organisations to service it. The story of NIBO is an interesting tale of the eventual triumph of chains of office over an objective good.

By the mid-1960s, the economy had racked up almost a decade of growth. Confidence was on the up and new promotional institutions, such as the IDA and Córas Tráchtála, were working well. As, indeed, was the Institute. There was optimism that a brighter destiny lay ahead. Preparations for free trade were being advanced, even though Britain's entry to the European Economic Community — and Ireland's with it — was still being blocked by President Charles de Gaulle.

The Second Programme for Economic Expansion, which covered the years 1964–70, introduced the practice of central economic programming for the first time. It called for much closer interaction between industry and government than the first. Indeed, the programme could not work unless the key economic players took an active part in the shaping of policy. To formalise this, the Government in 1963 established the National Industrial Economic Council (NIEC). The council was partly nominated by the Government and partly by the trade unions, the employers and the semi-state boards; agriculture was added later.

Industry was expected to provide the lion's share of a 35 per cent real increase in GNP looked for in the period covered by the programme: industrial output was required to increase at an annual rate of 7.1 per cent, as against less than four per cent for the other productive sectors. Employment in industry was projected to grow by a total of 60,000 jobs to 334,000 by 1970. Industry's inputs to the NIEC needed, therefore, to be of the highest quality. Not everyone was happy that this was so.

Explaining to the IMI conference in 1965 the programming approach adopted by the Second Programme, its principal author, Dr T.K. Whitaker, Secretary of the Department of Finance, said:

> The first programme was mainly concerned with the Government's contribution to development. The second programme deals much more explicitly with the contribution of the private sector. It makes specific growth projections for each of the main economic divisions and breaks down those for industry into projections for individual industries and industrial groupings. These projections are not just forecasts of likely development resulting from the free play of market forces, but are rather objectives to be reached through influencing market forces by the purposeful application of appropriate policies. They require techniques of analysis, judgement, consultation and agreement as advanced as in any other country, and the provision of a broad framework within which Government and industry can achieve agreed objectives.
>
> Without these, however great the national need or however praiseworthy the objectives, the programme loses force and the economic realities it seeks to effect remain unchanged.

Whitaker told his audience that the Second Programme demanded a change of approach and attitude to their functions by government departments and state agencies. But, he warned:

> There must be a corresponding appreciation by industry
> of the significance of programming and what it requires of
> managements and trade unions. Experience after the first
> year of the Second Programme suggests that this under-
> standing is not yet widespread. The targets have not so far
> had a significant impact on industry and are not taken, in a
> sufficient number of cases, as the framework for planning
> by individual industries and firms ... Since economic ex-
> pansion is mainly the total result of a large number of de-
> cisions made by individual enterprises, it would be
> disquieting if industries and firms did not quickly base
> their policies and actions on the targets which they have
> had a hand in framing.

Whitaker was firm, if diplomatic, in laying the blame for the disappointing first year of the programme:

> The novelty of the procedure and an insufficient grasp of
> its purpose were, no doubt, in part responsible for this; it
> also appears that there was insufficient knowledge at in-
> dustry level of the problems and difficulties facing firms.

> These deficiencies amount to a weakness in communica-
> tion both within industry and between industry and Gov-
> ernment. They undermine the extent to which the
> successful resolution of industry/state relations at their
> present juncture depends on an adequate exchange of in-
> formation between the two sides and on each understand-
> ing the complementary functions of the other. They also
> demonstrate that while the broad structure of institutional
> arrangements to meet this need has been provided, it
> contains gaps at several points which have to be made
> good before it serves its purpose properly.

The pitch was clearly coming from the Government side of the table that its private-sector partners in the great enterprise of economic programming would need to sharpen their act and become
at least as proficient as the civil servants. Some business leaders
were already concerned about the ability of the existing industry
representation structures to deliver.

There were two main industry organisations, the Federation of
Irish Industry (FII), for economic and industrial policy, and the

Federated Union of Employers (FUE) for manpower and industrial relations issues. Some of the leading industrialists in the FII were becoming concerned that industry was not equipped to participate in national programming. In 1965 the NIEC issued 16 reports, many of which had serious implications for industry. FII had three representatives who were expected to respond to all these initiatives and to do so on behalf of industry as a whole. The unions, on the other hand, were well resourced with economists, statisticians and other specialists.

Early in 1966, Guy Jackson, managing director of Guinness, held a meeting in his office with Michael Rigby-Jones, chairman of the IMI; Sidney Gibson, president of the FII and head of Bailey Gibson, one of the top packaging companies; Don Carroll, of P.J. Carroll, governor of the Bank of Ireland; Ray Sellers, managing director of Cadbury Ireland, and Perry Greer, chairman of Unidare. They discussed the dispersed pattern of industry representation and the multiplicity of bodies to which they were expected to subscribe. They decided to invite about 45 leading industrialists to a one-day conference, advertised as the '66 Business Conference, to focus on the problem with the object of rationalising the whole representational sector.

The conference was told that there were an astonishing 65 employer or management organisations in Dublin, none of which had an effective voice at national level. A short paper was considered proposing the formation of a confederation of business organisations, state companies and banks, as an initial step towards unity. It would harmonise and co-ordinate the policies of member organisations on major issues, carry out special studies of areas under scrutiny by the NIEC and act as a coherent voice for business. The conference agreed to fund a £40,000 study by the management consultants, Harbridge House Europe, to consider how the business sector "could be more effectively represented in Irish national affairs generally and in relations with the Government and trade unions in particular".

The move had the private support of the Taoiseach, Sean Lemass, who months earlier had called on business to assume a broader role in public affairs. Harbridge House approached the brief in the knowledge that their client, the '66 Business Conference, had already decided that the answer was not simply to strengthen existing institutions. What they set out to test in a series of interviews — with leaders of industry, services, the trade unions, politics and the Civil Service — was a more radical proposition: the creation of a new entity to represent business at a level of capability appropriate to its place in the economy. The core structure would be formed by combining the strengths of the FII and the FUE. To enhance the claim of the new organisation to be the voice of united business, other, even less well endowed bodies, like the Association of Chambers of Commerce, the Federation of Builders, Contractors and Allied Employers of Ireland, the Federation of Trade Associations, the Irish Exporters' Association, etc., would be subsumed into the new organisation.

In June 1966, the consultants spent two hours with the director of the IMI, Ivor Kenny, and his deputy, Brian Whelan. Clearly, the IMI would add significant capability to the proposed body in developing its members' entrepreneurial and managerial skills. But there were constraints. The IMI's position was different from others: it was not a representative body; its job was to raise the standard of management, not just in industry — it had members in the public and educational sectors also. The consultants would have been told that the Institute was heavily reliant on government funding and would not want to be seen biting the hand that fed it. Of course, the IMI would not have been unmindful that, if it remained aloof, a powerful new business body might get into competition with it.

When the consultants came back to the steering committee, they gave a generally positive account of the attitude of Irish business to the proposal. But recognition of managers' responsibility to contribute to national policy-making was "not generally apparent". Those who had little involvement in national affairs saw such a role as, at best, a necessary evil and, at worst, a distraction from their responsibility to their companies. This view was widespread among small enterprise managers. Business people who were already involved with government wanted to see others carrying their share of the load.

By the autumn of 1966, the process had advanced sufficiently for the chairman, Sidney Gibson, to begin briefing the main institutions about it. In October, he talked to the IMI council, of which he was a member. Denis Hegarty told him that some council members worried about rumours that the Institute might "be drifting into a situation where decisions might be taken about [its] role without reference to council". The point was made more than once that the IMI was not representational; as Michael Dargan put it "the Institute's members came together to exchange experience and to learn". While members of council might have welcomed the development (and, by and large, they tended to do so), by the end of the discussion there was a clear feeling that the Institute should not do so officially and should keep its distance.

In a nutshell, the consultants' report recommended that employer and industry and trade bodies — beginning with the FUE and the FII — should be integrated into a Nationwide Irish Business Organisation. NIBO would formulate policy on economic, labour, social and commercial issues, advance the case of Irish industry in regard to those issues and "serve as a national resource to those seeking the views of business generally". The range of committees suggested reflected the reach of the new body's proposed agenda. Policies, once established, would be binding on the entire business sector.

The consultants had taken account of the IMI's sensitivities. Provision would be made for some form of IMI participation so that NIBO could use IMI resources without compromising IMI's business relationship with other sectors. The formula would place it at arm's length from the core NIBO organisation. There would be a "committee for business education and training" that would "establish sectoral policies for meeting the education and training needs of business". It would determine long- and short-term educational and training needs; develop internal resources to meet those needs, and "co-ordinate external resources such as the IMI, universities, etc." But the principal educational resource would be the IMI. Both the IMI and NIBO councils would exchange representatives and, in return for an annual payment to the institute, NIBO's members would be considered members of IMI, except for voting rights.

The state boards were also sensitive about full involvement with NIBO. They were, after all, part of the public sector and had direct policy links with government and the Civil Service. On the other hand, they represented a substantial part of the industrial base of the economy; a central business organisation that did not include them would lack completeness. The consultants were instructed to revisit these issues and to test the proposed organisation design extensively with business. They were to look at how the integration and affiliation might be tackled in detail and how the transition might be managed.

To keep the project moving, a feasibility committee was set up. It included the original promoters, representatives of 12 of the core business organisations (including the IMI) and the state companies. The momentum was maintained by the frequency of the committee meetings — eight plenary sessions in a 16-week period. An abundance of optimism was generated; the idea seemed unstoppable.

In July 1967, when Harbridge House reported back to the Business Conference, there were no doubts. The message was unequivocal: NIBO was feasible. It could be a legal entity by March 1968 and would begin operations immediately under a transitional council, starting with the integration of the FII, the builders federation, the motor traders organisations and the Exporters' Association. The state companies and banks would join later, followed by the Association of Chambers of Commerce of Ireland, the Federation of Trade Associations and the Printing Federation. There would be a "formal liaison" with the management institute. When completed, NIBO would have a nucleus of 2,250 corporate members and 12–14,000 affiliated companies.

The Institute submitted a paper on how the relationship with NIBO might develop — a close working association, but with the Institute maintaining its separate identity. The argument ran:

> The IMI's function was an educational one. It was significantly different in its objective and in its work from NIBO. The Institute would require continuing substantial government subvention; it would be undesirable for a branch of NIBO to be subvented by government.

NIBO members would have access to IMI information services, library and journal. For the IMI, this was a good bargain: it would have a much wider market for courses and, in a stroke, triple the circulation of *Management*.

So what happened to NIBO? In the earlier phase, there were many who, although convinced that it was needed, did not expect that existing organisations would, in the final analysis, agree to be swallowed up by a new entity. Yet, when senior representatives of the targeted organisations came together in the feasibility committee, the consultants found no such caveat:

> We were most pleased and encouraged by the conclusions of the feasibility committee that an integrated organisation was both possible and necessary. The time and effort put into the realistic assessment of the NIBO proposals by this group of executives currently familiar with Irish business organisations augurs well for the successful formation of a NIBO.

The euphoria was short-lived. The reason for the collapse is probably to be found in a disclaimer in the consultants' preamble to the feasibility committee's report:

> It should be emphasised that these committee members did not serve as official spokesmen for their various institutions and that they were in no way asked, expected or empowered to commit their institutions on the various proposals under discussion. Rather, they served in personal capacities with the objective of evaluating the proposals with due regard to the policies and practices of their respective institutions.

The project's momentum made it difficult for members of that committee to keep their organisations fully informed. The "bandwagon effect" took over, a shared dream outpacing back-home reality.

A serious fault-line showed when the FUE decided in the spring of 1967 to pull back and not merge with FII. With that decision, the project ran out of steam. Various other organisations balked at losing their identity in the cause of unity. The IMI's involvement was always conditional on union being achieved between the FUE and the FII. When informed of the FUE's decision, the executive committee noted bleakly:

> The proposed arrangements for a link between the Institute and a Nationwide Irish Business Organisation do not now arise.

With the failure of the Harbridge House design, the FII decided to salvage what it could of the concept. The need was still there and the requirement to strengthen industry's representational ability was no less urgent. Don Carroll chaired a working party that came up with an alternative proposition — the forging of a loose confederation of business organisations, without the FUE. They would retain their identities (and chains of office) but there would be a central council, which would receive the views of the sectoral groupings and develop a common position on the national front.

The president of the FII, Guy Jackson, and the director-general, Ned Gray (both, tragically, to be victims of the British Airways Trident crash at Staines in 1972) briefed the IMI council about this "plan B" in March 1969. They got good support. Frank Lemass, who chaired the meeting, suggested the FII should, for a start, change its name: Federation of Irish Industry was too much associated with the protectionist regime of the past. The FII council had, in fact, already decided to launch the new initiative under the name Confederation of Irish Industry.

Sir Geoffrey Thompson of Guinness contributed some final, thoughtful and, indeed, prophetic, observations on the NIBO project:

> Of course, it had been the right thing to do. There should be a single strong business organisation to interface with government. The difficulty was that the NIBO idea had taken Irish industry by storm. Industry was asked to act too suddenly; sufficient account was not taken of vested interests. There should, instead, have been a gradual evolution. The FII and the FUE should now, in the first place, seek common ground on which they can co-operate. That might well evolve into sharing a common secretariat and, finally, into a single organisation.

There were many who, with Geoffrey Thompson, regretted the lost opportunity represented by the failure of NIBO. Perhaps Tony O'Reilly was right when he quipped at that 1970 conference: "Maybe if they called it FIDO, it might have come!"

CHAPTER SIXTEEN

"CRASH WIDOWS SLAM PLAN"

In autumn 1971, Ned Gray, director-general of the Confederation of Irish Industry, called to see Ivor Kenny at Orwell Road. He told Kenny that he intended to leave the CII soon and that now might be a good time to talk about a closer integration of the confederation with the Institute. Although it had been five years since the NIBO adventure, he did not think that the time was yet ripe for another try at integration with the FUE. But other aspects of the concept could, perhaps, be advanced — with EEC entry less than 18 months away, the resources problem was even more pressing.

Kenny discussed Gray's approach with his chairman, Ronald Nesbitt, who agreed that the discussions should continue. Michael Sweetman, business policy consultant with the confederation, was also involved in the talks. A committed European, he was a leading contributor to the IMI's EEC preparedness programme, and to the success of the national referendum for EC membership.

By the spring of 1972, the talks were running out of steam as both directors-general identified barriers ahead. The IMI was now less sure of the benefits of such a liaison. It was in the middle of a fast growth phase, its market multiplying; a re-opening of the NIBO issue would be a distraction. Gray and Kenny agreed to let matters rest for a time and talk again later.

In mid-June 1972, Gray and Kenny were at a function in Dublin. Gray suggested a resumption of the talks. Kenny agreed. Three days later, on Sunday, 18 June, Ned Gray, Michael Sweetman and ten other Irish business leaders were on their way to Brussels to discuss issues connected with Ireland's entry into the EEC. After a short stop-over in London, they took off in a British Airways Trident.

Ninety seconds later, the aircraft crashed at Staines, killing every-one on board. At a stroke, the CII lost its president, Con Smith, immediate past-president, Guy Jackson, director-general Gray, business policy expert Sweetman, economics and trade officer, Fergus Mooney, and council member, Michael Rigby-Jones — a former chairman and president of the IMI. Also killed were the president of the Dublin Chamber of Commerce, M.W. O'Reilly; Ivan Webb, chairman of the Employers' Confederation; Melville Miller, a former vice-president and deputy chairman of the FUE; Owen Lochrin, vice-president of the Association of Chambers of Commerce of Ireland; Hugh Kilfeather, assistant general manager of the Irish Export Board and Edward A. Coleman, deputy general manager of Irish Steel Holdings.

The shock reverberated through Irish business. In a commissioned memorial piece in *Management*, titled "Requiescant", the poet Basil Payne wrote:

> The headlined horror
> Sickens the stomach as it rips the memory
> The jagged odds-and-ends of reminiscence.

Ivor Kenny called Peter Keehan, the vice-president of the CII, to offer the Institute's sympathy and any help he needed. After an emergency council meeting in the CII the same morning, Keehan called back to ask if the IMI could supply an acting chief executive, their most acute need. Two weeks later, Liam Connellan, head of the small business division, was seconded to the role. The arrangement was for six months to allow the CII to recruit a successor to Gray. Connellan was 36. An engineer with industrial experience, he had been six years with the IMI.

In August, Kenny and Keehan met to discuss the void left by the air crash, particularly in the light of imminent entry to the EEC, now only six months away. The tragedy had been a stark reminder of the scarcity of business leadership in a small community. They talked about the need to revisit the notion of strengthening business's representational arm and a possible integration of CII and IMI. The latter seemed to offer the best and quickest solution to CII's crisis. In a phrase that was to be used many times by the protagonists of the idea: it made sense.

Why did it make sense when, albeit in different circumstances, a few short months earlier, the IMI's attitude towards a merger had been cool? According to Ivor Kenny:

> There are two distinguishable, but inextricably inter-twined, strands running through the saga. The first is the fundamental purpose of an organisation, the *raison d'être* which gives it its legitimacy and commands support suffi-cient to maintain its existence. This is the objective strand. The subjective strand lies in the motivations — and emo-tions — of stakeholders and particularly office-holders. The more benign manifestation of this latter is a concern for the freedom of action of an organisation: its ability to attain its objectives unencumbered by constraining rela-tionships with — or, worse, subordination to — other or-ganisations; in a word, elbowroom. The less benign manifestation of it is job-protection.
>
> Ned Gray genuinely felt that the CII had reached a pla-teau; with Sweetman, he was vividly aware of the changes the EEC was going to wreak in Irish industry — the objec-tive strand. But it is doubtful if he would have opened dis-cussions with the IMI had he not already decided to leave. His leaving freed up the situation; it made change possi-ble — the subjective strand.
>
> I find it impossible to unravel which concern predomi-nated: the unheroic one of job protection or the more de-tached one of doing what was right for the IMI and, through it, for Irish industry. The truth is probably that it was a mixture — a sometimes competing mixture. The IMI's coolness to the CII's overtures was certainly influ-enced by it.

What then had changed?

> First, there was the emotional impact of the air crash. It left a feeling of vulnerability and impermanence. The reaction was a desire for renewal and strength and a belief that here was a new opportunity. There was the feeling that, at such a time, personal motivation would have been shabby. But, secondly, there was the fact that the IMI was now the organisation with which the initiative lay. The CII had been

wounded. The IMI was the stronger, continuing organisation. The CII's president was the catalyst. That was critical.

Against this background, arguments for a joint body were developed. Kenny discussed progress with his chairman. Nesbitt approved, provided the academic independence of the IMI — about which he felt deeply — could be adequately safeguarded. Connellan, although still formally on loan from the IMI, had quickly taken the CII perspective; even as head of the IMI's small business activities, he had always believed in closer integration of management development with business development generally. The integration proposal to him, too, "made sense".

The minimum necessary commitment of the honorary officers and the chief executives of both organisations was achieved. To this inner circle was added Michael Dargan, vice-chairman of the IMI, who was due to succeed Nesbitt as IMI chairman the following year. As well as being vastly experienced in the IMI, he was also a member of the CII council. His support, which would be essential, was given only after deep consideration. His opposition would have put a stop to the proposals.

The first step would be to get together a small working group of CII and IMI senior staff to formulate an outline proposal for the executive committees of both bodies, and, then, to the councils. The final decision would rest with extraordinary general meetings of both. Along the way there would be consultation with other organisations and individuals. Early in September, a timetable for implementation was prepared, a schedule that was to end neatly with the first meeting of the new joint council on 31 October.

There was little doubt that the timetable would be followed. The idea was sound. Its pedigree stretched back to the NIBO adventure. It had been given impetus by rapid changes in the business environment in the interim, and now by imminent entry to the EEC.

Kenny recalls:

> As the circle of consultation widened, confidence grew. Influential figures were impressed by the timeliness of the proposals and their decisiveness. This growing confidence was to inhibit hearing what Igor Ansoff called the "faint signals", something to which the antennae of the effective corporate planner are sensitive. The first of these

signals was when the IMI senior staff were informed of the proposals early in September. The CII senior staff — of whom there were indeed few — were not informed, at least officially, until four days later. The latter had more to gain — or lose.

The CII executive committee was to meet on 11 September for the first formal ratification of the proposals, the IMI's executive committee the following day. Keehan wrote as follows to the CII executive council:

> On Sunday June 18, the President and Director-General of the Confederation of Irish Industry, together with other leading industrialists, died while on their way to Brussels for discussion on Ireland's future within the enlarged Common Market. Their loss to Irish industry was tragic and severe. It came at a vital time for the country, with accession to the Community on January 1, three months from now. It cut short a process of expansion and development within the Confederation essential if we were to cope with the rapidly expanding problems facing the whole business community in Ireland: problems which were changing not only in degree but in kind.

> Against this background it was necessary to think rapidly about the Confederation's future. A permanent leader within the Confederation of Ned Gray's capabilities was not going to be easy to find, and even when found was going to need time to assume full responsibility for the representation of industry's interests. Yet time is in short supply. We are undergoing the most fundamental change in our economic and industrial development: it is now that we need to be strong and decisive and united in every move we make. Because of this I sought the views of a number of leaders of our business community on how best the interests of that community could be served in the difficult times that lie ahead.

> The proposal that emerged from these talks was that the Confederation of Irish Industry and the Irish Management Institute should be united to form a Confederation of Irish Business.

The advantages are many. I list here some of the more important ones:

1. **Strength**: The bringing together of two powerful organisations both working, though in different fields, for the direct benefit of business in Ireland will immeasurably strengthen the voice of business in public affairs. It is strength derived partly from the increase in size of membership and therefore in financial resources. As well as this the Confederation of Irish Business will work from a much broader base, one that combines strong representation with a strong, well-tried management training organisation with effective research and development resources.

2. **Broader Role**: A direct result of the strengthening of the voice of business by the merging of the two organisations will be the Confederation of Irish Business's ability to play a much broader role in public affairs. This was the primary aim of the '66 Business Conference, supported not only by leading industrialists, but also by government ministers, the civil service and trade union leaders. It was foreseen that the contribution would be a positive and far-ranging one, backed not so much by the business community's desire to look after itself in the narrow sense, but by the feeling that the complex problems facing the country then would benefit from a more positive, more flexible approach in which the representational work on behalf of businessmen would be supported by well-researched, well-informed understanding of the needs. The primary reason for NIBO's failure was not the lack of seriousness in this objective of a broader role in public affairs, but the choice of the work mixture with which to achieve it. The FUE, with its difficult and precise role in the field of industrial relations, was not ready for a marriage with the then FII. I believe, together with a number of colleagues drawn from the Executive Committees of the CII and the IMI, that the right mixture is presented to us in the amalgamation of these two organisations into a Confederation of Irish Business.

3. **Leadership**: The tragic losses of last June cannot be made good. Nevertheless, the work of representation, of planning, of training, must go on. The close ties between CII and IMI were demonstrated immediately after the air crash by the secondment at my request of Liam Connellan as director-general for a six-month period. What will now become available is the pooled talent of both organisations, with leadership spread over a wide range of matters of vital importance to businessmen in this country.

4. **Potential Expansion**: The broader base and the greater strength of a Confederation of Irish Business will attract wider membership. I believe that it will encourage other business interests to give greater support, and will bring in groups that up to now have remained separate and divided. The regional structure of business in Ireland will be strengthened.

I believe it is fair to say that these objectives closely parallel those of the '66 Business Conference, and that the proposed organisation will go a long way towards achieving what NIBO failed to become. They were also the firmly held objectives of a number of the men who died, among them Ned Gray, Guy Jackson, Michael Rigby-Jones, Con Smith and Michael Sweetman. This has been considered seriously, at length, and by many people over a considerable period of time. There is now, however, a particular element of urgency with our imminent entry into the EEC. It is for this reason that I send you this letter, which I trust you will treat as very strictly personal and confidential to you as a member of the Executive. I ask you to give the most serious thought to an event that could be crucial for every businessman in this country.

Keehan had emphasised the urgency of the situation, the advantages of the new organisation, and the fact that it was in line with the objectives of those who died. The document that accompanied his letter stated:

The Confederation of Irish Business will be organised to provide for effective and positive participation by Irish business in national and European affairs. It will have strong supporting services including policy formulation, research and information. The Irish Management Institute, with its key role of management development, will be integrated into the Confederation, but will maintain the autonomy necessary for objective research and training.

Seven distinct functions were proposed: national business policy, sectoral affairs, regional affairs, international affairs, management development, training and research (the IMI), communications and administration. A staff of 156 in 1972/73 was envisaged, with an annual operating budget of £900,000. It was, on paper, an attractive package. The national executive committee of the CII seemed to think so. On 19 September 1972, it passed unanimously the following resolution:

> That the National Executive Committee of CII gives its support to the proposal to merge with the Irish Management Institute in order to form a Confederation of Irish Business and that it recommends this decision to the National Council for adoption.

The resolution was proposed and seconded by two past-presidents of the CII. The support at the meeting was unequivocal. Keehan said there was a remote possibility that the grants to the IMI might be reduced, but that it was unlikely, as they would be used solely for management education. He had discussed the proposal "in depth" with the Minister for Labour, the secretaries of the departments of Finance, Industry and Commerce and Labour. They had all supported it. He had been assured that the confederation could pursue an independent line (uninhibited, presumably, by government funding for the IMI).

It was agreed to have a press statement prepared, for use only if there were enquiries. A formal announcement would have to await the council meeting to consider the executive's proposal. At the close of the meeting, Sidney Gibson, who had been president of the FII at the time of the NIBO proposals, congratulated Keehan "on his depth of thinking and initiative".

Ivor Kenny continues:

> The IMI, for its part, had to ensure that integration in a business representative body would not affect its gov-

ernment grant — the other side of the coin of freedom. On 19 September 1972, the chairman and I met with the Minister for Labour, Joe Brennan, and the secretary of the department, Tadhg O Cearbhaill. We came away with their support and an assurance that "the proposed organisation would not interfere with the present form of State subvention". The minister mentioned that he had informed the Government of the proposals at their last meeting and would do so again. The same day I saw the secretary of the Department of Finance, C.H. Murray, and the assistant secretary, Michael Murphy. My minute conveys a slightly (and understandably) more guarded attitude from that department, but records that "a possible formula mentioned was that subvention would be given to the Confederation of Irish Business for the Irish Management Institute".

The formula would be worked out with the Department of Labour. The Finance representatives agreed that there was need for a strong business organisation whose submissions were based on research and who did not indulge in "tip and run" comment. They probably had in mind a recent criticism by CII of a "proliferation" of state bodies, unaccompanied by any constructive proposal. Officials would have spent many frustrating years in the early stages of economic planning dealing with business organisations that seemed to make up policy as they went along.

With government support assured, and the CII executive committee unanimously in favour, it looked like plain sailing for the IMI executive committee meeting. There was, however, one note of opposition. Frank Lemass, chief executive of CIE and a former chairman of the IMI, was chairman of the Institute's Founding Fund.[1] It was an unqualified success, bringing in the largest sum ever raised voluntarily from Irish business and that success was due in large measure to Lemass. He was someone to be listened to. He wrote to Nesbitt:

---

[1] Established to finance the building of a new national management centre, then being planned by the Institute (see Chapter Seventeen).

While I accept that there is a certain overlapping of membership, I do not agree with your view that there is a wide area of common ground between the two bodies. In fact, I can find little, if any. Neither can I agree, I am afraid, with your dictum that a fusion is good management. You will be aware of some disastrous mergers in the business world! ...

The recent high level of support for the Founding Fund by the bulk of the corporate members makes it imperative, I feel, that they be consulted and their approval sought ... the matter should not be rushed.

The more I think of it the more I am against the idea, I think it just would not be a success.

For Lemass, at least, the proposal did not "make sense". However, plans went ahead as arranged. The IMI executive committee met the day after the CII meeting. They decided unanimously to recommend the proposals to the Institute's council.

It would have been unusual for the council of either body to go against the considered recommendations of the executive committee. That was what executive committees were for: to make recommendations on matters of fundamental policy and to get on with the job of running the organisations. Only once had the IMI council thrown out a recommendation of its executive committee (and that, oddly enough, was also a proposal for a merger — with the Institute of Public Administration in 1959). The way was clear, therefore, for wider consultations.

Ronald Nesbitt wrote to council members of the IMI:

With our imminent entry to the EEC — when we shall all face a totally changed trading environment — Irish business needs a strong, united organisation to represent it effectively in national and international affairs and to serve it adequately through policy formulation, through research, and through the training and development of managers.

The proposals are a logical outcome of the policy approved by the executive committee and endorsed by the council on 11 April 1972. At that time, we emphasised that the Institute was set firmly in the context of growth as a national objective. We also emphasised that our work must be directly related to the immediate problems of business. We must not be academic and aloof.

The new organisation will provide an environment for the Institute which will ensure that all its work is, and is seen to be, directly related to business's problems, while maintaining the impartial, professional character of the IMI. The proposals envisage an IMI stripped of its ambiguities — those membership activities more appropriate for a Business Confederation. The Institute will now be clearly seen to be dedicated to the single objective of raising the standard of management in Ireland through training and research. It will retain its individual membership structure. It will retain unchanged its Members' Founding Fund for a management training centre. The proposed organisation will not interfere with the present form of State subvention. Firmly set in a strong united business organisation, its role unambiguous, the Institute will develop an independence to research and comment that its present structure can inhibit.

I have regarded it as my prime responsibility as your Chairman to ensure that the Institute retained these essential characteristics. I am satisfied that the proposals before you achieve that end and that I shall have discharged my responsibility. I shall now be happy to stand down to clear the way for whatever new appointments are agreed for the Confederation of Irish Business.

But having said that, you will agree that the Institute has responsibilities wider than merely ensuring its own integrity. The proposals before you present us with an opportunity to serve Irish business with a new, strong, outward looking organisation. Some of our colleagues, including our past President, Michael Rigby-Jones, died in this service and with this vision.

At a time of change, I believe we owe it to their memory and to Irish business to take this initiative and to act decisively.

I am sending this letter to you personally and confidentially as a council member. I know you will understand the necessity for strict confidentiality until the councils of both organisations have taken their decisions.

Ivor Kenny comments:

> Nesbitt put the proposed merger in the context of devel-
> oping IMI policy. The points about loss of integrity and
> government funding were met. His offer to stand down
> was a strong indication that there was no doubt about the
> proposal going through. There was, as there was in Kee-
> han's letter, an emphasis on confidentiality: a concern that
> the right information should get to the right people at the
> right time.

The confidentiality was shattered a week later by an article in *The
Irish Times*. It was surprising in a close community that the press
had not got hold of the story earlier. The article, by Andrew
Whittaker, *The Irish Times*'s business editor, described what he
called "this extraordinary proposal" as less a merger, more "an
IMI take-over bid".

Michael Dargan called a meeting of the heads of state-
sponsored companies. Connellan and Kenny attended, leaving
when they had answered questions. The meeting agreed that, while
there were inherent risks in the merger for both parties, the new
organisation would "provide a more powerful instrument for influencing government policies and public attitudes in support of
measures likely to produce increased business activity and national prosperity". State-sponsored bodies represented at the discussion would support the new organisation. While they "would not
have much to gain, they could have much to contribute". The proposals had secured the backing of another powerful constituency.

Because of the EEC dimension, Peter Keehan went to see the
Minister for Foreign Affairs, Dr Patrick Hillery. Hillery knew both
the CII and the IMI well, having been both Minister for Industry
and Commerce and Minister for Labour. He welcomed the proposal, as did the secretary of the Department of Industry and
Commerce, J.C.B. McCarthy. Michael Dargan for the IMI (Nesbitt
was away) and Keehan saw the Taoiseach, Jack Lynch. He had to be
officially neutral, but expressed approval. They saw the Minister for
Finance, George Colley. He had been concerned about the subvention issue but seemed satisfied with their answers.

Ivor Kenny had a second meeting with the Minister for Labour
on 5 October and prepared a note for him for a meeting of the

Government. A brief was sent to opposition leaders, Liam Cosgrave, Fine Gael, and Brendan Corish, Labour, and to Dr Garret FitzGerald of Fine Gael, a former consultant to the CII and former council and executive committee member of the IMI. Kenny also met the officer board of the Irish Congress of Trade Unions, who seemed benevolent.

A joint CII/IMI memorandum to the Taoiseach put the case for the CIB in a way that would appeal to the Government:

> Since Ireland's entry into Europe was first mooted over a decade ago there have been many studies and reports advocating "adaptation" to totally changed trading conditions. Despite these studies and continuous exhortations by government ministers and by business leaders, many businesses are ill-prepared. The most serious symptom of this unpreparedness is the growing number of redundancies. Over the next few years, these redundancies will give rise to some of the gravest economic, social and political problems to face the country.
>
> While government action is the single most powerful force for change, it has been demonstrated over the past ten years that government action by itself can be limited in its reach. It has not been sufficient to have elaborate incentive schemes, capital grants, export tax relief, CIO, COIP, NIEC reports. What has been missing is a strong, genuinely representative business body with which government can collaborate. The pace of economic and social change is accelerating. The pace of adaptation is not. The urgency of the situation calls for decisive action by business unfettered by any forms in which it has organised itself in the past.

The paper described the CIB as "an organisation as much *about* as *for* business", its objective being to participate in the development of an environment for enterprise, "where essential economic progress will be reconciled with the dignity and values of the individual". It would help business in a practical, pragmatic way to cope with change in international and internal trading relationships, in attitudes and expectation, and change caused by technological development:

An organisation focused on the narrow interests of a particular group is bound for ultimate failure . . . the challenges to Irish business, many of which come from outside the country, could ill be faced by an organisation that was negative, protectionist and divisive.

How would it relate to government?

Co-operation rather than criticism will be the keynote of the relationship. It is not to say that the Government with its much wider, and ultimate, responsibilities will always see eye to eye with a Confederation representing one sector of the community. It is to say that Government policy for business will be that much more informed if it has a strong business organisation with which to consult in the formulation of policy and a genuinely representative body to participate in the consequent implementation of that policy.

A key factor in the new CIB would be the interlocking of the IMI role of the development of managers "with the pragmatic CII objective of ensuring the survival of industry in a changed trading relationship by the formulation of business policy derived from practical experience":

At a time when business faces a turbulent environment, for which there is no precedent, for the IMI to remain aloof, dedicated to the pursuit of management science as an end in itself, would be a good recipe for the IMI to become irrelevant. If the IMI were not relating directly to the immediate pressures on business as identified by business itself, it could quickly lose the substantial commitment it has built up over twenty years: this at a time when all sectors are agreed that ineffective management is the most important blockage to industrial progress.

To have one organisation for the development of practical business policy and another for the development of business managers in a small community where resources of money and intellect are very scarce is now not simply wasteful, it does not work well. Integration of the two is now essential. It can be achieved only if there is unity at the level of overall policy and direction. Where there are two organisations, they go their separate ways, developing different policies, with more or less the same group of businessmen attending twice the number of meetings, considering related policies in an unrelated form. The lack of unity of policy and action was tolerated at a time when business was to an extent cushioned from the realities of a competitive environment. It cannot be tolerated now.

The paper then addressed the most sensitive issue: while its IMI component would enjoy government patronage, this "strong, genuinely representative business body" must, at all costs, avoid the accusation of using government money in its representational role.

> The IMI and the CII agree that government subvention to a body that is solely representative in role can be inappropriate both in itself and *vis-à-vis* other bodies, in particular the trade unions . . . Government subvention has been found necessary for management training. The IMI is satisfied, following consultation, that a formula can be worked out which makes clear that government funds are devoted only to the management training activities of the CIB.

In what looks like straw-clutching, the paper pointed out that the IMI would retain its name, individual members and Founding Fund; that its training centre would be separate from the headquarters of the CIB with an "academic policy board [including] representatives of the Departments of Finance, Labour, Industry and Commerce, Public Service, subject to the agreement of the minister concerned, representatives of the trade unions, representatives of AnCO and of the educational bodies". The Institute would "continue to develop the participation in its work of civil servants, both to give its staff a greater understanding of how the civil service works and to help bridge the gap between civil servants and businessmen".

As part of the bargain, the "institute of managers" would disappear:

> It will be stripped of the ambiguities of its present structure where in fact its membership activities — council, regional and national conference, etc. — cause it partly to be perceived as a representative body. It will in future be perceived as a professional management training centre,

but one whose work is integrated into a broader structure concerned with the development of business as a whole.

The memorandum to the Taoiseach claimed:

> The councils of both the IMI and CII — comprising over 60 chief executives of Ireland's principal businesses in the public and private sectors — have given serious consideration to the merger of the two bodies. The unanimity of support for the merger is impressive . . .

This was to prove a premature claim. It did not take account of the confederate nature of the CII. Not all members of the council, particularly the sector members, favoured the proposals. They were uncertain about whether they needed to check back with their sectors before they could support the proposal and were uncomfortable with the haste, the secrecy and the whiff of "IMI take-over".

The crucial council meetings were carefully arranged for the same day, Tuesday, 10 October 1972. The plan was that the CII council would meet in the morning and take what would be the critical decision. The IMI council would meet in the afternoon and give its blessing. Then a joint press conference would be held.

Doom awaited, however. On Sunday, 8 October, two days before the councils were to meet, the *Sunday Press* front page screamed across eight columns:

"CRASH WIDOWS SLAM PLAN"

Under this banner, the paper printed a letter from Una Gray and Barbara Sweetman:

> It was with great concern that we learned of the proposed merger between the CII and IMI to form a new Confederation of Irish Business and feel we would be failing our husbands if we did not make our voices heard. We know that neither of them would have supported this merger because it goes against everything they worked for within the Confederation and would not be in the best interests of Irish industry. For this reason we are very disturbed to hear that their names are being used to support the merger.

Writing in the *Sunday Independent*, the business editor, Colm Rapple, was unequivocally against the merger. The CII would lose its ability to criticise government because it could not bite the hand that fed it. The IMI would have its academic freedom stifled within "an unashamed pressure group". He concluded:

> The pity is that the executive committees of neither body has seen fit to outline the doubtless logical thinking behind the proposals to which they have given their stamp of approval. The result is that many are left with the impression of a needless and perhaps damaging merger of two organisations which as separate units have been operating exceptionally well in their individual spheres.

Mrs Gray was reported in *The Irish Times* as saying that both women were "disturbed by the secretive character of the proposals". She "felt the original proposal had been shelved and that it was resurrected following the death of her husband and Mr Sweetman". The government subsidy to the IMI threatened "the independence of the Confederation and its obligation to speak fearlessly on behalf of its members". Her present action in speaking out was being done "for the sake of my husband and for no other reason".

Peter Keehan, the president of the Confederation, asked to comment on RTE radio, said:

> I would, of course, regret if any distress was caused to the relatives. I am not certain I would agree with what their husbands might have recommended. For one thing, the situation is obviously so different from what it was before their husbands unfortunately died. The situation is so different that they would not have been looking at the same problem.

Press comment reached a peak that Monday with articles in *The Irish Times*, both on the front page and in the business section. Whittaker quoted from the confidential documents that had been circulated. The tone of the articles was against the merger:

> The merger body would lack the hard, cutting edge that CII was developing in representing the private sector in the Irish economy.

At 11.30 am on Tuesday, 10 October 1972, the council of the CII met in the Burlington Hotel, Dublin. There were 34 members present, of whom 14 were from industry sectors. The following motion was passed:

> It was unanimously agreed that the proposal to effect the merger between the CII and IMI in a new organisation to be known as the Confederation of Irish Business be examined further in depth and considered again by Council following consultation with the members.

But that was no more than a face-saving formula. The merger notion was damaged beyond recovery. The decision was telephoned to the IMI. Its council met at 3.00 pm. Twenty-one members attended. There was an air of anticlimax. Seven members, including Peter Keehan, had been at the CII council meeting that morning. IMI council minutes are almost verbatim. They give accurately not only the content but the flavour of the meeting.

> The chairman, Ronald Nesbitt, began by outlining the extensive consultation that had preceded the meeting. He mentioned letters of support from several members who could not be present. He informed the council of the CII's decision. Disappointment was expressed. There was a slight but discernible shift on the part of some members: their earlier enthusiasm for the merger had lessened a little. Others vigorously defended the concept and searched for a means to pursue it.

> Arguments from a purely IMI viewpoint were raised. No matter what was said now, the merger would have led inevitably to diminished government support. The benefits to the IMI were doubtful, the benefits to the CII considerable. The objects of the CII were about the politics of business while those of the IMI were about the management of business.

When a member asked if any other link-ups were considered other than the one with the CII, Nesbitt replied: "When contemplating marriage you do not consider matrimony in general, you consider someone in particular."

The meeting agreed unanimously to issue a press statement jointly with the CII, giving the text of the CII's resolution and adding that the IMI were following a similar procedure.

In a radio interview that evening, Kenny said:

> I think perhaps it moved at a speed which was too fast and did not take into account that, towards the end of the process, there were many people who felt they had not been consulted as fully as they should have been. At first there had been an absolutely overwhelming degree of support. As we came nearer the shore we found that some rocks began to appear.

It is impossible to measure the effect on the events of press comment. Kenny does not believe, as was claimed by some, that the newspaper articles forced a rethink of that whole proposition:

> On the other hand, to say that the councils were not influenced in any way by the publicity would be too large a claim. The truth is probably that the protagonists of the merger were unmoved and that the antagonists would have had their views reinforced. Press comment would not have changed the views on either side: they were deeply held.

Three weeks later, at a meeting of the CII national executive committee, it was decided that further examination of the proposal was to be undertaken "though not in haste". The important thing was to appoint a permanent director-general and strengthen the organisation. The position was offered to Liam Connellan, who accepted.

That ended talks of any association between IMI and CII — or any other body for that matter. Eventually, the push for an alliance between the two main industry organisations, CII and FUE — the main motivation for the NIBO 1966 project — reached a long-delayed dénouement with the birth in January 1993 of the Irish Business and Employers Confederation (IBEC).

CHAPTER SEVENTEEN

THE HIGH GROUND

Meanwhile, the IMI was immersed in plans to move to extensive new premises. The steady rise in demand, such a feature of the mid-1960s, had accelerated greatly at the end of the decade: the 1968/9 season, for instance, saw attendance grow by 40 per cent over the previous year. The multi-module courses that had worked well for production managers were extended to finance, personnel and marketing. The Institute was able to offer longer courses in computers and operations research for systems analysts. The small business unit was involved in a programme with the IDA. The in-company unit was working with over 20 large businesses. It used the management-by-objectives method: the IMI team helped the company identify corporate goals, install systems to achieve them and monitor the results. It was painstaking and labour intensive. Every manager set out his basic work programme in writing. Using that information, the Institute's specialists designed group workshops on problem analysis and decision-making, based on the type of issues likely to arise in the business. Later, help was available to sort out any implementation difficulties encountered back on the job. Demand was such that the council was told in 1968 that, with current resources, there was sufficient work in hand for over three years.

Spurred by strong demand across the board — and knowing that it was about to be boosted further by state incentives — the IMI simply kept growing. As long as anyone recruited made a contribution after his/her own costs, it made sense to expand the teaching staff. For a time, this expansion could be accommodated in temporary buildings in the grounds of Errigal at Orwell Road.

When that space ran out, the Institute bought an adjoining house, Lisheen. However, given the predicted upward demand curve, the capacity of the combined Errigal/Lisheen grounds was quickly reached. The choice then was either a high-density redevelopment at Orwell Road or a move to a new site with adequate potential to meet any imaginable future expansion. The snag was that, as usual, the Institute was without capital.

Because of the constant stream of submissions for grants, the traffic between the IMI and the state was then at its most intense. The need for a new, national centre for management training was first raised in a letter to Tadhg O Cearbhaill in September 1968:

> The Institute is faced with a pressing problem of accommodation. The projection of activity shows that by 1971 the annual programme will include 320 courses with 6,500 participants. This is an increase to 2½ times the present level of activity. The existing facilities of three temporary classrooms are inadequate, even for the present needs. Our architect has recommended strongly against the construction of further temporary buildings, and has recommended putting up a permanent building to meet the needs for conference and office accommodation, which would cost in the region of £300,000. At 31 March 1968 the Institute had no reserves whatsoever for further investment.

The initial plan was for a relatively modest construction on the Orwell Road site. It called for a deposit of £75,000 for the construction phase and £15,000 for equipment. The letter asked for reinstatement of a £34,000 cut in that year's grant. That, and the funds already requested for the following two years, would suffice for the redevelopment. The letter argued with Jesuitical point that this was not a request for capital; it would, rather, allow the Institute to accumulate a surplus on the revenue account that could then be used for capital!

At a meeting in the Department of Labour to discuss the request, the assistant secretary, Jack Agnew, patiently briefed the IMI supplicants on the facts of state funding: the Department of Finance was boss; it was "a first principle" that unexpended portions of subvention must be returned to them; it was "against principle" for voted money to be used for capital — the Government could not be expected to borrow money to give to the Institute, a non-state body, to invest in assets. However, Agnew was sympathetic to the IMI's predicament and suggested alternative ways of tackling the funding issue to allow for greater flexibility. The Institute's delegation came away better informed and with fresh options to pursue. Available resources at the IMI were deployed to produce within months a five-year plan for 1969–74. It was an intensive exercise. The heads of section not only had to extrapolate the likely growth in demand for current services, they had to estimate recruitment needs and the technological and other facilities required to support a broadening of the Institute's role, sectorally and geographically.

To help, they had available an assessment of the management development needs of the manufacturing sector. The data, although not current, had been compiled relatively recently in *The Management of Irish Industry*. But there were other sectors of economic activity besides manufacturing that were of interest to the Institute — utilities, commerce, financial services, communications, transport and logistics. Estimates were needed of the numbers and types of managers in these businesses and their training needs. The 1966 Census of Population was a source of rough data, not precise enough to be of much use: it included under "managers" every sub post-master/post-mistress in the country. But it was a start. First, more than half the managers over 50 were discounted on the basis that they were unlikely to bother with courses. Half the self-employed in industry were eliminated — they were mainly in repair work. The census reported that 40,000 managers were employed in distribution. However, anticipating the impact of supermarkets, the IMI team halved that number. Leaving aside 4,500 taxi and lorry owner/drivers, they concluded that the IMI's effective manager "universe" was 40,000.

The heads of the four training sections took a view on how much of the market they would be able to reach over the following five years. Longer programmes were expected to grow by 70 per cent, short courses by 100 per cent, and distribution by 40 per cent. The most spectacular prediction was for the new small industries section. The small industries division of the IDA had great plans for the sector; influenced by this, "participant days" for small business were forecast to grow from zero to 6,000 in five years!

On the qualitative dimension, it was decided that, if the standard of management was to be raised to, and maintained at, a higher level, every manager must be given "an opportunity to attend courses appropriate to his needs":

> After his initial training, a manager will need to attend courses of different types: longer ones whenever there is a major change in his job, in his work within that job, or in the knowledge related to that work, and shorter ones to keep him up to date with more limited or specialised developments.
>
> Because there is no such thing as a once-for-all education, a constant renewal of the manager's knowledge will be necessary throughout his career.

Having witnessed, in this heady exercise, projections close to infinite growth for the organisation, Jim Darlington, secretary of the Institute, doodled: "IMI — Ireland, My Institute!"

The five-year plan with detailed financial projections was submitted to the department in May 1969. Possible new sites were looked at, including Rathfarnham Castle and St Killian's School. But, when the planning office of Dublin Corporation indicated that a four-storey development might be permitted in Orwell Road, plans switched to redevelopment there. The architect, Arthur Gibney, of Stephenson Gibney, devised a three-block design; one for conference rooms and catering; one for offices and a 60-bedroom residential building, at a total cost of £800,000. A member of the council, Bob Willis, wrote to the chairman, Frank Lemass, criticising the architect's outline as "exceptionally extravagant" and saying that he was "left with the impression that we are attempting to provide a university-style palace on a very limited area".

The Department of Labour referred the funding aspects of the five-year plan to the Department of Finance. At the time, Finance had before it a submission from the Institute of Public Administration seeking a grant for a centre of public administration at St James's, Clonskeagh. The secretary of the department, C.H. Murray, put the IMI's request on hold pending the outcome of a study into the feasibility of a joint IMI/IPA development.

Through the second half of 1969, the Institute waited tensely for a government decision, its future hinging on the response. The Exchequer was not in good shape, so the attitude of the Department of Finance would be crucial. The Institute was confident that it had a sound ally in the secretary of the Department of Labour. Tadhg O Cearbhaill had consistently supported its requests for subvention. He threw his weight behind the five-year strategy, telling Finance that management training was at the heart of his department's industrial manpower policy, under which AnCO was committing massive investment to training at lower levels. Full value would not accrue from that investment without a marked raising of the performance of managers. The technical assistance grants scheme, which covered as much as 50 per cent of the cost, was fuelling demand for management training. Its successor, the levy/grant scheme, would put further pressure on the system. He argued that it was essential that the resources of the IMI be expanded to meet the needs. He also reasoned that the Institute had embarked on programmes that could not be expected to be self-supporting, including the small industries training programme undertaken at state (IDA) request.

At last, in November 1969, O Cearbhaill brought the welcome news that the government had agreed to continue subventing the IMI's programme and would support the building project. This would be done "on the basis of an increased annual subvention to meet the cost (i.e. interest and sinking fund) of servicing borrowing of not more than fifty per cent of the total cost involved or £400,000, whichever is the lesser". Effectively, the "no grants for capital" barrier had been breached.

Informing O Cearbhaill of the decision, C.H. Murray had written:

> I think it would be opportune to return to the general question of state subvention of the institute's other expenditure in the five-year plan. We concede that state support will have to continue but we hope this rate of subvention will slacken off after some years and that the institute will keep in mind the necessity of achieving self-sufficiency, not as a long-term objective but in the medium term. We would hope that, after termination of the Institute's five-year plan, state support will diminish until eventually only

the subvention towards the borrowing for the new accommodation will remain.

Although the decision included the usual caveat that future payments under the agreement were conditional on the state of the
Exchequer, this was the closest the IMI had come to certainty
about the continuance of government financial support. The council now felt confident that they could give the construction project
the go-ahead. Coincidentally, they did so at a meeting in November 1969, which opened with a tribute to the memory of Sir
Charles Harvey who had recently died and who had done much to
see the Institute established.

Introducing the discussion on premises, the chairman, Frank
Lemass, said that before bringing the proposal to the council, the
executive committee had taken note of the report of the working
group on co-operation in business education, which recommended
a joint campus with UCD. He reminded the council that the college
president, J.J. Hogan, had ruled this out.[1] The possibility of a joint
campus with the IPA had also been examined; this had failed to
identify any synergies. It was now time for the Institute to proceed
with its own plans. Colm Barnes, chairman of the consultative
board, led a supportive response from council members. He said
that the most recent information available to the board was that
demand for business education would increase rapidly to a very
high level. It would not be met by any one sector but the Institute
would have a key role and should proceed with its plans forthwith.

Despite the refusal of the UCD authorities to entertain the notion
of a joint campus, some members were concerned that the project
might signal a divergence from previous IMI policy of close co-
operation with the universities. The director, Ivor Kenny, said that
the working group's recommendation of a joint UCD/IMI business
school campus had been referred by the Government to the newly
founded Higher Education Authority. The Institute had informed
the authority that a joint campus, though desirable, was not critical
to its plans. Hinting that the Institute's view had hardened further in
the meantime, he told members that, if there were to be equal or
proportionate development of business schools outside Dublin, it

---

[1] See Chapter Thirteen.

would be inappropriate for the Institute to be associated with a particular Dublin university. Further, he could not see the members of the Institute "finding it attractive to contribute to half the cost of a joint campus".

The council heartily endorsed the proposal to build. There was a slight demurral, but not on the substantive issue: Sir Basil Goulding, a distinguished patron of the arts, had a comment on the aesthetics of the plan for Orwell Road. It was a mistake, said Sir Basil, to put such a large project on "such a mundane site". However, Dublin Corporation decided in June 1970 to attach a crippling condition to its planning approval for the Orwell Road plan: a height restriction of 25 feet. This, in effect, removed the possibility of longer-term expansion there. The Institute would have to look elsewhere. It was not unhappy to do so, because it had become clear that courses could not have continued in Orwell Road during a quite lengthy construction period.

Jim Darlington was appointed project manager and was asked to find, within a two-mile radius of Belfield, a site that could accommodate any possible future development. The stipulation about proximity to Belfield was to keep open the option of a future link with the UCD business school, or the mooted successor, a joint UCD/TCD school.

The estate agents, Lisney, found the ideal location. The Myerscough residence, "Clonard", in Sandyford was for sale. It was on 12 acres at the foot of the Dublin mountains, yet within five miles of the city centre. It would easily contain any future expansion of the Institute, including a residential block[2] for participants on extended courses. Arthur Gibney was excited by the potential of the undulating site with its backdrop of the Dublin mountains. Sir Basil Goulding, also, was happier with the grander setting of Sandyford. Dublin Corporation gave outline planning permission in December 1970 and the purchase of the site was completed in August 1971.

The staff associated with the Institute's longer courses were keen on having a residential facility. Residential courses had to be held in hotels in the Dublin area, an arrangement far from ideal.

---

[2] The five-year plan 1969–74 stated that almost half of the 25,000 "participant days" forecast for 1974 would be residential.

Custom-built accommodation on the Sandyford site that did not have to share space with weddings and other functions was the aspiration but a further feasibility study ruled this out; it would have added about 30 per cent to the construction costs, plus £20,000 annual running charges. The funds were simply insufficient.

Staff proposed a bold alternative: a take-over of the 48-bedroom Opperman's Hotel at Kilternan (now the Kilternan Golf and Country Club Hotel). They mounted their own enquiry and reported that the hotel was making a reasonable profit before interest. With full occupancy in the off-season — which the IMI courses could guarantee — the residential facility, far from being a drain on resources, would in fact yield a profit. To help cover the capital costs, the group proposed the sale of the bulk of the land surrounding the hotel, the balance to be financed by the Institute's pensions fund. However, the executive committee was cool on the proposal and decided that "the staff should study further the question of residential accommodation related to the Clonard centre". In case the financial circumstances changed, Arthur Gibney included a residential block with 60 study/bedrooms in his model for the National Management Centre. But that was as far as it got until the Institute's Golden Jubilee in 2002.[3]

The Institute's general finances, under heavy strain from salary inflation and the rapid expansion of the organisation, encountered a windfall when the Orwell Road premises were put on the market in 1974. When the estate agents, Lisney, announced the forthcoming auction, there was prompt interest from an unexpected quarter: the government of the USSR. The IMI's secluded site — once lyrically described in the *Irish Press* as "poetically landscaped with green lawns and soaring trees which sing with birdsong" — was ideal for its new Dublin embassy. The Soviets refused to participate in a public auction and, instead, put in an early bid of £550,000, described, with heroic understatement in the minutes of the executive committee, as "substantially in excess of the auctioneer's current valuation". The Soviets liked their missions self-contained, capable of housing *in situ* expatriate personnel, including drivers and cleaning staff. The IMI happened to have what may have been the

---

[3] See Chapter Twenty-three.

only available site matching their demanding criteria. The Russians were determined to have it.

The deal was not without a glitch. The Kremlin lawyers, perusing the deeds of the site — which like most urban properties of the time was not freehold — discovered that a "fee farm grant" conferred on the legal descendants of the original landlord rights of access to the lands for fishing and hawking. The Russian lawyers blanched at a vision of unknown numbers of people arriving at the gates of the embassy, during the prevailing Cold War, asserting their legal right to roam over its grounds. The IMI's lawyers pointed out that, under Irish law, ancient rights could be extinguished easily by application to the relevant branch of the Irish courts, which dealt with such issues as a matter of course. Moscow refused, as it was Soviet policy not to engage in litigation in a host country. The impasse worried the Institute, which had seen the market for prime property plummet in the meantime. An impossible alternative would have been to track down every legal owner of the rights — estimated at about 80, scattered around the globe — and persuade them to sign a consolidation deed, waiving a "privilege" of which none of them would have been aware.

Eventually, the Kremlin offered to proceed with the purchase but, regarding the ancients rights clause, £30,000 would be retained because of the lease restriction. In addition, the Institute must indemnify them against any lawful claim to exercise those rights for a period of 20 years. The IMI accepted at once and effected a bond, for a single premium of £250, indemnifying the Institute in turn to a maximum of £50,000 against any such claim for the period in question. A good bargain.

The total estimated cost of building the national management centre in Sandyford was £1.2 million, including provision for inflation. A total of £200,000 was available from the residue of the sale of Orwell Road. With a £400,000 state grant assured, the Institute turned to the members for the balance of £600,000. As appeals for funds went, this was a formidable sum, unprecedented at the time. Professional fund-raisers, a United States company, the Wells Organisation, was hired to plan and administer the campaign. To invest it with an appropriate level of patronage, the executive committee appointed a number of eminent members to a Founding Fund committee. Dr J.F. Dempsey and Frank Lemass — former chairmen of the Institute and both with excellent contacts in business — became co-chairmen.

The consultants advised that the 80/20 rule applied to fundraising: 80 per cent of the target would come from 20 per cent of the corporate members. A "hierarchy of gifts" was drawn up. The leading donors would set the tone of the campaign: the response down the pecking order would be determined by the size of the top donation. If the leading gifts were pitched too low, the fund's financial goal would not be achieved.

Instead of one major giver, it was decided that two large corporations would jointly lead the fund with £50,000 each. The four on the next level of the pyramid would each be asked for £25,000. The following eight would be expected to subscribe half the second-level donation, and so on down the widening pyramid. It did not work quite as smoothly as planned but steady and substantial progress was achieved. Frank Lemass, in particular, committed a lot of time asking business leaders to donate substantial sums to the creation of a national management centre, a considerable feat of persuasion. Sadly, he died in July 1974, two months before the centre opened.

The campaign moved on smartly; by September 1971, the Institute had pledges totalling £500,000 from 55 companies out of a total corporate membership of 750. The campaign directors were confident of reaching the target, a remarkable tribute to the IMI at a time when most businesses were under pressure to trim expenditure ahead of EEC entry, only a year away.

A great part of the construction costs had to be paid up front but, as the corporate donations and government grant were scheduled over five and four years respectively, there was a cash-flow problem to be dealt with. Jim Beddy of the Industrial Credit Company (ICC) suggested a five-year mortgage debenture. Even at the most favourable rate, this was a costly business. It did not make much sense to pay substantial interest to a state bank, effectively out of the state's own largesse, so the Institute asked for a meeting with the Departments of Finance and Labour and the ICC. As a result, Finance decided to pay the entire grant up front. The assistant secretary, Michael Murphy, conveyed the good news.

The architect, Arthur Gibney, recalls his first visit to the Sandyford site, 12 acres at the foot of the Dublin hills with a mid-nineteenth-century house, Clonard, more or less in the middle. Site studies showed that the proposed buildings would fit comfortably on it with ample room for expansion. Both architect and client were determined to retain the hundreds of mature trees as well as the house. Gibney:

> At that time in Ireland, nobody would have raised an eyebrow at the idea of knocking this building down. But both the IMI and we, the architects, decided that Clonard should be kept. That constraint as well as the mature trees, the rocky nature of the site, the need for an entrance road and extensive parking dictated the position of the new building.

An important influence on his design was the IMI's stipulation that it not be a typical office construction but a corporate building of character:

> From my point of view it was a new concept: the headquarters of a national business institution, with an educational campus and a library. Nobody had built management institutions which could be defined as typical. We looked at a few management schools in the US and Scandinavia but they did not match the IMI model.

> The rising site was a difficulty. It was not a typical location in Ireland for a major edifice. It was full of granite boulders. With rock, you have to blast it or work with it. Blasting was out because of cost and probable damage to surrounding property. We decided to apply as much imagination to the development of the design as possible. We looked for examples of similar construction that would typically be seen in hill country in Italy, Switzerland and northern Europe, and more pertinently in America. We were influenced by certain buildings, in particular the Oakland museum, near San Francisco, designed by the Irish-American architect, Kevin Roche, at that time not well known. The museum site was slightly hilly so he used a system of step terraces. That was one of the influences on our design.

> Back on site, we decided, instead of a longish structure going up the hill, to build along contour lines and step it

up, building on the shelves of rock to avoid expensive ex-
cavation and blasting. This gave the structure its length
and terraced appearance.

The early 1970s was a precarious time to build. Inflation was rising
steeply, doubling from 8.6 per cent in 1972 to 17 per cent in 1974.
The budget was tight for the amount of accommodation required,
90,000 square feet. Every cost item was checked. The construction
was achieved for a little over £9 a square foot, lower than for a
standard office block at the time. Air conditioning was not considered because it would have added 20 per cent to the cost; with the
airy and quiet location it was not a priority. The design team opted
instead for mechanical ventilation of the deeper spaces.

The building in its hilly setting has been described in architectural parlance as romantic. Gibney is at pains to point out that it
was dictated by the most rational of considerations: function and
cost.

> The teaching accommodation and the staff building are
> linked by a concrete podium, beneath which are the res-
> taurant, library and communal accommodation. The whole
> concept worked out logically; it is a "rational" building for
> its site. We adopted reinforced concrete because it was
> the most appropriate, most economical material to com-
> plement the granite "shelves" of the site. This was not ex-
> pensively shuttered concrete, quite simple off-the-shutter
> concrete. The internal spaces were based on a single cell.
> Two of these cells formed a teaching space. Between the
> teaching rooms there were smaller cells for equipment
> and services. Spaces were left to allow unknown future
> technological developments to be plugged into the build-
> ing, with minimum disruption. The cellular design was
> used horizontally along the contours and vertically to cre-
> ate a series of overhanging terraces. That, in a nutshell, is
> the genesis of the design.
>
> The IMI was an excellent client. They wanted an exciting
> imaginative building which would answer their functional
> needs but which would also stand as a symbol for what
> they were about, which was helping to build a new Ire-
> land. The design team was given a reasonably free hand.

The construction contract went to MJ Davis & Company on the basis of a competitive tender of £722,000. The builders moved onto the site in July 1972. Despite the extent of rock the construction proceeded on time and substantially on budget. Council members were taken on a tour of the site at the halfway stage in March 1973. Some sections of the new building were ready for occupation by June 1974 and the move from Orwell Road proceeded before the end of July.

The auguries were positive as the new centre began to take shape. The mood in Ireland was buoyant, despite the depressing intensity of the conflict in the North and a worrying inflationary trend in the South. Having said no for almost a decade, France cleared the way for Britain's entry to the European Economic Community, along with Ireland and Denmark. Members of the IMI celebrated the day of Ireland's accession, New Year's Day 1973, with lunch in Jury's Hotel. Guests included the ambassadors of the eight other member countries. Brian Lenihan, Minister for Foreign Affairs, intoned:

> This is no imperial grand design resurrected from the past. It is a Community uniquely suited to enabling small countries to protect and promote their interests.

Altiero Spinelli, an Italian member of the Commission, in a message to the lunch, promised that the enlargement would do away with the handicaps of small markets, parochial attitudes and expensive inefficiency. Ireland could now "compete on an equal footing with the industrial giants that threaten to dominate our economies". He said the Institute would play an important a role in bringing about

> the necessary adaptations of managerial skills that are a precondition for making full use of the opportunities of the new, large, unified market.

The French Ambassador, Emmanuel d'Harcourt, on behalf of the six founder members, proposed a toast to the nine-nation Community. Any executive who may have missed the lunch because of a business trip to Europe was, according to *Management* magazine, able to join in a toast to the grand European adventure: passengers on all Aer Lingus flights had their glasses charged with champagne and were invited by the captain to "drink a toast to peace, prosperity and happiness for all the peoples of the world".

Frank Lemass, who presided at the lunch, hit out at the negative attitudes of some businesspeople who hankered after the old days:

> We, the managers, whose decisions have such a direct effect, not only on the destiny of our enterprises but on the standard of living of our own community, must ensure that our attitudes are based on a true awareness of reality. We are now equal partners, not poor relations, in a nine-member European Community. We are part of the elaborate network of consultation and evolution. We have a voice in future planning. We must make sure that it is clearly heard, and that its demands are based upon a thorough understanding of what is good for Irish business. Irish business must be positive, vital, energetic and well informed.

To address a widespread ignorance of the European project — even among managers — the IMI had unveiled a special programme of briefings on what Irish business needed to know about the Community. They covered the impact on specific industries, harmonisation of tariffs, social and labour policy, transport and distribution regulations, purchasing and licensing procedures, and how to appoint agents and distributors in Europe. In a wake-up call to Irish managers, an opinion piece in the February 1973 edition of *Management* pointed to the "primitive attitude generally" to management training in Ireland:

> One rather startling measure of what we are up against in the EEC is that the Paris Chamber of Commerce subvents its management training centre to the tune of £40 million a year — not francs, pounds!

The final report of the COIP,[4] with its catalogue of management deficiencies, gave little comfort to those who contemplated the decimation of tracts of the existing industrial landscape. Old family businesses were particularly prone:

---

[4] Committee on Industrial Progress (COIP), set up in 1968 to monitor progress in product development and marketing.

> Capable salaried managers are often impeded by owners
> or directors who resist change; where this occurs it will of-
> ten be found that a major factor is the advanced age level
> of the owners or directors.

The IMI would agree; it often encountered cases where the founder of a business was succeeded by less able family members who
took the security of the enterprise for granted and who felt that to
take a management course offended their status. A 1972 analysis
found that only 30 per cent of chief executives in firms with more
than a hundred employees had any formal management training.

Reviewing its mission around then, the Institute experienced a
Pauline realisation that management training was not necessarily
for everyone; not every Irish business could, or should, be saved.
The director-general, Ivor Kenny, told the 1973 national management conference: "We know that now. We didn't once. We thought
our mission was to every manager in Ireland."

The Institute had finally freed itself from AnCO's grand scheme
of endowing every manager in Ireland with four days' training,
every year. Still, the IMI's reach had been extensive enough. Ten
years earlier, about a quarter of managers had some minimal training from the IMI; that had climbed to about one half of an increased
number. And in the country's small businesses — those with fewer
than 100 employees — penetration had grown from nothing to
about 40 per cent. Of the 5,000 managers then attending IMI
courses, some 3,300 were from firms employing 100 or more and
the rest from small business.

So what about the effectiveness of what the Institute was doing?
The director-general said:

> To argue that we must have played *some* part in raising
> the tempo and skill of Irish business is neither convincing
> nor of practical use in our development. It would be satis-
> fying to relate participation in IMI courses directly to im-
> provements in company performance. Our experiments in
> this direction so far have confirmed the difficulty of being
> fair and accurate. The variables are infinite. No company
> is ever going to say "We owe it all to the IMI." But there are
> other kinds of measures, which, though less than scien-
> tific, are indicative. One is the crude degree of growth: if

we have not attracted everyone, we are not cold-shouldered. The rate of repeats tells us something more encouraging: in the firms with over 100 employees, managers have come to us three times on average. Those in the bigger companies have come back even more often. Consumer response is a measure not to be despised. For example, from our latest sample of more than one thousand participants, we find that nine out of ten would recommend a course to people in their own kind of job and seven out of ten could foresee examples of increased efficiency arising from what they had learned.

At the time of entry to the EEC, a survey showed that in Belgium 70 per cent of managers had third-level qualifications, in France 50 per cent and in Ireland less than 40 per cent. The Institute's own data on its market were now almost a decade old. It decided on a follow-up study to *The Management of Irish Industry*. The new survey would be under the direction of Liam Gorman, co-author of the book *People, Jobs and Organisations*. It would involve interviews with chief executives and senior managers in the transportable goods sector. In spite of the uneasy relationship between the two bodies, AnCO funded the study without strings of any kind. As Gorman says:

> What I find interesting is that, even in a lot of turbulence, you can find areas of co-operation. Without the support of AnCO that study and the books which sprang from it would not have happened.

The fieldwork was completed in September 1973, nine years after the Tomlin study. It covered all 80 businesses employing 500 people or more and about 50 firms each in the medium and small ranges. The results were published in two books, *Managers in Ireland*[5] and *Irish Industry: How it is Managed*.[6] The first, dealing with

---

[5] Gorman, Liam, Handy, Ruth, Moynihan, Tony and Murphy, Roderick (1974), *Managers in Ireland,* Irish Management Institute.

[6] Gorman, Liam, Hynes, Gary, McConnell, John and Moynihan, Tony (1975), *Irish Industry: How it is Managed*, Irish Management Institute.

the characteristics of managers, was described by Paddy Moriarty of the ESB[7] as

> a kind of "Guinness book of facts about managers in Ireland" — their average ages, their nationality, technical, academic and professional qualifications, training, mobility, proficiency in languages, etc.

The second was about management practices in manufacturing firms in Ireland. Both compared the managerial scene in Ireland at the point of entry to the EEC with that of a decade earlier when the economy had just about emerged from protection and isolation. *Managers in Ireland* reported only a small increase in the proportion of managers holding degrees but a significant growth in professional qualifications. Marketing was a case in point: this new management tool showed a marked advance but, in view of the increased need for exports, the researchers questioned whether this was enough.

In the decade since Tomlin's report, manufacturing had become more sophisticated, with a marked increase in the use of management techniques. To the Institute's great satisfaction, the research found a strong causal link between this finding and greater participation in management training. The picture was, however, uneven. Bigger tended to be better: large, publicly quoted firms, both Irish and foreign-owned, had the best practices. Sadly, the mainly Irish-owned private companies made least use of management systems. Few small and medium-sized companies bothered with any sort of planning; those that did, however, performed better financially. Outside the top 80 companies, marketing hardly existed: most dealt with their customers *ad hoc*. The COIP[8] had also spotted this weakness, which it put down to:

> an inheritance from the protected era when management and workers came to regard capacity to manufacture as largely entitling them to have the home market . . . reserved for them.

---

[7] Moriarty, Patrick J. (1974), "Managers Now", *Management*, October, p. 81.

[8] Committee on Industrial Progress, report (1972).

In many businesses, financial information was not widely shared within the company; thus, decisions were frequently made without reference to their true financial consequences. Quality control was to say the least haphazard except, again, for the top size segment. But the results were also reassuring; while there was a long way to go, the work of the past ten years was having an effect. The Gorman study team, like Tomlin a decade earlier, did a service to industry in confronting it with its still considerable managerial shortcomings. The continuing deficiencies were highlighted as well as the types of businesses in which they were likely to exist.

Both IMI studies have become benchmarks for measuring progress in a number of dimensions, including the education of managers, practices in organisations, the participation of women in management and so on. In many respects the data are unique: nowhere has business been studied more closely in that period than in Ireland. Nothing was being left undone which might shock Irish industry out of its passivity and prepare it for the realities of global competition. Bit by bit, the insularity was being chipped away, leading one impassioned conference contributor, overcome by his own rhetoric, to exclaim: "No man is an island; indeed . . . no island is an island!"

The new centre in Sandyford represented to some a confident statement that Ireland was now a participating member of a new economic age. The centre was designed to accommodate 350 participants per day, rising to 500 at a pinch. There were ten teaching rooms, four syndicate rooms for break-out discussions, and a large open plan area. All teaching rooms were linked to the Institute's computer, a Digital PDP 11, and equipped with the latest technology — a projection booth with overhead projector and wired-in stereo sound. The showpiece was the TV studio, designed by Philips in Eindhoven to IMI specifications. It, also, was linked to the teaching rooms and was much in demand for role-playing sessions and personal skills training. The first course held in the new management centre, a week before the official opening, was a three-day course led by Donal Wills, mundanely titled "Managing the Workshop".

Because of the large numbers attending courses and its remoteness from restaurants, the Institute had for the first time to get into catering.[9] The architect's brief included a 400-seat restaurant and kitchen. Catering was contracted to professionals to provide all meals and refreshments. JS Caterers, a company founded and managed by John Swords, has, apart from a short contract with another company, been catering to the Institute since.

The benefits of the investment in the new management centre were addressed in an apologia in *Management*:[10]

> The physical background for good communication is of primary importance. In conventional teaching situations, the surroundings are so ritualised that they are taken for granted — and consequently ignored. It may be reasonable to expect a group of adults to sit in a conventional classroom for one or two hours but not for a week of intensive concentration. The precise arrangement of the teaching accommodation at the new Centre was developed from a close study of the factors that influence group behaviour. The total environment is also important. The emancipation of the student from dependence on the teacher develops maturity and responsibility. But it is an intensive process and also an exhausting one; dreary surroundings and dull architecture do not help to solve the problem.

On Wednesday, 25 September 1974 the National Management Centre was opened, without excessive flourish, but with much satisfaction that the project had been delivered on time and on budget, in a period of rollercoaster inflation and generally unstable economic conditions. A silver memorial medal had been struck as an acknowledgement to the founding donors and others who contributed to the project.

The opening marked the Irish Management Institute's majority: 21 years that had seen very considerable progress — a transformation, even — in the way Irish business was managed. Neither the

---

[9] In Orwell Road and previously, lunches were taken in a nearby restaurant by special arrangement.

[10] *Management*, October 1974 (p. 17).

private nor the public sectors could have achieved this change in managerial attitudes and practices unaided. The Institute's partnership with successive governments in the difficult first decades harnessed the drive, innovative capacity and market knowledge of enterprise sector to the resources and authority of the state. The imposing new management centre in Sandyford could be regarded as a monument to that uncommon, mould-breaking partnership.

Michael O'Leary, the Minister for Labour, representing the IMI's substantial financial partner in the enterprise, did the honours at the opening. The chairman, Michael Dargan, acknowledged the generosity of successive governments to the Institute.

Apart from its symbolic impact, the building itself attracted much favourable comment. Arthur Gibney's response to the challenges of the rising tract in the foothills was a building unique both in concept and design. In due course, the centre was awarded the triennial gold medal of the Royal Institute of Architects of Ireland reserved for a building of outstanding merit. The jury's verdict:

> The Irish Management Institute complex at Sandyford is a distinguished group of buildings, which provides for the education of managers in Irish industry and commerce. The architect's response to the managerial brief is impressive and has resulted in a scheme of quality and sensitivity. The positive use of a sloping, rocky site provides for the sympathetic retention of the existing house and the integration of the new buildings in a manner that is thoughtful and stimulating. The broadly treated landscaping of grass, boulders and trees, combined with the simple materials used in the buildings, all contribute to a complex which has been skilfully handled to achieve good massing on the site and appropriate scale in the setting.

> The discipline of the strongly expressed cellular structural form is used to produce buildings of restraint and dignity. Internally the buildings are well planned and carefully detailed. The imaginative use of levels and lighting, particularly in the main concourse and dining areas, coupled with the quiet sophistication of the services and equipment throughout the building, provides an environment of high quality appropriate to the purpose of the institute.

> Altogether an imaginatively conceived and well-executed design in which planning, materials, functions, forms, atmosphere and landscape are brought together in harmony and delight.

A final observation from the architect:

> It was an interesting brief and we were proud of the building and pleased when it was awarded the gold medal of the Royal Institute of Architects in 1975–76. That puts it in exalted company. It was very favourably written up in the UK's *Architectural Review* in 1977.[11] I was glad, for the Institute, that it was received so well. This was a risky project on a very difficult site but the Institute had guts to commission something that was different.

Twenty-two years later, the building featured in an exhibition of leading buildings in Paris and is now deservedly recognised as part of Ireland's architectural heritage. (See the architectural photograph of the National Management Centre on the next page.)

From the beginning, it was apparent that the quality and form of the building provides ideal space for the display of contemporary works of art. With the early encouragement of Sir Basil Goulding and Gordon Lambert, both council members and distinguished patrons and collectors of art, and under Nóirín Slattery's informed care, a fine collection was accumulated, based on the work of exciting, emerging artists. Viewing one of the more abstract paintings, a bemused member asked Sir Basil to explain what modern art was about. "Making the incongruous congruous," was the quick reply.

Supplemented by loans from the Contemporary Irish Art Society (CIAS), the collection grew steadily until 1986. Acquisitions resumed in 1996 with Barry Kenny's appointment as chief executive. The latest commission is the powerful sculpture, *Dolmen*, by Michael Warren, dominating the entrance to the building. The work, reminiscent of some of the great stone structures of neolithic Ireland, is intended by the artist "to convey the feel of receptivity and communication like the familiar angling of solar panels, satellite dishes, etc."

---

[11] Wright, Lance (criticism); Snoek, Henk & Donat, John (photography); *Architectural Review*, March 1977, pp. 166–171.

The National Management Centre, headquarters of the IMI, at Clonard, Sandyford

Of the art collection, Patrick Murphy, president of the CIAS, writes in the Institute's catalogue of works:

> The IMI has given the lead by introducing contemporary art to all who pass through its portals. It is my wish that all who come to learn and look will go on to enrich their lives by a lifetime pursuit of the visual and spiritual pleasures of art. If they succeed they will be less likely to be bored, eat bad food, drink inferior wine, wear ill-designed clothes, live in poorly designed houses, or work in shoddy office buildings.

As far back as 1959, the Institute was advocating the benefits to industry of a closer link with the visual arts with the help of the eminent Professor Thomas Bodkin of the Barber Institute in Birmingham. Bodkin criticised advertising and packaging at the time, saying that the emphasis seemed to be "on untruthful verbal propaganda rather than a visual appeal".

In 1974, the new national management centre symbolised what was now a mature institute, unique in Europe. The IMI had successfully achieved a synergistic fusion of its dual mandate: prime promoter of the interests of the new "profession" of management and creator of an internationally recognised institute of management, research-based, delivering a broad portfolio of training from two-day seminars to programmes at master's level.

At the moment of significant achievement — the opening of its national management centre — the Institute itself was facing its gravest challenge. Behind the outward show of confidence at the launch of the splendid premises lay deep worries about the viability of the entire enterprise. The recession into which the economy had plunged following the 1973 oil crisis was as serious as it was sudden. The country's newfound optimism was an early casualty. Business had to apply the brakes to the momentum of previous years.

In normal times, the opening of a national centre for management would be an occasion for a government to celebrate the country's achievement and potential. Instead, it was anxiety over the growing mood of pessimism that dictated the theme of Minister

O'Leary's speech, as well as the headline of the *Irish Times*'s coverage of the occasion:

O'LEARY WARNS BUSINESSMEN NOT TO THINK THEMSELVES INTO A SLUMP

The minister counselled: "We must not become over-panicky; the way out is to maintain investment programmes." He asked the banks to hold their nerve "by not foreclosing on productive investments". Michael Dargan, the chairman, took his cue from the minister to remind fellow business leaders that talk of recession was almost as harmful as recession itself. He took the opportunity of promoting the IMI's stock-in-trade, management training:

> The role of managers is crucial, perhaps never more so than now. We need to increase our investment in people. Confidence, which is now in danger of being eroded, comes from knowledge, which in turn is obtained from training.

But the fact was that confidence had deserted the business sector in the face of light order books and sudden tightness of credit. Businesses, far from seeing the recession as a time to invest in management development, were letting managers go. Recalling the opening ceremony a quarter-century later, Ivor Kenny said that his predominant feeling at the time was not of achievement, but of gloom:

> We faced extraordinary difficulty. We opened the national management centre on 25 September 1974 and, with most exquisite timing, we made 11 staff redundant just before Christmas. We couldn't have timed it better.

CHAPTER EIGHTEEN

CRISIS

A year earlier there had not been a cloud in the sky, nor a sign of the crisis to come. The Institute was a substantial organisation with a total staff of more than 130. The 30 management teachers had each been with it an average of two and a half years. A typical specialist would have over 12 years' business experience — equally spread between service and manufacturing — a substantial part of it at senior level in large and medium-sized businesses. All had degrees and/or professional qualifications: ten at masters' level, two with doctorates and four were completing doctorates. By European standards, the IMI was a substantial management centre. But there was no complacency. A root-and-branch review of its policy and organisation had addressed itself again to the question: what business are we in?

> We are in the business of helping firms cope with change. One of the tools to cope with change is knowledge. We are, therefore, in the knowledge business: knowledge of the business environment, knowledge of the process of managing people and resources, knowledge of skills and techniques in the functional areas, self-knowledge.

There were stresses arising from the Institute's national role. It had to "ride successfully the two tigers of independence and state subvention" and, as well as providing a service for its members, it had to help shape national policy and be organised to do so:

> Most of our policy has been formulated in documents addressed to the Department of Labour looking for govern-

ment subvention. In asking for taxpayers' money we had
to relate to the total problem, expressed as the total number of managers in the country.

However, the council was told, market penetration was a problem:

The Institute has been learning with increasing force that
a key factor in management development is the individual's motivation and the organisation's receptiveness to
change. Some evidence of this is the relatively slow increase in the proportion of managers who participate in
our work.

The 1970s had opened brightly. The pace of world economic growth
was so strong that it had become the focus of concern by the Club of
Rome — a think-tank, founded by Giovanni Agnelli, chairman of
Fiat, and a group of other industrialists, scientists, philosophers, and
economists including Bertrand de Jouvenel. The Club of Rome defined what it called the *problematique*: how accelerating industrial
production, largely uncontrolled, threatened the viability of the
planet itself. Economic expansion in the developed world had been
fuelled by cheap oil. The Club of Rome commissioned the Massa-
chusetts Institute of Technology to look at the implications. The main
thesis of the resulting book, *Limits to Growth*[1] attracted copious media attention: if the Armageddon of cataclysmic resource depletion
was to be avoided, governments must, forthwith, impose strict limits
on the use of fossil fuels and other natural reserves.

The Club of Rome's admonitions dominated economic debate in
the following months. Nevertheless, economic activity accelerated.
Even as late as May 1973, experts at the Killarney conference —
including the doyen of futurologists, Herman Kahn — predicted
sustained growth. Asked how the energy situation — a key deter-
minant of industrial progress — might change over the following
25 years, Kahn told the conference that the barrel price of oil
"would go to $5 and even out there"! No-one predicted that within
months the growth cycle would come to a shuddering stop as
OPEC nations, for their own reasons, cut production and prices

---

[1] Meadows, D.H. (1974), *Limits to Growth: A Report for the Club of Rome's Project on the Predicament of Mankind*, Universe Books, New York.

escalated to more than $20 per barrel. For Ireland, importing two-thirds of its fuel, the effect on the economy was rapid and catastrophic. Frank Cunnane, executive director of the IMI's business management programmes, writing in *Management* in January 1974, painted a disheartening picture of the reality on the ground:

> The rather ridiculous unpreparedness for the situation had left governments and industries grappling with the problems of scarcity and cost of a basic resource (energy). The extent of our dependence is shown by the fact that in 1970 we generated six million kilowatts of electrical energy compared with 2.2 million kilowatts in 1960. The proportion of electrical power dependant on oil has increased from 20 per cent to 60 per cent in the same period.
>
> A second and more immediate problem for many Irish companies has been overshadowed by the energy situation: raw material procurement. The prices of nearly all raw materials shot up last year to an unprecedented extent. And, while some respite could normally be expected after such dramatic rises, the oil situation has served to disrupt the production of basic raw materials and normal cyclical trends. . . . Many native companies have been badly hit by cost increases and by very long lead-times on delivery.
>
> What are the net effects of these problems on management? Taking production as an example, the old performance criteria for this area — the right goods, at the right quality, right time and right cost — have all been affected. Time is not controllable because of raw material scarcity, quality takes a knock for the same reason — a slightly substandard material will probably be more acceptable than no product at all. As for price, one company had a material price increase of 1,000 per cent since 1 March 1973.

For the Institute, the foundering of demand for management training as a result of the crisis — except for the topical workshop *Managing the Energy Crisis!* — could not have come at a worse time. It had been geared up to meet high demand generated by the state's incentives packages and by a more aware business universe grappling with the fact of EEC membership. Staff numbers had reached a peak of 135 during the last days in Orwell Road. Cushioned by grant income from the state and from an unexpected new source — the European Social Fund (ESF) — the Institute was able to invest like never before in research, development and ancillary areas. It had recruited support staff not directly fee-earning but whose work helped improve the quality of teaching and provide enhanced services to members.

The ESF was a bonanza for the IMI. A month or two before Ireland joined the EEC, the Department of Labour copied to the Institute a complex memorandum about the Social Fund. Frank Cunnane, who was given the job of deciphering the dense document, discovered that the IMI might meet the criteria for substantial funds focused on reducing unemployment in areas of the Community suffering from a lack of economic development. As soon as Ireland joined in January 1973, the IMI applied to the Social Fund, via the Department of Labour, for £300,000, claiming that it met the Commission's criteria on the grounds that:

> . . . the operations of the Institute are concerned with the training of business to develop existing enterprises and create new enterprises.

The following autumn, the Commission authorised a grant of £295,000, boosting the Institute's budgeted gross income for the year by over 20 per cent. The IMI, announcing the news, said that it reflected the Community's concern for better management as one means of closing the gap in living standards between Ireland and other European countries. The grant endorsed the importance of management training in achieving social objectives such as the maintenance of stable and productive employment, the encouragement of new enterprise and the raising of personal incomes. The Institute's press release said:

> In past financial conditions, the IMI has found it difficult to undertake special projects which yield no immediate financial return but which are essential to the effectiveness of its work and to the longer-term success of Irish business. We have in practice mounted investigative projects of this kind, even at substantial cost and risk of deficit. The ESF grant will provide a new impetus.

That impetus was seriously disrupted as the oil crisis took its toll. The Institute suddenly found itself overstaffed, in the jaws of steeply rising wage inflation and sharply falling demand. The ESF grant, regardless of the comfort it brought in the immediate situation, had to be considered a one-off injection of funds. There was no guarantee that it would be repeated. Urgently revised financial forecasts showed that, as things stood, unless it cut back severely on its overheads, the IMI would be facing substantial and unsustainable losses. As a labour-intensive organisation, its biggest overhead was people. Salary inflation was leaping ahead at a rate in excess of 20 per cent per annum. If necessary cuts were to be achieved, people would have to go. For the management team, this realisation clouded the final days of the move from Orwell Road; hence the low-key opening of Sandyford.

The problem came into sharp focus when the management committee (director-general and heads of division) met in October to consider the 1975 budget. *Discontinuity* had been the theme of the 1974 national management conference; it could not have been more descriptive of the context in which those budget discussions were held. The 1974 national pay agreement had resulted in an extraordinary wages increase of 29.4 per cent. For business, retrenchment was the order of the day and spending on training featured high on the hit-list for cutbacks. Because of the poor state of the national finances, the Department of Labour grant was held at £300,000, losing over 30 per cent in value through inflation. The Institute had been lucky with the ESF: it was the only management centre in Europe to access the fund. It had been quick off the mark early in Ireland's year of accession when the desire to "do something for Ireland" was particularly strong but there were serious doubts whether the Institute would qualify for future support. The IMI's market share had dropped from 86 per cent in 1972 to 61 per cent in 1974 because of increased competition.[2] The budget arithmetic was ominous: the IMI was in crisis. The meeting concluded that major surgery was unavoidable.

---

[2] The main sources of competition in the mid-1970s were the Regional Technical Colleges, the National Institutes of Higher Education and a growing number of training consultants. Larger companies were also beginning to provide more training from their own resources.

The director-general briefed the executive committee on the situation on 19 November 1974. There could be no question of the Institute, a non-profit-making body, running a large deficit: it must budget for break-even. General approval was given "for any steps to this end the director-general finds necessary, with specific approval on matters of policy to be given at the next meeting".

So, cuts it was. The management decided that they would be made in support activities that were not directly revenue earning; the brunt, therefore, had to be borne by research, information, member services and administration. Ten jobs had to go. The directors of the affected departments drew up a list; and the management committee prepared to give effect to a decision that was to induce trauma throughout the organisation, not only among those who were to lose their jobs.

The ten were seen individually and given three months' notice. A small surplus carried forward in the accounts from the previous year was used to construct severance terms in excess of the statutory requirement, including an offer of early retirement to those over fifty. Following the discussions with the ten, the director-general informed the executive committee members by memo:

> It has been possible to initiate action without raising any policy issues, i.e., at this stage there is no proposal to discontinue any major Institute activity.

He told the committee that the people affected had been informed, that their professional competence was not in question and that a committee had been formed to help them get new jobs. Among the staff, however, the response was not as phlegmatic as the note implied. As soon as the ten had been seen, the director of each of the units called a meeting to explain what was happening. As the news sank in, the organisation reacted with shock: the dismissals were outside the culture of the IMI. The fact that job losses were widespread in business — due to the same causes — did not lessen the dismay at the unexpected departure of ten close colleagues. The director-general called a meeting of all staff to explain the reasons for the decision and the way it was communicated: "When discontinuing activities and, consequently, staff, there is no way of doing so by consensus." He wanted to allay anxieties that this might be just the first phase of an even greater jobs cull. The meeting was stony. The following day, Saturday, the staff, excluding the management group, met to discuss the situation. They offered to set up a support group to act on behalf of the people who had been given notice. The offer was accepted and a "Committee for the Ten People" was formed. More dramatically, however, they resolved:

> To propose changes that will make the IMI more effective and enable those within the IMI to get on with their jobs in the confidence that the IMI is adequately managed.

The resolution was fleshed out in a memo to the director-general a week later, announcing that the staff had set up an "organisation reform committee" to propose "effective criteria for effective structures and roles to secure the future of our Institute and the people who work in it".

That decision sparked a year of self-analysis and organisation disequilibrium. The whole process has been referred to as "the revolution". If so, it was bloodless and the denouement, when it came, was by agreement. It led to substantial change in the way the Institute managed itself and how leadership roles were filled and exercised. What emerged was a structure that allowed staff at all levels to participate in the management of the Institute, including the nomination of people to leadership roles, other than to the positions of director-general and the statutory position of company secretary.

It is difficult to assess the opportunity cost of the intensely inward focus of so much energy over a substantial period. The ten redundancies which gave rise to the "revolution" proceeded as planned. Two took early retirement, others had their notice extended to allow projects to be completed, and some found new careers immediately. They left behind an organisation in some turmoil as it struggled to address a difficult proposition: how to create a structure for the effective management of an organisation whose "foot soldiers" were, themselves, expert in management. This unique organisational reality may well have underlain a smouldering discontent for some time, for which the redundancies had provided the catalyst.

Months later, council member John Byrne asked the director-general how the morale of the Institute had withstood what he called "the upheaval". Had creativity been affected? Were "pride and excitement" still there? Ivor Kenny assured him that, although the new matrix structure of the faculty was only three months old, it had "released creativity and motivation not there under the old hierarchy structure". Supporting that point, Pat Rock, the first head of the faculty appointed by the new consultative process, said that he expected the budget for the first six months of the new regime to be achieved because of "substantial response" of faculty members to tough trading conditions.

Reflecting on the "revolution" almost two decades later, one of the participants commented:

> The organisation matrix that evolved was an interesting one and ahead of its time. It was a form of participative management being espoused by some leading thinkers but practised by nobody!

There was one final outcome to the tremors that stemmed from the IMI's own redundancies and the subsequent restructuring. The tensions that inevitably follow substantial organisational change gave rise to internal conflicts, which led six very senior staff to join a trade union and eventually resign in November 1976 as a result of disagreement on policy. This ended what had been a somewhat unhappy term in Sandyford.

CHAPTER NINETEEN

MANAGING OUT OF A RECESSION

Inflation peaked at 21 per cent in 1975, creating real difficulties for management, in particular financial control. Pricing — indeed all budgetary decisions — were made tougher than usual. Don Carroll, a former governor of the Bank of Ireland[1] and head of the Carroll tobacco group, decided existing accounting practices were inadequate to deal with hyperinflation. He campaigned for the adoption by the accountancy profession of a system of "inflation accounting", to record more accurately the underlying financial realities of a business at a time when currency values were volatile. He and the bank's chief executive, Ian Morrison, who at the time was chairman of the IMI, suggested that the Institute develop a course to help financial controllers and senior managers deal with inflation-based issues. "Inflation workshops" made an appearance in the prospectus for a time in the mid-1970s. They were put together by the IMI's Ciaran Walsh and Morgan Sheehy, with help from the consultants McKinsey, the CII and the Institute of Chartered Accountants. About 400 managers attended the courses in 1975 and early 1976. As inflation was brought under control the need vanished and so did the workshops. But the tough times remained. The high rate of personal tax was hurting the Institute's membership and making it difficult to reward managers financially. The Institute added its voice to those appealing for relief in the 1977 Budget; the Minister for Finance, Richie Ryan, had a torrid time at the previous year's national management conference on the issue. Following the Budget, the Institute acknowledged as

---

[1] He was to serve a second term as governor from 1983 to 1985.

"a courageous political step" the reduction of the top marginal personal rate from 77 to 60 per cent. A year or two later, Paddy Hayes, then managing director of Fords of Cork and a former chairman of the Institute, used his shopfloor workers to make a point on the then crippling national debt:

> They have to work the first hour and 32 minutes [of an eight-hour day] to earn the money to pay their income tax, virtually all of which is needed to meet the interest on borrowings which successive governments should not have borrowed in the first place. In addition they must work another two hours and 34 minutes to pay for government-imposed VAT and excise duties.

An economy in turmoil has many human casualties. Businesses, gearing up to capture their share of the fruits of earlier buoyancy, had from the mid-1960s invested heavily in management. Organisation structures grew more elaborate, even luxurious. Over the following decade, the resulting growth in overheads, swollen by spiralling salaries (up by 29.4 per cent in 1974 alone), was to an extent masked by the rising tide of revenues. When the boom was lowered, though, a lot of companies found themselves with unsustainable costs. There was a surge in layoffs and redundancies. Jobless numbers soared by 45,000 between March 1973 and March 1977 — a major social calamity. The Government mobilised its agencies, principally AnCO, to cushion the blow and make available a countrywide training programme for displaced workers.

For the first time, the job cuts included significant numbers of managers — as many as 4,000 found themselves on the dole. The psychological effect on executives was even greater than on others who, through bitter experience, had lower expectations of job continuity. The IMI felt it had a duty to respond to the plight of its hard-hit members. A programme to address the predicament of redundant managers was urgently put together by Gay Redmond and Ruth Handy. Funded by AnCO, it was offered, free of charge, to the affected managers.

Careers taken for granted had been ended with cruel suddenness. It quickly became clear that the participants needed first to have their self-confidence, damaged by the loss of position, restored. Lifestyles built on an expectation of job security were ruptured by abrupt discontinuity. Many felt that their status had been damaged in the eyes of their families. The six-week course, called the Career (later, Management) Development Programme, aimed to rebuild self-esteem and strengthen their skills as managers so that they would be better placed to regain employment as soon as possible. They were given advanced management training, advice on improving personal skills and help with career/life planning. Also included was a job search on behalf of the people concerned. Many, more familiar with interviewing than being interviewed, were apprehensive at the prospect of a return to the position of interviewee. So the course included practice in being interviewed.

For many, the trauma of job loss is exacerbated by a feeling of shame and self-blame. In some cases, those who lost their jobs told their spouses but not the children. Appearances were kept up in front of the neighbours. So heading out to the IMI every morning with a briefcase was a God-sent cover, even if the case held only the bus timetable. One of the first sessions on the course was about home economics — how to maintain lifestyle externals by cutting out non-essentials. The IMI course leaders found themselves in the role of personal counsellor. The challenge was to get participants to rely on their own judgement and resources rather than become dependent on their teacher/counsellors. The IMI experience helped these victims of recession maintain contact with a work environment and prepared them, with a restored sense of purpose, to find new careers. Some used the period of unemployment for a mid-career re-evaluation: to consider what they really wanted to do rather than what circumstances had sent their way.

The success rate of the rehabilitation programme was remarkable. By the end of February 1976, when the first three programmes had been completed, only one in four of the "graduates" of the first programme remained unemployed, half of the second group had got jobs and a third of the participants of the most recent course had been placed. The chairman, Ian Morrison, told the council that the Minister for Labour, Michael O'Leary, had sat in on part of a course and been impressed by its positive impact on the unemployed managers. But the personal reaction of the participants was like nothing the IMI experienced before — touching gratitude for the help they got when they were traumatised by rejection and emotionally at their lowest. An anonymous graduate of the course penned this verse as a tribute to the IMI:

> You stirred a new awareness of
> Self worth and quantified
> The talents overlooked
> Buried by time and relentless conformity.
> Listing them with reawakened pride
> We came to understand our true worth
> Emerged better equipped to market
> The precious commodity of self.
> So much to repay.

Notwithstanding AnCO's bullish projections, the emphasis within the IMI in the tough years of the middle 1970s was back on survival. The cut in staff in 1975 lightened the ship enough to help it remain afloat. But there were other forces at work also — increased competition and cuts in government grants — which led to further trimming in 1976. In the high inflation years of 1973–76 — when one wag said, "Money no longer talks, it goes without saying" — direct income from course fees fell by seven per cent in real terms. Government grants declined in value. By December 1976, staff numbers had fallen below 90 from 130 three years earlier.

All the while, competition was intensifying. Some companies set up their own training departments. Market share was being eroded by new entrants to the burgeoning third-level education system — the Regional Technical Colleges and the National Institutes of Higher Education — and from private firms attracted into the business by the handsome array of government incentives. For years, short courses for medium- and small-sized companies in manufacturing and distribution had constituted the Institute's volume market. These sectors were grant-aided and the level of activity in any one year was to an extent governed by the volume of grants dispensed by AnCO under the technical assistance scheme.

Services, other than internationally traded services, were not eligible for grants. The rationale for this was sometimes explained with an analogy, beloved of bureaucrats, in which, parable style, the service sector was personified by the village chimney sweep: "Grants may encourage a second chimney sweep to set up. But, since the number of chimneys is finite, all that happens is that the incumbent's market is halved." Encouraging manufacturing and distribution, on the other hand, would bring about net growth in economic activity. The exclusion of service companies was a bone of contention with members in that sector, particularly smaller companies, which constantly asked the Institute to lobby for change. The IMI went through the motions but without conviction — the policy was too strongly entrenched to allow any chance of change. Only about 20 per cent of the Institute's business was in the services area, mainly banks and insurance companies, which were not grant-sensitive.

The grant-assisted market attracted the most intense competition because it was relatively easy for predators to enter. In 1972/73 the IMI had 61 per cent of the market, dropping 14 points to 47 per cent in 1975. It was still the market leader by a long way, no competitor having more than three per cent. In December 1975, in the course of a review of strategy to address the competition issue, the faculty segmented output into product/market groupings. The aim was to identify where the Institute had the greatest competitive advantage, and where it might be most vulnerable to competition. Every product group was scored for "competitive intensity" (amount of competition on the ground) and its "cost/ability barrier" (how difficult it was, in terms of finance and resources, for competitors to enter that market). There were eight product groupings. The most vulnerable were, as expected, the short seminars and courses in personal skills. Medium-length training courses and in-company development programmes were assessed as moderate risk; safest from threat were the degree courses, in-company workshops and, in general, the long multi-module programmes.

The outcome was a decision to concentrate on areas where the Institute had a cost or ability advantage over existing or potential competition, particularly its ability to design and run long development programmes. The vulnerable short seminars would be strengthened by pointing them more specifically at managers' problems. Courses in personal skills would have more behavioural sciences input — an IMI strength — and their impact would be enhanced by role-playing, using the advanced audio/TV facilities at Sandyford, not easily duplicated by the competition. Longer programmes would be extended to allow for more one-on-one time with senior managers. In-company work would be strengthened by a greater emphasis on the introduction of new corporate planning techniques in the more sophisticated firms.

Another IMI strength was its position with small businesses. The first venture exclusively for small business owners was a week-long residential course in 1966. A special unit was set up in 1968 under Liam Connellan, later succeeded by Neil Dean and Gerald Smyth. By international standards, most Irish businesses would have been classified small but, for the IMI, small meant fewer than 20 employees. The IMI helped owner/managers develop their businesses, set goals and broaden their understanding of the key skills needed for business survival.

An ingredient in this was "achievement motivation", a concept developed in Harvard by David McClelland, professor of psychology, and an associate, David Berlew. McClelland was well known to the IMI since the 1960s when Dermot Egan and Liam Gorman first came across his work in this field. Fifteen IMI teachers attended a training course with David Berlew in Dublin, following which the topic was integrated into IMI courses, particularly for small business clients. In 1966 there was a week-long residential course for owner/managers — many of them entrepreneurs — although they would not have recognised that description.

The IMI continued to build a strong niche in small business development. Special attention was given to the needs of the small business owner who, in the words of one, has to be "a bit of an expert in everything". Larry MacMahon, IMI's colourful marketing specialist of many years and now an international consultant, wrote a jargon-free book on marketing for the owner/manager: *If You Can't Sell It, Don't Make It*. A consistent success during the recession years was the Business Development Programme (BDP). Two senior specialists, Tony Moynihan and Chris Park, created the 18-month pilot programme, launched in November 1977. A boldly innovative concept, its appearance in the IMI syllabus in 1978 was timely. A difficult employment situation put the spotlight on the creation of new enterprises. Small new businesses are notoriously vulnerable in their early years, so both the Government and the European Commission targeted the sector for special attention. The IMI had been accumulating, since 1966, unique experience in small business survival; when the spotlight was shone on the sector, the Institute was in a good position to lead the campaign.

The BDP was an expensive commodity requiring closer interaction between the course leaders and participants than was the case on any other management development programme. Clients were owners of small manufacturing companies, with between ten and 60 employees, who were willing to make a commitment to expand their companies and increase employment in the short to medium term. Participants in the initial programme were recommended by various state help agencies. Eighteen were selected, their average age 38. Most had been craftsmen in similar businesses and decided to set up on their own, some because of redundancy. Two were women, one in engineering and one in clothing. Because of the relative inexperience in company management of most clients, there was a strong emphasis on one-to-one counselling and problem-solving. The IMI's normal pricing criteria could not apply to such labour-intensive work and, in any case, the client businesses could afford at most a nominal fee. There was, however, no shortage of sponsors for the balance, including the European Social Fund, Allied Irish Banks, the Bank of Ireland, Guinness, P.J. Carrolls, the Jefferson Smurfit Group, the IDA and AnCO.

The directors of the programme were of necessity drawn into operational detail of the client's business in a way unthinkable in any other context, sometimes to the extent of helping the client on a Tuesday make a case to his bank to cover Friday's wages. This mix of training and handholding was the secret of the programme's success, word of which rapidly spread internationally. In the 1980s, the BDP was franchised to Austria, Greece and Denmark, establishing the IMI as an international market leader in small business development and Chris Park as a guru on the topic.

The IMI's competition strategy worked well, helped by an early recovery in demand. As the shock of the first oil crisis abated, confidence returned and with it the need to step up managerial performance, as the effects of EEC membership began to impact. The end of the worst part of the recession was signalled at the December 1976 meeting of council, which heard a buoyant year-end report: the number of courses had increased by 26 per cent and profitability had grown by 44 per cent, a remarkable productivity performance by a smaller faculty, helped by increased use of outside lecturers. A trimmed-down membership services division had also moved from deficit to surplus.

When grants from the state and the European Social Fund were included, there was a swing from a deficit of £23,000 in 1975 to a surplus of £58,000 in 1976 despite the fact that the state grant had been pegged at £300,000 for three years, a significant percentage of its value eroded by inflation.[2] The 1976 productivity surge had improved the ratio of grant to earned income, from 53 per cent in 1973 to 35 per cent. But when the European Social Fund was taken into account, the Institute was still receiving £2 in grants for every £3 it earned in fees. There was a major drawback to the ESF grant: its deplorable pay-up record. At one point, the IMI was owed £640,000 by ESF, costing it £9,000 a month in overdraft charges. Later, the state grant increased but not to the levels of the early 1970s: the 1980 grant of £520,000 was, thanks to inflation, worth half the £294,000 received in 1973.

Demand remained reasonably strong in the late 1970s. Relying almost totally, as the IMI did, on direct mail marketing, the 1979 postal strike — which lasted from February until June — had a greater impact on revenue than the second oil crisis of that year. But the early 1980s saw a return to difficult trading as inflation began to soar again and, with it, unemployment. The worsening Exchequer position brought renewed fears of cuts in the grant. Michael Woods, the Minister for Health, deputising for the Minister for Finance, Michael O'Kennedy, came to the Institute in May 1980 to present diplomas at the end of a course in applied finance. In the course of his speech — doubtless prepared by the Department of Finance — he dropped a heavy hint:

> An essential element in increasing employment, or indeed in retaining employment, is a well-trained workforce including managerial and supervisory staff. Those who established the IMI were well aware of this. The Government

---

[2] It could have been worse: the Institute learned in September 1975, in the midst of its woes, that the Taoiseach, Liam Cosgrave, had intervened and instructed that the grant be cut to 60 per cent. When the implications were explained, the grant was restored.

has recognised it explicitly by subventing the Institute's operations, although I'm sure the Minister for Finance would hope that he will not have to do so indefinitely.

This induced in his hosts the intended frisson, particularly as a meeting had been arranged with Gene Fitzgerald, the Minister for Labour, for the following month to discuss the Institute's needs. The message was reinforced by the Minister's next remark:

> Our commitment to increased employment remains full and unwavering as shown by our decision to provide above-average increases for both the IDA and CTT, which are central to this country's employment strategy.

The chairman, Ian Morrison, was abroad but a letter from his deputy, David Kennedy, was on Gene Fitzgerald's desk the following morning:

> We find disturbing the inconsistency that management training is "essential", while contemplating a further diminution in Government help, and the acknowledgement of the "centrality" of the IDA and CTT by above-average increases. We would hope that, at our meeting, we can work out with you a formula which is seen as fair and reasonable by everyone concerned and which enables us to continue our work with some assurance of continuity.

Tadhg O Cearbhaill and the assistant secretary, Ian O Fionnghalaigh, reiterated the Department of Labour's belief in the centrality to economic growth of a strong management cadre. The severe cuts sought by Finance were successfully resisted and the 1980 grant was approved with a ten per cent increase. The first act of the new chairman, Mark Hely Hutchinson of Guinness, was to give dinner in St James's Gate to Gene Fitzgerald, after which there was a lengthy and constructive discussion about the role of the Institute in the Government's economic policy. Once again the Institute had been able to demonstrate a synergistic connection between its work and the Government's economic objectives. It had, through regular contact with the senior officials of the Department of Labour, ensured that its training policies were as far as possible in harmony with the manpower development goals of the department.

When Tadhg O Cearbhaill, the founding secretary of the department, retired in 1982, the council deservedly awarded him Life Fellowship of the Institute. The minute reads:

> In the unique partnership between the state and a private organisation, the Institute's greatest advocate was Tadhg O Cearbhaill, who in many ways encouraged successive executive committees in directions which were complementary to national policies for economic development, and who presented the IMI case for decision to many different ministers and governments over the years.

In the early 1980s, what became known as the Telesis report was published. Commissioned by the National Economic and Social Council,[3] its aim was to inform a new debate on industrial policy. It generated plenty of controversy, challenging as it did the bases of existing policy and the strategies the development agencies were employing. Joining in the fray, Charles Carroll, the IMI's senior marketing specialist, was highly critical in *Management*[4] of the central tenets adopted by Telesis. The report, commissioned as "a practical exercise designed to assist policy formulation", had stated:

> Greater wealth for each person in a nation is created by increasing the value-added per work hour embodied in the goods and services produced in the country. This can be accomplished both by improving productivity for existing industrial activities and by shifting resources across industrial activities towards those that can command a higher international price per hour of labour.

Using evidence from an international database, Carroll warned against the dangers of businesses aligning their corporate strategy with those of inappropriate peers:

> Our businesses must avoid the "imitate the leaders" illusion. It may hurt our pride but we are "followers" in most markets. The posture of the *successful* follower must be

---

[3] National Economic and Social Council (1982), *A Review of Industrial Policy*.

[4] Carroll, Charles (1983), "Has anybody really read the Telesis Report?" *Management*, April, pp. 36–40. See also, by the same author (1985), *Building Ireland's Business: Perspectives from PIMS*, Irish Management Institute, Dublin.

the one we seek to emulate. . . . There are and will be no-
table exceptions and it should be remembered that skilful
"followership" requires an R&D effort easily more than
double the current average of our industry.

How to achieve high value-added per increment of investment is equally as important as higher value-added
per employee. The consequence of ignoring this balance
could mean a business sector over-burdened with debt
and, by extension, a state over-burdened with debt. It is
from this situation that we are trying to escape.

Officially, the Institute steered clear of the Telesis debate, although it did contribute to the subsequent White Paper on Manpower Policy which followed the Government's long-delayed and
largely negative response to the disputed report. Even though its
main prescription was rejected, Telesis had, however, demonstrated that indigenous industry was still very much behind in its
attitude to technology and best management practice. The IMI had
not worked itself out of a role.

It was, however, conscious of its own shortcomings in the research and development field. The pressures of running an organisation struggling to break even rarely allowed funds to be put
aside for reinvestment in the development of the product. A research unit had been created in the good times of 1972/3, only to
be decimated by the events of 1974. The relationship between the
specialists and their client businesses did, of course, ensure that
the content of courses continually evolved to reflect the changing
context in which their clients worked. But, because of funding ups
and downs, research in the formal sense was only fitfully pursued.
What was needed was a dedicated funding source, outside the Institute's core finances, to afford the research function the level of
financial support it needed for innovation in course design and
content, and the testing of new teaching concepts.

With the help of the best available legal and tax advice, a
Members' Fund for Management Development, later simply the
Development Fund, was created to fund the evolution of new management training "products". It was a separate entity at arms-
length from the Institute, with an autonomous board to manage the
investment and rule on project applications from the Institute. This

arms-length arrangement ensured that the fund did not affect the IMI's entitlement to state grants, which, in reality, were a form of deficit funding.

When the proposal was first put to the council in March 1981, the economy was again on a downturn and some members felt that it would be wiser to wait for better times. But the need was urgent: with the real value of grants continuing to fall, the Institute was in the throes of further belt-tightening, with a pay freeze in place for all staff. At the council meeting, the strongest support for the proposal came from the chief executive of Córas Tráchtála, Sean Condon. It was the experience of both his organisation and of the IDA that nothing was harder than persuading Irish firms to invest in the future. In a revealing comment on contemporary managerial attitudes eight years after EEC accession, he said:

> The two greatest constraints on export performance are the shortage of truly professional, internationally minded chief executives, and product obsolescence: most firms have entered the 1980s with the products of the 1970s because chief executives have little conviction of the need for research.

The export sector, according to Condon, needed all the expertise the Institute could make available to it. It was taking as long as four to six years to convert graduates into effective managers. This had to be shortened and, in his view, the only way to do so was through more intensive management training. There would be real concern, he said, if the IMI was forced to slow down its research programme in this area.

When David Kennedy took over the chairmanship of the Institute in the summer of 1981, he asked his predecessor, Mark Hely Hutchinson, to take charge of the fund-raising. The project was launched in 1982 and it is a tribute to Hely Hutchinson's zeal and the standing of the Institute with leading businesses that, in two years and despite hard times, the fund was close to its formidable target of a million pounds. It was time to announce the members of the board which would rule on priorities, satisfy itself as to the *bona fides* of projects, allocate funds and monitor the progress of funded projects. Arguably the most prestigious board of directors in the country, it involved leaders of banking, industry and distribution: Jim Culliton, Cement/Roadstone; Niall Crowley, Allied Irish Banks; Mark Hely Hutchinson, Bank of Ireland; Tony Halpin, Beamish & Crawford; J.H.D. Ryan, Carroll Industries; P.J. Moriarty, ESB; Feargal Quinn, Superquinn; and Dermot Whelan, Howmedica. The executive committee decided that it would be chaired by Michael Killeen, vice-chairman of the council. The chief executive would be a member ex-officio.

The Development Fund was the final act of Ivor Kenny's 19-year term as director-general. On his retirement, he was conferred with Life Fellowship in recognition of his far-sighted leadership. David Kennedy, announcing the decision, said that twenty years earlier, Ivor Kenny had launched the Institute in a new direction with his exhortation that it grow its own timber. Since then, the IMI had outgrown two premises. In his continual concern for standards, he had involved the state and the European Commission in "a unique partnership with Irish managers in developing an enviable managing training resource in this small country".

To ensure a smooth transition, Kenny had signalled his intention to move on two years earlier. A "search committee" was set up of honorary officers past and present to find a successor. A number of people were invited to apply. However, none emerged who met the exacting specification the committee had set. The horizon was expanded to include Britain. A high-profile Irish manager working there at the time was Detta O'Cathain, later Baroness O'Cathain OBE. She had begun her career with Aer Lingus and later held senior appointments in such diverse sectors in the UK as the automobile industry and the Milk Marketing Board. She met the search committee and was offered the job. Having initially accepted it, she had second thoughts about a move back to Ireland and informed the committee that she had changed her mind. The search was renewed, this time with a definite result. Brian Patterson, the 37-year-old personnel director in Guinness, had built a reputation in St James's Gate as an effective, tough manager, at a time when his department was at the centre of the brewery's productivity strategy. He joined the Institute in January 1982, taking over as director-general on Kenny's departure in April. Patterson's relationship with the Institute — as a consumer — had been positive:

> For about ten years I had been involved with the IMI and had taken a number of programmes, including a residential course in Killarney which had been very formative for me. Indeed, about four years before my appointment, I very nearly joined as a specialist. I had even signed the letter but Guinness came up with an attractive offer, so I stayed. I came to the Institute as a huge supporter of what it was doing, having benefited from it myself. For me, it was a fascinating, interesting, challenging place.

The economic signs were not good. In the year just ended, the Institute had run a deficit of £176,000. A product-costing analysis showed that, when overheads were allocated, none of the Institute's programmes made a profit. The dependence on government and ESF money was extreme:

> The Institute would obviously have been better without that dependency. It was the issue that engaged me for most of my time there — trying to reduce that reliance but also having to wrestle with the complex, difficult process of maintaining the funding in the interim. It was soon clear that the Institute could be made viable only by taking out still more cost and making the remaining cost structure more flexible.

With the new chairman of the faculty, Howard Greer, Patterson began his war on overheads by initiating a programme of voluntary redundancy in the faculty. Specialists wishing to review their careers were encouraged with generous severance packages to trade full-time, pensionable jobs for part-time contracts, with the freedom to develop a non-conflicting client base outside the IMI. Many continued to run their programmes as independent contractors, enabling the Institute to retain their skills and embedded knowledge but on a leaner and more flexible basis. Within five months of taking office, Patterson told *Business & Finance* that this strategy had reduced the number of full-time staff from 85 to 67 at a one-off cost of £250,000, without seriously affecting output.

Patterson, coming from the hard knocks school of big business management, found it difficult to relate at first to the soft-focus IMI staff structures:

I was appalled by it; wrongly, as it transpired. There were still about the Institute echoes of the mid-1970s "revolution"; the structures were a by-product of it. I had come from a fairly conservative organisation, Guinness, which then had an almost military way of doing things. Once, in the course of a rather heated discussion, a senior faculty member leaned across the table and said "you are not dealing with kievesmen[5] here!"

Of course I had to change: I was dealing with very bright people who knew a thing or two about management. The structure, with leaders being part-elected and so on, was difficult. But, together, we learned over the years, with some flexibility on both sides, to work the system. The cost-reduction exercise, with some people leaving, some returning as contractors, changed the culture somewhat. But the decision-making processes remained largely as they were. I had learned by that stage that, in any case, it would be wrong to try to micro-manage the specialists; they knew what they were doing and they had to have a structure that let them to get on with it.

The pressure for more productivity was relentless, not only in the operational sphere but in sweating a better return from the Institute's substantial physical assets. As staff numbers fell, considerable administrative office space, generous to begin with, became surplus to requirements. As a result, an entire floor of 8,000 sq. ft. in the administration block was let from January 1985, contributing substantially to the bottom line.

In his first major report to the council in November 1983, Patterson took members through the scenario facing the IMI. Government grants as a percentage of total revenue had declined from 45 per cent in 1975 to 25 per cent in 1983. The managerial population was shrinking in line with general employment. At the same time, the Institute was facing increased low-cost competition. Information technology and the trend towards leaner organisations were likely to mean proportionately fewer managers in the future.

---

[5] Burly, onetime Guinness operatives who, stripped to the waist, entered the kieves (large mashing vessels) to shovel out the steaming spent grain.

Some of the council's comments on his presentation were quite
radical, one member questioning whether the Institute was not
overly concerned with its own survival! However, there was consensus that any retrenchment must not compromise its position as
the national leader in management training and development.
There would, indeed, be a renewed emphasis on the twin motifs of
relevance and quality. Financial pressures, of course, demanded
quantity also. Although, according to Patterson, output per IMI specialist was about twice that of their counterparts in the university
business schools, the 1984 budget looked for an even more demanding performance.

There was one bright patch in an otherwise forbidding financial
outlook. The Development Fund, under Hely Hutchinson's guidance, was moving satisfactorily towards its £1 million target and the
board was now in a position to accept applications from the Institute's management for the funding of projects. So at least some research and development could proceed. Patterson:

> The development fund was a very important initiative.
> Great credit is due to Mark Hely Hutchinson, Michael
> Killeen, David Kennedy and the others who got it going in
> difficult times. It is one thing to raise money for a building,
> it is quite another to put a case for funds for something
> you cannot see or touch, like research.

Six months after his arrival in Sandyford, in an interview with *Management*,[6] Patterson was asked what percentage of IMI resources
was committed to R&D:

> The short answer is, not enough. Whereas, say, ten years
> ago we would have been devoting 10–15 per cent of our
> resources to innovation and research, recent pressures on
> costs and revenue have led us to the position where we
> are trying to do our innovation on a shoestring. The fact
> that there are 57 new courses in our range of 220 this year
> is a great tribute to the Institute's staff.

---

[6] "IMI — Researching and Developing for the Next Thirty Years", *Management*,
December 1982, p. 30.

On his priorities for the use of the research money that was soon to become available from the development fund:

> First, we must stay abreast of the work we are doing. There are many changes occurring in the environment. Changes such as new patterns of authority offering challenges to managers. There are dramatic fast moving changes in technology. There are special problems of older industries in the recession. We have what has been called gymkhana management: every time you go around the course someone puts the hurdles up and changes the fences. The IMI is like any other business; one of the keys to its success is market-led innovation.

The Development Fund helped re-establish research and development as an ongoing part of the Institute's programme. It was used for research on management-related issues not being addressed by the universities and research institutions. It made a significant impact on the Institute's ability to innovate, testing new courses and upgrading established programmes.

The application of information technology to business was at the top of many agendas at the time so it is no surprise that the first project sanctioned by the board related to the application of computers to small business and to office administration. Projects subsequently approved were curriculum development for a primary degree in management, a new approach to changing organisation cultures, fresh initiatives in industrial relations and the creation of a range of Irish case studies in management. In the pipeline were an international master's degree, an experimental self-taught course, a number of research projects and a new export marketing programme with Córas Tráchtála, supported by the European Social Fund. The Development Fund also helped to finance the recruitment of research assistants.

The EU also helped the Institute innovate in how it reached its market. Since 1989, the IMI has offered a limited number of courses via the "open learning" method. This is not a cheaper option to standard classroom-based courses, but an alternative, flexible way to learn at a time and place suitable to the individual. There is support in the form of fortnightly tutorials, which help the managers apply the principles to their work situation and provide the contact with fellow learners that would otherwise be missing. For most of the courses, the IMI acts as "agent" for Henley Management College, a pioneer of open learning for managers. There is a management diploma, the equivalent of two-thirds of the Henley MBA course. "Open learners" who achieve the diploma have an option to complete the MBA, although the final year must be taken in the traditional way in college. The IMI added its own open learning courses, including a National Certificate in Business Studies (Customer Service). Research and development for this innovative course — the first qualification available to people working in the expanding field of customer services — was completed with the help of EU funds. The open learning modules are supported by fortnightly tutorial sessions in Cork, Galway and two Dublin locations as well as on an in-company basis. The Higher Education and Training Awards Council (HETAC) validates the award which, unusually, is determined not by examination, but by a novel assessment of work assignments in which participants apply what the Institute describes as a "robust theoretical framework" to real job situations. Although still a relative newcomer to the IMI prospectus, open learning is likely to extend its range as the flexibility it offers becomes more widely appreciated.

The Development Fund continues to provide resources for the Institute's ongoing innovation programme but there are occasional projects, the scope of which puts them outside the reach of the fund. This was the case in regard to what the Institute's chief executive, Barry Kenny, calls "the most important and ambitious project ever conducted into management in Ireland" — a National Action Learning Programme (NALP) which began in 1997 and still continues. Despite a long involvement in action learning, the Institute had never before attempted anything on this scale. Twenty companies were chosen to participate in the programme, grouped according to their prime interests. The aim is to identify models of best practice in areas critical to business success in Ireland. For example, subsidiaries of multinationals have focused on "securing and expanding the mandate of the multinational subsidiary"; growing enterprises have been grouped around the proposition "developing and managing a high growth SME"; established indigenous companies have been assigned the theme "rejuvenating the mature organisation" and another group "adopting world-class practices in the well-established organisation".

NALP was approved for funding under the European Commission's ADAPT programme and assigned the substantial budget of £2 million.[7] The model being developed in Ireland will be replicable in other member states of the EU. In a review of progress after the first phase, participating managers — all at chief executive/top policy level — reported that it had already yielded considerable benefit to their companies in enhanced strategy development, greater objectivity in decision-making and a comforting realisation that their problems were not unique![8] Two of the three phases of NALP were completed by 2001; the third — the dissemination of the results of the research throughout the EU — began in 2002.

---

[7] Includes fees to third party contractors.

[8] Liam Gorman and Tony Dromgoole, "Developing and Implementing Strategy through Learning Networks", in Patrick C. Flood, Tony Dromgoole, Stephen J. Carroll, Liam Gorman (eds.). (2000), *Managing Strategy Implementation*, UK and US: Blackwell Business.

CHAPTER TWENTY

FOOTPRINTS ABROAD

The IMI took its first tentative steps overseas in 1973. In that year, Harvard's David McClelland was asked by the Governor of Ohio to help address inner city unemployment. Lack of motivation in the inner city population had been blamed as the core cause of the problem. At McClelland's suggestion, Neil Dean went to Cleveland to run the IMI course, "Developing a Small Business", for inner city participants. The Governor reckoned that the IMI course was the most fruitful of his inner city initiatives, thus consolidating McClelland's high regard for the Institute. When later that year he was asked by the International Management Development Institute, a non-profit US organisation specialising in training for developing countries, to recommend a training programme for owner/managers in Africa, McClelland referred them to Gerald Smyth, Neil Dean's successor as head of small business. As fees for small business courses, at home, had to be pitched at about half the rate for standard courses, the prospect of topping up revenues with some overseas work in the slack summer months was attractive.

A team was assembled and set about briefing itself on the economy and culture of Kenya and Tanzania, the first countries to be visited. Missionaries of different religious orders were a valuable resource, explaining how they taught in Africa: what worked, what did not. The team read any literature they could get their hands on — even essays and plays — to help understand the culture.

Smyth spent ten days in Nairobi, the location of the first assignment, visiting participants in the proposed programme. What they needed most was help in accounting, business policy and long-term planning: clearly, the IMI's expertise was as relevant in Kenya as in Ireland. Three IMI specialists flew out to conduct the courses. Afterwards, the clients were visited back at their businesses to help them apply the material. Subsequently, a local industry body evaluated the Institute's work. The verdict was that the programme "was at the grass roots and attacked reality in their businesses".[1] They wanted more.

When the oil crisis recession hit in the mid-1970s, the Kenya experience — an opportunistic response to a chance enquiry — encouraged the IMI to develop alternative overseas markets for its product during the slump in demand at home. Questioning the basis for the emphasis on overseas work in the 1975 programme, council member Norman Kilroy was told by the head of the faculty, Pat Rock, that it was driven by the need to maintain revenue and critical levels of staff, for whom it was also a valuable training opportunity. During the worst of the slump, overseas work was generating up to £100,000 annually. In the process, the IMI accumulated unique experience and understanding of the management development needs of emerging nations.

In some instances, the IMI overseas teams were dealing with the most basic deficiencies. In Tanzania, following a reorganisation by McKinseys of the vast state-owned trading corporation, the IMI was asked to train its top management and regional chief executives. Ray Fitzgerald and an IMI team discovered that the company, which was operating in about 24 regions, was entirely without financial or other management information systems. Every senior manager in the group had to be trained in basic systems in order that they could generate the data essential to the control and management of the business. The Irish government agreed to fund this and other projects from its foreign aid vote.

When the bad times at home abated, the Institute continued to build on what was then, in volume, a substantial export business. The target was no longer just the Third World. In Africa, the mar-

---

[1] Denis Murphy (1973), "Management Training in a Developing Country", *Management*, November.

gins were equivalent to those earned at home, so, for a time, the Institute sought business in the more lucrative markets. Contracts were won in Canada and Saudi Arabia. Strangely, the Middle East was disappointing. According to Gerald Smyth, there was little interest in management training in Saudi Arabia: it was too easy to be rich! However, the Institute eventually "struck oil" there. Through an introduction from DEVCO — the association of Irish state-funded overseas aid agencies — the IMI ran a course in Dublin for the Saudi banking sector. This led to the Saudi central bank commissioning a one-year programme in Dublin for its senior team, at the time the Institute's biggest single overseas commission.

The Institute has also worked overseas at the request of the European Commission. One of the first was a contract to create a Civil Service training centre in the Caribbean. Bert Walls, a veteran of many overseas projects, went to Curaçao to direct it. He and Donal Wills made the Caribbean their base for an extended period, becoming expert in the analysis of the management development needs of the region.

Later, having examined the real cost of keeping teams abroad, it was decided in the mid-1980s to switch the work to Ireland. Instead of training third world businesses directly, trainers from those countries come to Dublin for intensive briefing on the Institute's methodology and then return to work with local businesses. Apart from making economic sense for the Institute, it is a better way of achieving long-term change in developing countries. The Institute has also offered a course on how to create and manage a management centre, using the development of the IMI as a case study. This was a "world first" and brought a lot of interest. Participants attended from Mauritius, Lesotho, Uganda, Nigeria, Zambia, Malaysia, Israel, Tanzania and Kenya. Each client was required to write a strategy for a management centre back home.

Currently, the Institute hosts top management courses for senior executives of important enterprises in the developing world. These courses incorporate visits to Irish companies to help the overseas executives benchmark their own businesses against Western norms.

For a time, overseas markets constituted for the IMI a profitable niche in the wider world, which helped it lessen its dependence on government subvention at home. It was not just a useful add-on, a financial makeweight; it was for a time part of a survival strategy. Later, in the mid-1980s, there was an effort to expand into the Single Market of Europe. Only one American MBA programme was available in Europe, at Heidelberg, but it was for US Armed Forces personnel only. The IMI decided to test the market for an IMI-based, American-accredited MBA for European managers. It concluded an agreement with Fordham University in New York. The new MBA would offer Irish participants the chance to rub shoulders with peers from leading Western European corporations. It was a high-risk enterprise, with the substantial asking price of £10,000 per participant. The international response was disappointing and, of those who did apply, some failed to reach Fordham's entry standards. It was also a tough sell at home. Nevertheless the programme ran for a few years, not very profitably, before changed circumstances, both at Fordham and at the IMI, saw it discontinued.

During the same expansionary phase in the 1980s, the IMI took a tentative step into the UK. The initial signs were positive enough to prompt the setting up of a separate company, IMI Executive Development Centre Ltd., with an office in London, staffed part-time. The early promise was short-lived, however. A considerable contract with one of the Home Counties' local authorities was at the point of signing when the IRA blew up an army mounted unit in St James's Park. The local authority broke off discussions, as did three out of five other potential client companies. The IMI cut its losses and retreated.

Northern Ireland is a happier story. Even though "just up the road", its market potential was not fully considered until comparatively recently, mainly due to a preoccupation with the South's management deficit and the dependence on Irish government funds. The relationship with the Northern Ireland branch of the British Institute of Management was cordial and resulted in occasional joint events. When the conflict in the North was at its bleakest in the early 1970s and North/South business transactions were at their lowest, the two institutes decided to hold a one-day conference in Omagh in 1974 for businesses from both sides of the Border on a theme of mutual interest — *Enterprise*. The attendance was understandably sparse because of the tense atmosphere at the time. Throughout the years, IMI courses attracted a reasonable number of managers from the North but it was not until 1988 that a break-through was made in the North itself. Shorts, the aerospace company, then on the road to privatisation, employing 6,500 people, engaged the IMI to identify a cohort of people with senior management potential in the company and to bring them through an intense process of development. The programme earned a British management training award for "an original company training intervention" and was the subject of an article by the IMI's programme leader, Michael Keogh, and others in the *Journal of European Industrial Training*.[2]

This contract led to a three-way "learning alliance" between Shorts, the IMI and the University of Ulster, Jordanstown (UUJ), involving six in-house diploma programmes focused on Shorts' manufacturing division. The relationship with the company continued to the mid-1990s and led to in-company work with other significant NI companies. Subsequently, the IMI landed a contract with the North's Training and Employment Agency to supply a substantial part of its management development portfolio. As a result, the Institute decided to recruit an executive in the North to continue that initiative and build for the future.

The Institute's biggest overseas client has been the European Commission. It and its affiliated organisations constitute a vast management system. The IMI targeted it as a client in 1990, forming a consortium with French, German and Italian companies to bid for a project to teach time management to heads of units and middle managers generally throughout the EU establishment across Europe. The group lost the bid to a Dutch company. However, within nine months it was back on the market. This time the IMI went on its own and was rewarded with a substantial contract, involving work in Brussels, Luxembourg, Munich and the Netherlands.

The Commission funds a range of development programmes in Eastern Europe, not only in applicant countries, but farther afield. The IMI went after one of these, a large contract in Ukraine — to restructure the state's savings bank, a corporation of 65,000 employees. Given the size and specialised nature of the assignment,

---

[2] Humphreys, P., McAleer, E., Wightman, S., Keogh, M., Manson, B. (1995), "Customer-focused Management Development: A Case Study", *Journal of European Industrial Training*, Vol. 19, No. 5, pp. 26–32.

the Institute introduced AIB International Consultants as a partner. Three specialists were assigned full-time to the client bank, at the time close to bankruptcy. The IMI-led team developed a new strategy and structure, installed a risk appraisal system, built a training centre, and trained trainers to direct a core programme of specially designed courses. Other central European projects, closer to the IMI's core business, followed in Poland, Hungary and other applicant countries — projects such as the setting up of centres of management and the introduction of programmes for small and medium-sized enterprises.

The Institute undertook an unusual brief in Romania as part of an assessment of the country's state of readiness for entry to the EU: to examine the role and performance of the ministry of industry and commerce, its relationship with enterprise, and the support institutions it needed to develop the economy. This £1.75 million project included helping 30 state-sponsored organisations prepare for privatisation. The IMI put together a multidiscipline, international team including experts from Bossard, a European consulting group, the French centre of management at Jouy En Josas, the Stockholm School of Economics and Manchester Business School.

During the second half of the 1990s the overseas work was run as an independent operation by IMI International, with a brief to contribute to the Institute's bottom line. The work was mostly subcontracted. Eventually, the market was oversupplied, the rates became less attractive and the Institute, in common with some other suppliers of overseas training, disengaged.

CHAPTER TWENTY-ONE

SEPARATE TRACKS

For 30 years the prospect of a union between the Institute of Public Administration (IPA) and the IMI was canvassed and rejected. The core — and still unresolved — propositions driving the matchmakers were, first, that the terms "management" and "administration" were interchangeable and, secondly, that a more integrated training regime for public and private sector managers would dispel the dysfunctional "them and us" divide. The IPA's founders were a visionary group of civil servants in the departments of Local Government and of Health, all of whom worked in the 1950s in the Custom House — Tom Barrington, Patrick Doolan, Brendan Herlihy and Desmond Roche. Concerned at the lack of advanced training for civil servants, they set up a discussion group within the Association of Higher Civil Servants. It was chaired successively by Doolan, Barrington and C.H. Murray. In 1953 they founded the journal, *Administration*. That same year, shortly after the launch of the IMI, Barrington talked to Denis Hegarty, a member of the IMI council, suggesting a union with the IMI. Hegarty raised the matter with the executive committee, which was underwhelmed:

> It was agreed that our connection with this body should be one of association by courtesy rather than affiliation. They should be welcomed to all public functions of the Institute and the secretary was instructed to write to them to this effect.

When the civil servants went their own way and, in 1957, formed the IPA, the IMI allowed them to use its address until they found a place of their own. Within two years, the IPA was again proposing integration, this time at the behest of John Leydon, the IPA's first president, who was, of course, influential also within the councils of the IMI. Leydon had made it a condition of accepting the IPA presidency that the merger proposal was reactivated. An exploratory committee was set up — Colm Barnes and Paul Quigley for the IMI, Ruairí O'Brolchain, Dublin assistant city and county manager, and Desmond Roche, Department of Local Government, for the IPA, with Sir Charles Harvey in the chair. Roche submitted a persuasive case for integration. Described by the committee as "an admirable statement of the arguments", it set out "the real values realisable from co-operation in a common task, and the fusion of elements in the community which have tended to be divided by differences of occupation and outlook, and, in some degree, by mutual distrust". Roche's main point:

> The IMI and the IPA have broadly similar aims. The object of one is to improve standards of management, to collect and disseminate information regarding the science and techniques of management, and to develop managerial ability by means of training and education. The object of the IPA is to do precisely the same things in relation to administration. If one accepts that management and administration are much the same kind of activity (and each consists essentially in running an organisation) we have a position in which two institutes are doing what amounts to the same job . . .

> It is frequently alleged that the public service is not, in fact, sufficiently concerned with efficiency, or cost-conscious, or business-like to make any comparison between it and business realistic. There is, however, plenty of evidence to the contrary, and the emergence of the IPA is strongly indicative of a newly awakened sense of the need to promote the acceptance of management ideas in the public service. There are nevertheless numerous critics who continue to assert that money is wasted in the public service through faulty organisation, failure to introduce business methods and bad management generally. Integration of the two institutes could provide a unique means of bringing business ideas and techniques to bear on the

public service. Properly operated, the unified institute could furnish to the business community an apparatus for obtaining a factual and accurate view of the workings of the public service and an opportunity for informed criticism such as has never so far been presented to any independent body. The institute would in short form a bridgehead in what is to many outsiders an unknown and to some supposedly a hostile country.

The committee pondered seven likely objections to the deal, mainly to do with the cultural impact of the new grouping on the existing IMI ethos. All but Colm Barnes were satisfied that these could be discounted. A separate study of the financial implications of the merger concluded that an additional annual income stream of £4,000 would be needed, to be met by membership subscriptions from the 14 government departments and 30 of the larger local authorities. The committee recommended integration of the two bodies. Colm Barnes refused to sign the report, however. The IPA adopted the recommendation. But resistance to it was beginning to build within the IMI, led by the chairman, Denis Hegarty, himself head of a local authority, the Dublin Port and Docks Board.[1]

Faced with this opposition, the executive committee asked a small group, chaired by the IMI's legal adviser, Denis Greene, to re-look at the report in the light of the objections. Hegarty told Greene that he was "wholly opposed to integration" but would favour a form of collaboration. Tom Barrington advised that, having decided on integration, the IPA would accept nothing less. Greene's group reported back that "in view of the conflict of views, reconciliation between the Joint Committee's report and the objections thereto did not appear to us to be possible".

---

[1] Not all the opposition had come from the IMI. The Civil Service Executive and Higher Officers' Association, which was already in dispute with the IPA over other issues, resigned their membership of the IPA, stating, inter alia:

> The association's view is that the proposed integration [with the IMI] would render difficult compliance with the Official Secrets Act on the part of those civil servants who were members of the integrated body. It also felt that the proposed integration would not serve either the interests of civil servants or the interests of the businessmen who are members of the Irish Management Institute.

It was back to the executive committee to decide. Normally, it did its business by consensus but on this issue there was a vote — nine to three in favour of the merger. The proposal then went to a special meeting of the IMI council in December 1959. By then it had become somewhat of a *cause célèbre*. Messages of opposition were read from individuals and from some of the regional committees. The case for a merger was led by John Leydon, with the support of Todd Andrews, Tom Laurie, Sean O'Ceallaigh and Sir Charles Harvey. Thirteen spoke against. On a show of hands, the motion was lost by a substantial majority.

On Denis Hegarty's instructions, Paul Quigley wrote to the IPA, conveying the council's decision, adding:

> It was clear that the majority of the council took this decision in the belief that it was best not only for the IMI but for both institutes. They also clearly expressed the wish that the IMI should co-operate with IPA in any way possible, and that the existing good relationships between both bodies should continue and grow stronger.

The IPA chairman, C.H. Murray, replied cordially that the IPA looked forward to reciprocating "now that our finances have been strengthened".

That was that — for the time being. But towards the end of the 1960s, the question of a merger was once more on the agenda — this time because of external pressure on both bodies. The IMI and the IPA were in urgent need of larger premises and had made separate overtures to government. Between them, they were getting substantial funding from the Exchequer and it was held in some official quarters that it was time to knock heads together. To paraphrase the argument:

> They may be operating in different culture systems, but the disciplines, the management processes are similar. Managing the Civil Service cannot be different from managing the Bank of Ireland. A merger will bring substantial cost savings and other synergies and, in the process, nurture better understanding between both cultures.

But, by now, there was little enthusiasm for a merger in either place. The IMI was fearful of diluting its "college of managers" identity: its members were required to be at manager level while IPA membership was open to "any person who is employed or was formerly employed in the public service".

Coincidentally, the secretary of the Department of Finance adjudicating on both applications, was C.H. Murray, who had been chairman of the IPA ten years earlier when the IMI council threw out the original merger recommendation. He now invited both councils to carry out a joint study under the chairmanship of the principal architect of the Office of Public Works, G. McNicholl, to examine "the possible economies in locating both organisations on a single site". In due course, McNicholl reported to Murray that no significant savings were likely. Given the lack of appetite for integration, neither body was upset. Again, they went their separate ways.

The topic was touched on a year later — albeit in the context of university education for management — when the IMI's Consultative Board on Education and Training for Management considered a submission from a university sub-committee. This argued against separate systems of education for business and the public service, although it did acknowledge the different contexts:

> The public administrator is not in precisely the same situation as that of the manager of a private business in that he is not concerned solely with guiding the fortunes of his particular organisation in a competitive environment to the achievement of goals set within the organisation, but rather with administering the affairs of the state for the public good ...

> The increasing interdependence of private enterprise and the state makes it essential that mutual comprehension be maximised. We would regard it as very undesirable if private enterprise managers and public administrators were to be educated in different places. Nothing would contribute more to the separatism that must be avoided.

But the issue was not taken up in the final report of the consultative board on which the IPA was represented.

In 1976 the debate surfaced once more. The IPA was in another accommodation crisis and Finance ruled that the option of sharing the IMI's new campus in Sandyford should be examined before

new expenditure was considered. Ivor Kenny advised his executive
committee that "even at the present depressed levels" the proposition was not on. Killing off any possible further pressure, he wrote:

> The Institute's main thrust has always been to the produc-
> tive sector. The problems are awesome in that sector. The
> Institute's ability to fulfil its mission towards it is limited. To
> dilute that mission by somehow taking on also the prob-
> lems of the public service would lead to a loss of identity
> (a particularly critical factor in a voluntary organisation)
> and would make the Institute quite difficult to manage.

Instead, there could be closer co-operation on topics such as the
relationship between the public service and the private sector, or
personal skills courses "which are culture-free and in which there
may be duplication of resources". The executive committee con-
curred and that seemed again to bury a topic that had materialised
with regularity from the conception of both organisations.

But no; there was one more exhumation — in 1988, in what became known as the Galvin Report.[2] In the course of a review of the
training environment at the time of the establishment of FÁS, Bertie
Ahern, then Minister for Labour, set up an Advisory Committee on
Management Training, under the chairmanship of E.P. Galvin, operations director of Guinness Ireland and ex-president of the FUE.
The committee included universities, departments of state, industry
bodies, FÁS and the trade unions. Bertie Ahern challenged the
Committee to fashion a system for developing Irish managers that
would be "respectable and far reaching" and that would achieve
for managers standards of training equivalent to those of the well-
established professions.

The Advisory Committee came to the view that the level of
commitment to management development in companies was still
"unacceptably low", mainly due to a lack of understanding of what
it involved; that managers from different backgrounds lacked a
common core of relevant business knowledge and skills and that
small business managers were the least likely to receive adequate
management development. The Committee proposed that the pro-

---

[2] *Managers for Ireland: The Case for the Development of Irish Managers* (1988)
Stationery Office, Dublin.

viders of business education adopt a common curriculum. Professional bodies which offered qualifications in subjects such as engineering and science were urged to include a "business education input". The Committee also found that separate training of public service and private sector managers was "not in the national interest":

> Increasingly, management within the public service is seen as having many aspects in common with management in the private sector — particularly in regard to the task of optimising the use of scarce resources and of relating output to customer needs. Increasingly also, there is a need for greater understanding between public service and private sector, so that they can interact most effectively for the national economic benefit . . .
>
> The present approach — with separate training for public and private managers — misses an important opportunity for mutual development.

Bluntly, the report recommended that a study group look for common ground in the IMI and IPA training activities and "develop a practical proposal to integrate these common activities within three years". The recommendation was discussed by both organisations and found not to be workable. John Gallagher, the late director-general of the IPA, commented:

> While the management principles are the same, the environment in which the average public service official operates remains so substantially different from that of his private sector equivalent as to make it virtually impossible to structure a wide range of courses that would be relevant to both. Neither body found this recommendation by the Galvin committee to be practicable. However, exchanges between senior managers and senior public service officials can be mutually beneficial and our institutes have organised joint meetings on topics of direct interest to both.

Today, when the public service is driven by the disciplines of strategic management and the private sector manager is burdened with greater public accountability, the management/administration dichotomy — if it ever was valid — no longer holds. The territory that once divided the public and private sectors is now much travelled. The sort of language heard today across the old divide is about "sharing best practice" and "exploring a community of interests".

Since the mid-1990s, the IMI has been engaging directly with the public sector. Participation by senior managers from the public service on IMI degree programmes is encouraging the long-sought exchange of experience between the sectors, based on a shared interest in the development and operation of economic and industrial policy. A National Management Forum, created out of a discussion in 1996 between IMI chairman, Dermot Egan, and the secretary-general of the Department of the Taoiseach, Paddy Teahon, provides a meeting place for peers from these diverse management backgrounds. As many as 100 high-ranking public and private sector managers attend meetings of the forum, which is directed by IMI specialist Andrew McLaughlin, himself a former senior public service executive.

Many current top managers of government departments are alumni of TCD/IMI degree programmes. The public service, notably the Department of Enterprise, Trade and Employment, is a significant client of the IMI's company-specific division on subjects like business planning and performance management. Not a few IMI specialists have joined the Institute from the public sector. There is, therefore, a heightened understanding at the IMI of the ethos of public service management and a deeper knowledge of where and to what degree translations of experience are possible between the two systems.

Relationships between the IMI and the IPA are cordial and co-operative but ideas of a merger are well in the past. There is no demarcation: both are free to find business in the other's territory. Integration of courses, even where they appear similar, is considered just not practicable.

The late John Gallagher put it this way:

> We did try [post Galvin Report]. The two institutes ran a joint meeting on a theme of mutual interest — the role of the non-executive director. The principles were the same; the speakers were excellent but, because the course had to take account of the different environments in which

each system operated, the result was almost bland. Take another example — the topic of motivation; an obvious candidate, it would seem, for a common approach; but with the constraints in rewards in the public sector, it make no sense to market a joint course with private sector managers, where no such curbs apply. The two institutes decided that the course integration proposal was just not on.

Barry Kenny:

Over the past decade the two institutes have developed along different paths. The IMI has gone on to become independent, market-facing and self-supporting, while the IPA pursues its mission within the ethos of the public service. The roles, rather than duplicating and overlapping, are different and complementary.

Although the Galvin committee recommendation for rationalisation of IMI and IPA courses came to nothing, the Institute was asked to help with another of its proposals. The committee had suggested an "action group for management development" to get more businesses interested in developing their management teams. Minister Ahern decided to give this job to the IMI rather than set up another agency. He asked the Institute for ideas. Over the following months, the director-general, Maurice O'Grady, put forward a number of suggestions. The favoured proposal was for a *Year of the Manager*. The event was launched in February 1991 under the guidance of the vice-chairman, Fergus McGovern. A lot of intellectual and financial capital was invested in the promotion, which consisted of a national awareness campaign, augmented by series of regional workshops. The Department of Labour negotiated a grant from the European Commission to fund the campaign.

The need to create popular awareness of the benefits of management training was not new: the IMI had struggled with the problem for decades. Twenty years earlier, in 1971, there was one of many attempts to persuade RTE to include a programme series on running a business. Farming was being well looked after with a number of how-to-do-it programmes and a popular "soap", *The Riordans*, which wrapped a core of benign farming propaganda in an appealing storyline. Business, on the other hand, felt it was getting poor press from RTE — one-off programmes triggered by industrial relations conflicts, polarising the issues and not reflecting the contribution of enterprise to society. The Institute wanted to see positive, helpful programmes, encouraging enterprise and creativity. It reasoned that, given their relative importance to the national economy, promoting efficiency in manufacturing and services was at least as important as in agriculture. It offered the expertise of its team of specialists as well as a contribution towards the cost. It even volunteered to find, through its network, markets for the programmes in other English-speaking countries, management being, after all, politically and geographically neutral. The proposition did not commend itself to the programme makers, for some of whom "management" may have been a tainted concept. Not too long previously, some senior RTE producers had become disaffected with the internal management ethos, which they blamed, in part at least, on the IMI's influence through its in-company work for RTE and the effects of its "systemised managerial techniques on creative people".[3]

The coverage given by today's expanded broadcasting system to business and business affairs has, of course, greatly increased, sparked by a heightened public interest in the central role which business plays in the new Ireland. For instance, RTE's economics editor, George Lee, based an entire TV series on the IMI's 2000 conference, *The Winds of Change*.

---

[3] Jack Dowling and Lelia Doolan (1969), *Sit Down and Be Counted*, Wellington Publishers Ltd.

CHAPTER TWENTY-TWO

A TALE OF TWO INSTITUTES

Back in 1952, T.P. Hogan's group, having decided in their Grafton Street lair to found an "Irish Management Institute" — before the entry into the picture of Sir Charles Harvey and his committee — mused on the sort of organisation it might be. They conceived a forum in which managers would organise study groups around developments in management and, through lectures and conferences, exchange experiences with colleagues. The early IMI was such an organisation. The members formed a "programme and planning committee", which picked the topics. Soon there was a basic library and information service. Within 13 months of the Institute's launch, the first copy of *Irish Management*, a journal specialising in management topics, reached the members.

In Paul Quigley's time, the IMI developed primarily as an institute of managers with an active committee structure of members, very hands-on, not only on policy matters but operationally also. This changed in 1962 when the review committee adopted the "grow our own timber" policy. Following the recruitment of the Four Horsemen and the reorganisation of the MDU along the lines of their respective disciplines, the initiative moved from the members to these young professionals. The operational committees appointed by the executive committee could no longer keep up with the pace of change; soon they became irrelevant and faded away. Exceptions were the powerful council and executive committee, where the members retained control on fundamental issues of policy and governance, and still do. Advisory bodies were created periodically to provide guidance to these governing committees on specific issues.

As the link between management competence and national economic development became more widely appreciated and resources flowed in support, management training became the Institute's prime mission. By the mid-1960s, the emphasis was on supplying a widening range of courses and seminars. Income from membership fees was dwarfed by growth in earnings from courses, including the training-related government grants.

Nevertheless, the Institute carefully guarded its identity as a private organisation, owned and controlled by its constituents, the business sector. It played this card with some skill whenever the occasion demanded, using it to differentiate the IMI from competing state agencies. The message to government and the civil servants was that the IMI was closest to the market: to discover what is good for industry, it needed only to look to its members.

The structures of the institute of managers were kept in place — the regional committees, membership services, conferences. There was also the ongoing public information role — interpreting for the public and, in particular, politicians and other groups the role managers played in society. Council member, Gordon Lambert, observed even as late as June 1982:

> There is a lot of ignorance among politicians at grass roots level about the role of business. The IMI has an influencing role here and should use every opportunity of increasing politicians' understanding of business and the problems of management.

Nothing trumpeted the institute of managers more than its annual "ard-fheis", the national management conference. Held in the late spring, usually in Killarney, the conference was the IMI's ritual show of strength. In its heyday, from the mid-1960s to the mid-1970s, it attracted a great deal of media attention. It remains the prime expression of the founders' aspiration — the collegiality of managers.

The economist, Louden Ryan, who has observed the Institute over its lifetime, comments:

> Before the IMI was founded, and certainly before the 1960s, managers lacked any sense of identity or self-confidence. They would not have regarded themselves as

> a group of people collectively doing a necessary and vital job. The Institute, perhaps mainly through its annual conference, played an important role in creating that sense of collegiality in managers, a communality of interest. This, of course, was in addition to its more central role of implanting the skills and the knowledge necessary to efficient management.

Through the years the annual conference paraded before Irish managers the icons of global business, and management theorists propounding the latest solutions to the problems of managing. It highlighted contemporary economic issues and acted as a forum for examining and expounding on the policy environment in which business operated.

In attracting big audiences of top managers, it incidentally helped Killarney become a prime conference venue. In the early days, the conference fitted comfortably in a modest-sized dining room of the Great Southern Hotel. Participants were accommodated two per twin room. This provided the ultimate networking opportunity. The first conference administrator, the late Des O'Brien, would receive calls from anxious manufacturers asking if Ben Dunne, the founder of Dunnes Stores, had booked and, if so, could they please share with him! As demand continued to exceed the hotel's capacity, the IMI encouraged the Great Southern to invest in a special conference centre. By the time it came on stream in 1964 with a capacity of 500, the event had grown to fill it. The problem then was finding enough bedrooms of a standard to meet the enhanced expectations of Ireland's management élite and their spouses for whom this springtime break in Kerry had become *de rigueur*. When completed in the mid-1960s, the well-appointed Hotel Europe filled that requirement. Often blessed with fine weather, the conference was a springtime fixture in Killarney for many years.

The 1969 conference, on the theme of *Leadership*, brought together one of the world's most powerful bankers, David Rockefeller, and the head of the Roman Catholic Church in Ireland, William Cardinal Conway. The sub-theme was the social responsibility of managers. If members of the Institute expected fireworks from the juxtaposition of God and Mammon, they were disappointed. There was, instead, a remarkable consensus. Rockefeller:

> We who occupy managerial jobs in private enterprise, regardless of our nationality, must continue to be profit-oriented, for it is upon profit that the survival of our enterprises — and, in my view, of our free societies — ultimately depends. At the same time, though, we must keep in close touch with men who are not essentially profit-oriented — that troublesome but creative minority of academics and intellectuals who can help us to identify emerging social problems before they reach crisis proportions. Above all, we must factor social considerations into every decision we make, for only thus can we hope to preserve the kind of stable social environment which is essential to the preservation of free enterprise.
>
> For the modern manager, in short, it is no longer enough to respond to the revolution of rising economic expectations. Today, if we are to perform our function fully, we must also respond to the infinitely more complex revolution — the revolution of rising social expectations.

Conway:

> There is always the danger of those who have responsibility for leadership taking too parochial a view, seeking solutions for their own problems merely within the terms of reference of their own particular sphere, for example within the industrial sector, and forgetting their responsibilities not merely to the wider national community but to the "one world" which is fast becoming a reality.
>
> In a word, I am suggesting that management should always have the larger picture in view and that, before posing the first question in the managerial catechism — "what are the objectives of the enterprise" — it should devote some thought to the question "what, at this point of history, are the objectives of the human race".

The protocol at conferences requires questioners from the floor to give their names and the businesses they represent. Professor Peter Dempsey, a regular at the conference, rising in his Capuchin robes to put a point to the cardinal, announced himself as "Dempsey, R.C., Cork branch".

Spanning a half-century, the conference themes are like benchmarks in the maturing of Irish management, from early discussions on the simplest management techniques to the latter-day complexities of competing in a global marketplace. When *The Entrepreneur* was proposed as the title of the 1970 conference, some council members demurred on the basis that few would know what it meant. This was sufficient reason, said others, to go with it. It was one of the landmark conferences, helping to define for the first time the characteristics that distinguish the entrepreneur from the manager. It sparked interest in the need to identify and nurture this attribute found sparingly in the population but crucial to the development of innovative, indigenous enterprise. Because of the demand, the executive committee even considered rationing places per company.

The 1970 conference had, unknowingly, a walk-on part in a national drama, news of which had not yet broken. The Taoiseach, Jack Lynch, had been invited, with his wife, Maureen, to join the conference speakers at dinner on Friday, 24 April. He would give the closing address the following day. Early that week, he had been made aware, privately, of the alleged involvement of some of his senior ministers in events that later led to the Arms Trial. Charles Haughey, the Minister for Finance and the most senior of those named, had, coincidentally, suffered a serious riding accident and was in hospital. Lynch asked the doctors for permission to visit him to discuss what he termed "an important matter of state". Permission was refused on medical grounds so the Taoiseach had no choice but to wait. Some 13 years later, he told the writer that he brought that burden to the IMI conference during what he described as "the worst week of my life".

> Because of the gravity of it all, I could discuss it with no one for almost a week, not even with my wife. I never before had difficulty sleeping; that week I did.

The star of the 1971 conference was the French publisher/journalist Jean-Jacques Servan-Schreiber, author of *Le Defi Ameri-*

cain,[1] that era's most talked-about book in business circles on both sides of the Atlantic. He was critical of what he characterised the imperial march of US corporations across global markets, devouring established local companies and "colonising" the European consumer, in particular, with American brands. Servan-Schreiber had agreed to give the main address at the IMI conference. Meanwhile, he entered French politics. The conference was an early sell-out on the strength of the star appearance. But a week before the event, the lead speaker reneged in order to attend a political rally in Nancy, his adopted constituency in eastern France. His decision was "not negotiable". But the IMI, having a contract to honour with its members, hired a Lear jet to fly him overnight from Nancy to Shannon. The arrangement wiped out the conference's surplus but at the appointed time Servan-Schreiber strolled onto the stage, electrifying an expectant audience with a memorable performance.

Prior to the 1973 oil crisis, bookings kept rising, often exceeding the substantially enlarged capacity. Again, the 1972 conference sold out within days on news that the world's best-known economist, J.K. Galbraith, would be the keynote speaker. It was a presidential election year in the US. Ten days before the conference, Galbraith told the conference director that the Democratic candidate in the primaries phase of the US presidential election, George McGovern — who had chalked up successes in the primaries — had foreclosed on Galbraith's promise to join him as economic adviser if the early campaign went well. It was a straight choice between disappointing the IMI or the then probable next president of the United States.

Not again, thought the director. As it happened, the Institute had hired from London a new communications technology miracle — an image projection system, capable of projecting a TV image of the speakers onto a large screen in the conference hall. Run of the mill now, in 1972 it was an astounding innovation. Embarrassed at having to break his commitment to the Institute, Galbraith agreed to videotape his speech in a Boston TV studio. When the conference chairman, Garret FitzGerald, introduced the video in Killar-

---

[1] Servan-Schreiber, J-J (1968), *The American Challenge*, (translated from the French by Ronald Steel), London: Hamilton.

ney, the audience enjoyed Galbraith's performance on the big screen, to such effect that a member was heard to boast months later that he had met the great Galbraith in Killarney!

The choice of venue and the time of year — late spring — provided managers with a welcome break from the rigours of winter. In its prime, the conference became an icon of the new Ireland. An old hand, whose admiration for the new breed of high-powered executive was tinged with acid, suggested a conference anthem:

> *Ring-a-ring neurosis*
> *Coronary thrombosis*
> *A seizure, a seizure,*
> *They all fall down.*

As affluence grew in the 1960s, more participants — then exclusively male — brought their wives. The IMI was soon under pressure to provide an alternative programme for what were termed progressively — as political correctness evolved — wives, spouses, accompanying persons, partners. First the choices were golf, tennis, walking, couture and cuisine. But, under Nóirín Slattery's deft management, the event evolved into a Women's Forum on a range of contemporary themes.

As the participation of spouses grew, so did the interest of the media's social correspondents. The picture coverage hinted at an élite disporting itself in a glamorous setting. Concerns grew at the impact on the Institute's image. The conference, though never less than serious in content, was in the eyes of some becoming damaged by its success. Criticism intensified in times of recession, questioning its future. Supporters pointed to its contribution in establishing the IMI as an important agent of progress, giving Irish managers direct access to intellectuals, innovators and practitioners at the leading edge of management theory/practice. It gave the Institute a platform to challenge and influence established national economic policy.

In 1983, during one of those cyclical recessions, the new director-general, Brian Patterson, decided on a root-and-branch review of the conference:

> I had some concerns about its image. I knew that the members valued it; that it had negatives for one of our

funding sources, government; and the media liked to
snipe at it as a junket. It had, to an extent, come to dominate the Institute's public profile.

With an eye to intense funding negotiations then going on with
government, Patterson decided to axe Killarney with its associated
negatives in favour of a one-day event, without the trimmings, in
Dublin. The result was not good: the attendance was intermittent,
many participants moving back and forth between their offices and
the conference. The networking dimension was lost. The following
year, it was back to Killarney, starring Tom Peters, author of the
then best seller, *In Search of Excellence*.[2]

In 1987, the incoming chairman, Howard Kilroy, asked for a study
of members' attitudes to the event. The head of membership, John
Dinan, surveyed chief executives — those who had not attended, as
well as those who did. Managers in manufacturing or retailing
favoured a shorter conference, but the services sector — banking,
insurance and professional services — did not. This reinforced a
view that there are two species at a business conference: the hunt-
ers and the hunted! The hunted won the argument; the conference
was reduced to two days, geared more to how managers manage
rather than to discussion of the national policy environment for
business — "back to the knitting", as Tom Peters would say.

The conference did move around in the mid-1990s. This was
part of a programme of change to strengthen the Institute's presence in the regions and in the North. The 1995 event was held in
Belfast on an all-Ireland theme: *The Island of Ireland — a National
Economic Zone for Business?* The board subsequently rated it "an
unqualified success". The following year, chairman Jerry Liston led
members to the splendid new hall in the University of Limerick;
again it was highly rated, with positive media coverage. Later, Killarney returned to favour for the modified-formula, more participative model of recent years. As mentioned previously, the *Winds of
Change* conference in 2000 inspired RTE's economics editor,
George Lee, to base a TV series on it. In 2001, foot and mouth re-
strictions, still in place at the decision deadline, caused a cancella-

---

[2] See page 288.

tion. But the chairman, Kevin Kelly, was quick to reassure Killarney: "We will be back in 2002."

Apart from the "flagship" event, whenever a topic emerges about which top management needs to be urgently and expertly informed, the IMI can quickly commission a briefing. Regional mini-conferences form part of the programme in the main provincial centres — now financially underpinned by ESB sponsorship and promoted by those pillars of the institute of managers, the regional committees.

The portfolio of services available exclusively to the "institute of managers" has changed little from the basic design of the founders — a library and information service and opportunities to meet and discuss topics of shared interest. The library dates from 1955. Its founder, Inagh Duff, although without training, had, in large measure, the essential qualities of a librarian: the knack of problem-solving and an infinite capacity for taking pains. Fond of quoting Samuel Johnson's maxim — "Knowledge is of two kinds: we know a subject ourselves, or we know where we can find information upon it" — she guided the reading of many a young manager over a long career with the IMI.

She established the basis of a library in quick order. Starting with empty shelves in the Merrion Square boardroom, she expanded the book stock, topic by topic. When it moved to Leeson Park two years later, the library had grown to 800 books and 1,000 periodicals. In 1958, Paddy Dillon Malone was recruited to coordinate and develop the information service and the journal. He concluded information exchange agreements with centres of management in the US and the UK, widening the IMI's trawl. Members were encouraged to bring queries of any kind relating to the job of managing, a valuable inducement to companies to join.

Today's library has 8,000 books. Regular culling keeps it to that number, ensuring that it remains current and relevant. The only library of its kind in Ireland and equal to the finest on management anywhere, it has a vast reach on behalf of its users through reciprocal links with the great library at Trinity College, the British Library and others. In addition to the books, an archive of as many as 150 journals is maintained, some going back to the foundation of the

Institute. Electronic technology has transformed access to this store of information. It is possible, for instance, under licensing arrangements with commercial databases, for members to retrieve, via the internet, articles from any of 1,000 journals world-wide. The catalogue of books and of the latest information carriers — electronic books and CD-ROMs — can be viewed and ordered online.

The journal *Management* was a popular periodical for managers for 40 years. Editorially, it had a challenging brief: to pursue in print the *raison d'être* of the Institute — raising the standard of management in Ireland. It helped promote awareness of the Institute in its formative years and spread knowledge of new management techniques and practices. It also addressed and commented on the social, economic, taxation and legislative framework in which managers worked.

Investigative journalism was not for *Management*! As the official organ of a membership body, it had to pick its way carefully so as not to tread on the interests of members or, naturally, of the Institute itself. An early editor encountered the narrow parameters of editorial "freedom". Much of the content of the journal was earnest stuff — the nuts and bolts of a manager's job. It needed the occasional lighter touch to help its appeal — a contributor who would cast a jaundiced eye on some of the nonsense that went on in business as elsewhere. A suitably cynical contributor was commissioned to write a monthly piece, protected by the *nom de plume*, Diogenes. His end-of-magazine "slot", with cartoon illustration, was soon the best-read part of *Management*. But he and his editor were quickly in hot water. In domestic dealings with the Dublin Gas Company, Diogenes encountered some ludicrous piece of red tape. The company's representative blamed it on "one of those cracked regulations made by head office". The company found itself lampooned in the Diogenes column. The general manager did not find it funny, contacted the IMI chairman and announced his company's resignation from the Institute, forthwith. The loss of such a large corporate member would have caused serious financial pain to the IMI. However, diplomacy and an abject retraction brought a reprieve.

A month later, Diogenes' displeasure alighted on what seemed, editorially, a safe target, well clear of the IMI's sphere of activity — the lifeboat service. He took umbrage at being asked on the street to subscribe to a flag day of the Royal National Lifeboat Institution on the reasonable grumble that "the cost of lifesaving at sea should be met by a levy on shipping at large and should not depend on charitable efforts to raise funds".

But he went deeper:

> In the second place, those who organise the fund-raising as a charity seem to be misguided in their efforts — they should apply their energies to genuine charity.

A vested interest lurked even in that unlikely place. Among the eminent patrons of the Royal National Lifeboat Institution was Sir Charles Harvey, then president of the IMI; his wife was one of RNLI's most dedicated fund-raisers. Harvey's long frame appeared at the editor's door: "Who is this fella, Diogenes?"

He was not mollified at being told of the guarantee of anonymity. As president, he could, of course, have demanded the file and found that the offending Diogenes was quite a senior executive in his own company, Guinness! However, he did not pull rank but pointed out that *Management* had insulted the voluntary commitment of many worthy people who had dedicated themselves to the welfare and safety of "they that go down to the sea in ships and occupy their business in great waters". A few issues later, *Management* published, free of charge, and without comment, a half-page fund-raising appeal for the Lifeboat Institution. The insult was forgiven and Diogenes remained undiscovered in his tub in St James's Gate.

Management was expected to cover its direct costs. Advertising was the only source of revenue to meet the cost of production and postage. (It boasted a notional cover price but, as it was free to members, its main market, little receipts accrued from that quarter.) In the 1960s, the editor read in *The Observer* that *The Manager*, the British Institute of Management's magazine, had been taken over by a Haymarket Press-led consortium, which was to relaunch it under the title *Management*. He went to see Haymarket's owner, Michael Heseltine,[3] pointing out that the advertising revenue base of the existing *Management* would be greatly damaged by such a clash of titles. Heseltine immediately offered to review

---

[3] The same!

the title, and later suggested *Management Today*, with which title the IMI was happy to agree.

When the journal was founded, there were few business publications in Ireland and those that existed had small circulations. The 1960s spawned a new breed of business journalist, specialist reporters who broadened coverage of business in the dailies with more in-depth reporting and analysis. One of its pioneers, Nicholas Leonard, was founding editor of the first business weekly, *Business and Finance*. Business monthlies proliferated. Some, in horseracing language, "flattered only to deceive" but all contributed to a competitively turbulent environment for *Management.*

If it was to compete with the newcomers, the journal had to have a full-time journalist and advertising manager, rather than the part-time attentions of the head of membership who doubled as editor. In 1967 Dominick Coyle was recruited from the *Financial Times* and became *Management's* first full-time editor. With Diarmuid Ó Broin's arrival shortly afterwards as advertisement manager, the magazine was in professional hands and better placed to contend in the newly crowded field of business journalism. Subsequent editors included Leslie Faughnan, Howard Kinlay, Alex Miller and Tom Curtin, the last of the in-house editors.

Mostly, the journal kept within its brief, balancing its "evangelical" purpose — promoting excellence in management — with livelier, newsier content. But there was an occasional lapse. One editor, tired of the constraints, decided, without bothering the chain of command, to liven things up by publishing a profile of Michael O'Leary TD, the Minister for Labour. The article included the following:

> Since his elevation to the government benches, Mr O'Leary has developed interests not entirely in keeping with his professed proletarian beliefs. He has been known to take to country houses of the actual landed gentry at weekends and indulge in a bit of grouse shooting. . . . His performance in government to date has been far below the standard which his genuine intelligence and ability would lead one to expect of him.

The anonymous writer went on to excoriate the minister's "lacklustre and incoherent" performance in a recent Dáil debate. The impact on the entire ruling echelon of the Institute was devastating. Here was its official government benefactor under personal attack from the Institute's own publication which boasted that its readership included all the decision-makers of Irish business. Because it was so much outside the brief of the journal to engage in abuse of anyone, much less a member of government on which so much of the Institute's ongoing public relations effort was focused, the top management was in shock. The chairman, Michael Dargan, immediately dispatched a letter of apology to the minister:

> I have just seen the article in the current issue of *Management.* I regard it as unworthy and offensive and I wish, on behalf of the council and the Institute, to convey to you our concern and our apologies. I am calling a special meeting of the executive committee to enquire into the wording and publication of the article and its implications and to consider, with the director-general, what action is appropriate.

The minister, in his reply, took the whole thing in commendably good part:

> Critical articles, however inaccurate and prejudiced one may feel these to be, are the occupational hazard of public life. In the case of *Management,* I would have felt that the article could have related to the work of my Ministry rather than flights of fantasy into my leisure activities. I believe that too little attention has been paid in this country to the question of relationships between the State and industrial relations generally and when I accepted the invitation to be interviewed by *Management* I thought it resulted from an editorial desire to answer questions in this area.
>
> These personal views apart, however, on reflection I see little to complain about in the article — it belongs to that general rash of anonymous and lazy journalism which is so much in vogue. Even if it does not do any good it can scarcely do much harm.
>
> I thank you for your expression of apology. There is a suggestion in your letter of further action being taken by your

executive committee. For my own part I would prefer that
this did not happen and that the matter be closed now.

Because of the minister's request for no retribution, a special
meeting of the executive called by Dargan to deal with the affair
was cancelled. But at the next scheduled meeting there was a general discussion on the journal and its editorial mission. A paper
prepared by Michael Viney, the Institute's head of communications, got in a pre-emptive strike against a possible move to emas-
culate the magazine:

> The journal has real value only if it is read. Editorial policy
> is now directed fully towards engaging the readership.
> The journal needs to provoke, inform and entertain. The
> first may seem inappropriate, but it does have some value
> where it is the drive behind factual, rather than opinion-
> ated, material, and analysis which is clearly authoritative.
>
> The journal has to compete for the work time and the lei-
> sure time of a heterogeneous group. Content needs to be
> to the point, relating to production managers in some re-
> spects and to personnel managers in others. It can also
> broaden its appeal by relating to the reader as an active
> agent in the socio-economic environment. It must be en-
> tertaining if it is to relate to the manager in his leisure
> time, rather than be relegated to the quick flick-through
> and the office shelf.

The executive agreed. It reiterated that the general objectives of
the journal were to help members identify with the Institute's aims,
to reinforce the IMI' s status "as the country's primary source of
management thinking and development", to underline the need
for management development and "to develop a surplus of income
over direct expenditure". The minute ended succinctly: "It was
agreed that there would be no point in publishing a journal that
was not read."

Ironically, in light of its origins, there was a growing view that by
the early 1980s *Management* had reached the limit of its development as an in-house publication. Coincidentally, Kevin Kelly, the
successful magazine publisher, suggested to the Institute a possible
deal that would take *Management*, which he described as "a sleep-

ing giant", into his stable of publications. The executive committee was sounded out but it was thumbs down; they would not countenance selling off, as they saw it, 30 years of history. A window of opportunity closed. In 1985, when the financial shoe was again pinching, *Management* was finally on the move. The executive committee approved Brian Patterson's proposal that Jemma Publications, publishers of a number of business-to-business titles, take over *Management* under licence from the IMI for a two-year period, with an option of then purchasing the title outright. In March 1987 the council was told that Jemma intended to exercise that option. The arrangement survived for ten years but the magazine failed to maintain viability and publication ceased in October 1996.

Publication as a discipline is encouraged within the IMI, not only for its contribution to the wider body of knowledge, but for the dividend of personal and professional development it confers on the staff. IMI staff contribute regularly to the national media and to significant international journals. The Institute has been a significant publisher of management books, research reports and commentary. It has co-operated also with other organisations in joint publications in the general field of management, sometimes acting as publisher of work outside its direct field but which it judges to be worthy of publication in the interests of managers. A case in point was a book in 1982 by the TCD economist, Sean Barrett, *Transport Policy in Ireland*. The IMI agreed to publish it, business being a significant "client" of the transport infrastructure. A pre-publication courtesy copy was sent to CIE as a corporate member and because of its dominant position in transport. The company reacted with outrage at some of the content and commissioned a British firm of transport consultants to examine the book on their behalf. CIE asked the Institute not to proceed with publication, threatening resignation. The Institute stuck to its position, pointing out that its aim was "to provide a forum for views and discussion". It published the book.

At one time, the most compelling incentive to companies joining the IMI was a significant member discount on the price of courses. But then came the state grants. The aim of the grants was to make access to management training as easy as possible for as many as possible. Reasonably enough, the state would not tolerate more than a token price differential for members on a product that it was subsidising with exchequer funds. With the major incentive unavailable, other ways had to be found to create an alluring bargain — a portfolio of self-financing services exclusive to members.

The first of IMI's surveys of executive salaries and fringe benefits — exclusive to members, telling them how they rate in the remuneration league — was published in 1968. The information officer, Frank McKevitt, had the formidable job of setting up the design. Companies were classified by trade category, turnover range and size. Executives were classed by no fewer than 12 levels and 14 functions. Everything had to be confidential. Not everyone was sure that the Institute should put the spotlight on managers in quite this way. The president of the Federation of Irish Industry, Guy Jackson, also a council member of the IMI, warned the Institute that the pending first report was giving rise to a great deal of concern in the FII:

> It will be appreciated that surveys that are either critical of management or show management in an undesirable light do not endear the IMI to its management members. I do not wish to question the right of the IMI to carry out surveys which will help it in becoming a more effective institute for management training. What I am questioning is whether surveys on fringe benefits and salaries should properly be a function of the Institute and whether the results of such surveys should be made available in a form which is accessible to almost anyone.

From the southern capital came a similar cry: Christopher Aliaga Kelly feared that "this sort of data" could be used "in a most damaging way and quite unjustifiably".

The Institute stuck to its guns. The chairman, Gunnar Larsen, told Jackson why:

> The reasons are that the Institute is a body of managers which if it is to have the respect and confidence of the community and Government should be prepared to publish objective information about management practice which is of national importance. It is to the advantage of the Institute and its members that they are seen to do this.

All was well; the press comment was even-handed and the feared backlash from the trade unions did not materialise. Ivor Kenny replied to Christopher Aliaga Kelly:

> We went to some pains to get the right impression across to the press and I think it has paid off. Like yourself, I was worried that we might get the headline — Irish managers get £15,000 a year.

In 1967, the Institute inaugurated the Executive Health Unit, a medical checkup service for senior management. Professor W.J. Jessop, head of the Moyne Institute of Preventive Medicine, Trinity College, Dr Jack Eustace, a specialist in industrial medicine, and the cardiologist, Dr Gerry Gearty of the Royal City of Dublin Hospital, Baggot Street, designed and tested an all-in-one medical checkup covering disorders likely to afflict the busy executive. The accent was on prevention, so care was taken with family history, lifestyle, exposure to stress. The attraction of the package was that it took only two hours. Stress counselling was included, unusual for the time. It was well received by business. The unit, shaped by its first physicians, Dr Jack England and Dr Philip Brown, played a part in early diagnosis, prevention and medical research. It continued under the IMI's management until 1987, when it was merged with Irish Health Care in Blackrock Clinic, the number of doctors doubling from four to eight. While the IMI conceded ownership of the service, it continued to promote it.

Some services endure. Others were transient responses to the needs of their time. During the pre-oil-crisis boom, an Irish-American counsellor, Eileen Kelly, provided career counselling for members, putting on a formal basis what had previously been *ad hoc*. Members at a crossroads had their skills and capacities professionally assessed and were counselled on where they were likely to find fulfilment. Those at career end were helped to plan transition to retirement.

When Ireland joined the EEC, report after report on competitiveness highlighted the inability of Irish firms to do business in languages other than English. The Institute felt it should do something about it and set up a language laboratory with Eithne Naylor in charge. Writing about the problem, she compared job advertisements in Irish papers with those carried on the same day in *Le Monde*.[4] Almost three-quarters of *Le Monde* advertisements looked for at least one second language; not one Irish advertisement specified proficiency in a foreign language. She made the reasonable point:

> It seems that the Irish still depend on interpreters and agents and on the willingness and ability of customers, suppliers and business contacts abroad to do business in English.

Her courses were slanted towards business topics, with marketing being the most popular. The service was discontinued in 1995.

In a surge of development in the brief, buoyant years of the early 1970s, the library and information services were incorporated into a new management development division. More professionals were taken on to extend the R&D capability. A special subscription service was set up, linking the Institute's membership with the international business information database of the *Financial Times*. In the cutbacks following the 1974 financial crisis, the information/research section was the first to be axed. The Institute was in future much slower to invest as heavily in work that was not directly related to its core activity, training.

Developments in company law in the 1980s put greater responsibility on boards of directors and highlighted the desirability of having an objective viewpoint at the board table. Member companies would ask the Institute to suggest people for non-executive directorships. The IMI was not keen to get directly involved but, when there was a proposal from Colm Barnes and Brendan Reville to set up a small independent organisation to promote the use of non-executive directors and establish a register of available people, the Institute supported it. The Boardroom Centre was set up in 1984 in the National Management Centre as an independent entity, with Reville becoming part-time director. He and his successors helped place many directors in Irish boardrooms. The Boardroom Centre has now been amalgamated with the Institute of Directors in Ireland.

---

[4] Naylor, E. (1983), "Mind Your Language", *Management*, March.

When the IMI was founded, membership was offered under four categories — corporate, member (for managers), associate (for interested non-managers) and affiliate (for "specialist organisations and other bodies or persons concerned with management"). The memorandum and articles of association today has seven categories, including two accolades by invitation of the council only — Life Fellow (LFMgtI) and Fellow (FMgtI). These allow the Institute to honour, respectively, "individuals of eminent achievement who have made an outstanding contribution to the advancement of any of the objectives of the Institute" (Life Fellow) and "individuals who are adjudged to have made an exceptional contribution to the theory or practice of management" (Fellow).

The roll of Life Fellows,[5] the highest honour in the gift of the Institute, includes past presidents, distinguished international writers on management and statesmen who have contributed to the Institute's work at home and abroad. The articles now also allow personal members to aspire to Certified Membership reserved for "practising managers with significant managerial experience and who have demonstrated their commitment to the Institute".

The most powerful assertion of the membership character of the IMI is in the council and the board, formerly known as the executive committee. The council is the "parliament" through which the chief executive and his colleagues account to the members. Part-elected, part appointed, it mirrors the spread of members and their interests. A council that was totally elected — as was the case at the beginning — favoured well-known candidates, the leaders of nationally prominent enterprises. Small and medium-sized enterprises were under-represented. The regional spread was also poor. To correct this, the right to co-opt was extended and used to ensure that smaller companies were given voice. To counteract the Dublin bias, leaders of regional committees were given council membership, *ex-officio*. This endorsed their importance as the standard bearers of the IMI through the country. The regional structure broadens the Institute's "constituency", ensuring that it does not become a solely Dublin-based centre of management. The board is

---

[5] See Appendix 2.

appointed by the council. With the chief executive, it implements policy and deals with issues affecting the viability of the organisation. Outside the formal structure, there is another key relationship: the day-to-day transactions between the chief executive and the chairman. This informal axis, while defying analysis, ensures that the "institute of managers" concept endures at the core of the Institute's decision-making system.

CHAPTER TWENTY-THREE

ACHIEVING, PURSUING

The predominant concern of most chief executives over the life of the IMI was its funding. Brian Patterson:

> It consumed more of my time and energy than anything else — the fact that the Institute was dependent both on government and the ESF, which had their own agendas, their own priorities and ways of operating. It was an uncomfortable relationship. I am sure that their, albeit unspoken, attitude to the Institute was, "If you're so smart, why aren't you rich?" I struggled to get away from that dependency.

In December 1984, presenting to the council a strategy to take the IMI through to the 1990s, Patterson described the continued dependence on uncertain external funding as a crucial issue for the Institute. Unlike previous strategies that took funding as the starting point and sought to shape the organisation's future in accordance with that constraint, his paper relegated the grants issue to last:

> With its present structure and role, the Institute is not and never can be a private, profitable business. The necessity for and uncertainty of funding are probably facts of life with which we have to live, so long as we maintain our present mission.

He concluded that, rather than continuing to agonise over the issue, the Institute should accept its dependence on grant income — with all its uncertainty. To that end, pressure would be maintained on the ESF — which had been showing signs of wanting to disengage — but alternative sources of funds would also be sought from private sector sources, including the larger corporate members.

The council was divided in its reaction. Howard Kilroy, president of Smurfit's, told the chairman, Michael Killeen, that he was concerned about the impact on the Institute's image of its chronic dependency on subsidy. He did not agree with funding being labelled the number one critical issue. In his view, if the product was right, other things fell into place. That was where the strategic emphasis should be: the Institute must aim to become a profitable business. Problems associated with funding and image would then fade.

However, Ivor Kenny, a former director-general, saw state support as positive: the Institute's financial link with government in his view strengthened its voice. It was unrealistic to expect the Institute to function without state funding, when AnCO, a competitor, was heavily funded. Tom Hardiman agreed: management skills needed to be developed in Ireland and it was the Institute's job to ensure that this happened — "the need for funding seems to be a reality". Tom Byrnes, Telecom Éireann's chief executive, supported the Kilroy view: the Institute should "free itself from funding and be more closely associated with private enterprise".

The dependency issue got another airing the following year at the first council meeting under Killeen's successor, Feargal Quinn. At this, as at other discussions on the issue, it was the private sector members of the council who were, in general, least comfortable with the Institute's being beholden to the taxpayer whether in the guise of government or the institutions of the European Commission.

When Howard Kilroy was chairman of the Institute in 1989, he delivered the keynote address to the Killarney conference. He took the opportunity to give public voice to the views he had been expressing to the council. In the previous year, the government grant had been cut by 41 per cent, down from £730,000. In an unscripted aside, directed at government, the chairman said bluntly that the IMI would be better and more businesslike without any grant. This sent a shudder through the current management — the state grant was still over £430,000. Even the civil servants present were taken aback, although a contemporary report of the Advisory Committee on Management Training[1] — of which Kilroy had been a member — had recommended a fundamental shift of government grants from the providers to the users of management training. The Advisory Committee had concluded that:

> State funding in the public service and the private sector be redirected from the present support of provision of management training, to the support of users and activities that will ensure the more efficient realisation of national objectives.

The IMI had welcomed the report despite its implications for future subsidy — not only from the Exchequer; John Corcoran, assistant secretary of the Department of Labour, pointed out to the Institute that a reduction in state funding would, in turn, affect the Institute's ability to draw down funds from Brussels.

This recommendation dominated a meeting with the Minister for Labour, Bertie Ahern, and his officials following publication of the report. The minister offered some comfort by promising continuing direct support for specific activities, such as research and small business development. Nevertheless, state grants declined steeply: from £730,000 in 1987 to £300,000 in 1990 to £67,000 in 1993 and to zero in 1996. The mid-1990s, therefore, saw the Institute, for the first time since the mid-1960s, having to plan without Lemass's ha'porth o' tar.

The board, in 1993, was in need of funds to refurbish the buildings at Sandyford, then about 20 years old and in need of a face-lift. The chairman, Fergus McGovern, asked Ivor Kenny to chair a steering committee for an appeal to members and invited Mark Hely Hutchinson to act as campaign director. Kenny and Hely Hutchinson decided, first, to take confidential soundings from business leaders on the likely response to a fundraising appeal. Finding stiff resistance, they recommended to the board that the proposal be put on hold. Some of the perceptions of the Institute uncovered in the course of their discussions were so negative that they urged the chairman to commission an external objective assessment of the Institute's performance. A concerned executive

---

[1] See page 256.

committee invited the Gemini Consulting group "to sharpen the Institute's strategic vision", measuring its performance against the best executive development centres.

Following the report of the Gemini study, a "reorganisation and change programme" was initiated. The elective component, which gave staff a strong voice in appointments to most managerial positions, had developed flaws, leading to some dysfunction. This practice was discontinued. The participative ethos introduced after the "revolution" 20 years earlier was maintained but, in the post-Gemini organisation, it was tempered with greater flexibility and a stronger emphasis on accountability for performance in the marketplace.

Coincidentally, a vacancy arose because of the retirement of the chief executive. The board, keen to maintain the momentum of the organisation and change programme, invited the chairman, Dermot Egan, to act as executive chairman pending the appointment of a new chief executive. Egan, recently retired deputy chief executive of the AIB group, knew the IMI well, having been one of the IMI's pioneering specialists of the 1960s. He became in effect acting chief executive for six months, guiding the organisational changes then in train, maintaining pressure on costs and successfully leading the search for a chief executive.

Barry Kenny was appointed in April 1995. An engineer and management consultant, he recalls that the IMI had been perceived as tending towards self-focus, due in part to its reliance, though to a lesser extent than of old, on grant income. On joining, he found the reality to be more positive but complex, nevertheless. He believed that a key to addressing any unfavourable perception of the Institute was to end the dependency. But he also had other concerns about the grant:

> At times in the Institute's life grants were clearly essential. But the criteria governing a grant may not always entirely match the aims of the organisation: they can be distortionary and push it in the wrong direction.

To achieve financial independence, the Institute would need to become more commercial in the sense that courses would be more market-driven in their selection and design. Some internal management practices needed to change. Aligning the output of the faculty with the organisation's revised goals, while respecting the professional autonomy it traditionally enjoyed, involved a change of some delicacy in the internal culture. A new incentive system rewarded people for running additional programmes, generating more revenue. As Barry Kenny says:

> With the co-operation of everyone, it worked; the new, more commercial ethos took root. Instead of being be-holden to others, we were able to generate extra cash flow from our own resources, which we could then re-invest in the Institute's future.

The fundraising plan that led to the Gemini project was still on hold. The new chief executive's view was that going to the members for donations would serve only to replace one sort of dependency with another. It was scrapped.

Under the canon of self-sufficiency, programmes are now required to cover costs, and generate a surplus for reinvestment. Enhanced utilisation of a very superior physical asset, together with a streamlining of the cost structure — involving smarter rather than harder ways of working — have brought significant improvements in the finances. Coincidentally, savings accrued when, as a result of a sustained sequence of shrewd investment decisions in the 1980s and 1990s, the need for annual topping-up of the Institute's pensions fund was significantly reduced.

Barry Kenny inherited a strong balance sheet. The Institute's financial reserves had been prudently managed over the years under financial controller, Jim Byrne. Membership revenues grew substantially with the economy's strong performance at the turn of the century, as did revenue from courses. The combined effect has been a sustained surge in the financial performance of the Institute over five years, making it possible for the chairman, J.V. Liston, to report in 1997 that it was fully independent, operating without state or EU subsidy and, indeed, in a position to lay aside surplus funds for investment in the future. External funding still has a place, but strictly on a case-by-case basis. For instance, available EU grants are pursued to step up research.

The effect on the Institute of the ending of its financial dependency on the state is seen by Barry Kenny as entirely positive:

It induced a changed emphasis in the Institute's approach to its market. The end of the state subsidy does not mean that the Institute will be self-sufficient in terms of its capital needs for the future. No organisation in its field — education and development — can be expected to generate development funds from its revenue stream without risking an unsustainable distortion of its pricing structure. Such institutions continue to be dependent on endowment funds for landmark projects. The IMI is no exception.

What of the Institute's client base? How has that changed in five decades? The businesses the IMI works with today are more complex, more sophisticated, more challenged by the pace of change and global competition. They grapple with elements that did not exist a generation ago, much less when the IMI was founded. The pace of innovation is a key difference: some sectors, notably information technology where innovation is the driver, work to unimaginably short product life-cycles, months even.

Though modern business structures are less hierarchical, the pressures on executives are considered greater. Cascading data create stress and anxiety which managers must cope with — in themselves and in others. There is more mobility; the career-long commitment of the past has been weakened by an easier job market and growing aspirations for a better life/work balance. As recently as the mid-1980s, it was the norm for people starting a two-year programme in the IMI to be in the same job when they graduated. Now the opposite is more likely.

Behavioural science has had a marked impact on the way organisations are managed. It is now recognised that the critical part of the strategic process is the implementation of change. It is here that behavioural science makes its greatest contribution. Managers are now more open to learning about themselves so that they may better understand others. "Command and tell" has yielded to a more participative style, reflecting changes in wider society.

The behaviour of organisations and their decisions are open to keener scrutiny than before. What amounts to a new bill of rights for employees and other company stakeholders — legislation covering consumers, equality, discrimination, behaviour in the workplace — constrains the actions of managers and demands a more sensitive exercise of that enduring managerial responsibility: getting work done through others.

Some management functions have changed more than others. Finance expert and writer Ciaran Walsh, from a perspective of over 40 years, 30 of them with the IMI, has observed big changes in the role of the financial manager:

> Prior to the 1950s, accounting was a statutory function: the accountant recorded all financial transactions and reported them to the fiscal authorities once a year. That changed with the introduction of "management accounting" in the US after the war. The accountant now had an additional responsibility — providing current, real information in a way that was useful to the company's management. The first IMI courses on finance helped to consolidate that change in Ireland.
>
> It was not until the 1960s, when the IMI pioneered extended courses in management accounting, that the strategic value of the finance function was recognised and the accountant moved from the backroom to the boardroom. The next change came in the 1970s with the growth of exports outside the United Kingdom, particularly after the 1979 break from sterling: currency and cash management — the treasury function — was added to the accountant's portfolio. Because the computer was initially introduced as successor to the calculating machine, the finance department inherited responsibility for IT. Then came the era of mergers and acquisitions and IPOs. Now, rather than the "goalkeepers" they were fifty years ago, accountants are key players in determining the profitability and growth of an organisation.

One of the striking changes is the profile of managers coming to the Institute on courses. Up to 80 per cent have third-level certification. Most have degrees. Nowhere has the change been more remarkable than at the front line. Thirty years ago, clients on supervisory management courses would typically be from the old indigenous industries such as footwear, textiles, food and tobacco, with job titles — now virtually disappeared — like foreman and charge-hand. Today, reflecting the changes in the role, the term supervision has given way to the more descriptive "frontline management". He or she can be "lead programmer", "team leader (quality)", "head underwriter", "project engineer", "technical administrator" — depending on the industry or service, the titles denoting a new professionalism and an acknowledgement that today's frontline manager is likely to be managing people with specialised skills, not the "general operatives" of old.

Organisations are now, in general, flatter, with fewer layers of management. This has been mainly at the expense of middle managers who have been replaced with more empowered first level managers, leading smaller, better educated, more skilled teams. The long-time head of the IMI's front-line management programme, Ray Leonard, notes the contrast with the old days:

> Then, it would not have been unusual for foremen to be in charge of twenty or more workers. The emphasis was on keeping production moving. Management issues, including personnel matters, were the domain of the middle management layer, usually the personnel department. Today's frontline manager is likely to have a team of from six to ten, is expected to sort out issues of motivation or discipline within his/her group, normally without recourse to personnel/human resources departments. Problem solving is firmly at the frontline.

American companies brought the team concept to Ireland in the 1970s. Quality — paramount in the knowledge-based industry — cannot be achieved by edict; the commitment to perform to high standards comes from within the individual. This ethos is reflected in a more egalitarian organisation system and an easier, more consultative management style. Them-and-us codes of address and, indeed, of dress are out. As the quality imperative spread in the 1980s, boosted by Tom Peters's timely book, *In Search of Excellence*,[2] so did the emphasis on the frontline — the shop floor in industry, the customer interface in services. The team approach has taken root.

---

[2] Peters, Thomas J. and Waterman, Robert H. Jr. (1982), *In Search of Excellence, Lessons from America's Best-Run Companies*, Harper & Row, US.

The portfolio of IMI supervisory training courses has evolved with that process, equipping a new generation of younger, better-qualified entrants to management — many of them graduates — for a more demanding, responsible role. The content of courses has long moved on from the old staple PLOC (planning, leading, organising, controlling) to reflect the modern figures on the management landscape: "world class management", "total quality management", "just-in-time", "customer care", and "standard operating procedures". The outline of a typical IMI course for the new-style frontline manager might include topics like: identifying key result areas; coaching, counselling and motivation; persuasive and influencing skills; employee relations, involving the handling of grievances and discipline; team leading skills, including insights into group dynamics and a team approach to problem solving.

Ray Leonard notes other signs of the integration of the old supervisory function into mainstream management. Thirty years ago, supervisors tended to align themselves with the workforce more than with "the bosses". If they worked late, they were paid overtime. A recent survey of participants disclosed that four out of five frontline managers worked longer than their standard contract hours, generally without overtime, and — a telling signal of their absorption into mainstream management — 55 per cent brought work home with them.

Attitudinal changes in the wider society have brought new pressures to the job of managing people. For instance, frontline managers may have to deal sensitively with on-the-job consequences of single-parent and two-parent-working households. The spate of canons governing the rights of the individual in the workplace — and the penalties for breaching them — provide plenty of human interest material for case studies and role-playing exercises on IMI courses. Managers must also contend with the on-the-job effects of legislation on equality, sexual harassment, unfair dismissal and other issues that never bothered their predecessors. The thin line between necessary management correction and illegal bullying has to be trod more gingerly than before.

A Ray Leonard anecdote shows that the subtleties of the anti-discrimination age have not yet been universally absorbed. He was on a job interview panel for a client company. One member of the panel leaned across in a pleasant, fatherly way to the young female applicant: "You wouldn't happen to be married, would you?" There was a startled silence from his colleagues on the board. The applicant, however, gazed serenely at her questioner and asked "innocently":

"Do I *have* to be married to do this job?"

"No."

"Well, why are you asking me then?"

"Old" industries now account for only a small part of the IMI's supervisory training market. Unlike the onetime supervisor who often got there through seniority, today's team leader is probably a graduate and as likely to be female as male, a balance not yet achieved at more senior levels. Another significant shift is from unionised to non-unionised companies. Today's frontline manager is expected to resolve issues of conflict on the spot, without recourse to shop stewards, once *de rigueur*.

While the greater numbers of participants come from frontline and middle-management levels, the IMI today is working more intensively than before with the top policy-making level, which accounts for the largest cohort of those taking masters courses.

From its beginnings in 1952, chief executives have been at the heart of the IMI's constituency; many IMI council members are CEOs whose needs differ from those of any other echelon of management. The then chairman of council, Ian Morrison, himself a CEO (of the Bank of Ireland), painted a picture of the manager's world for a special edition of *Management*[3] marking the Institute's Silver Jubilee in 1977:

> The computer has taken charge of bookkeeping and management struggles with intricate risk analysis in an inflationary environment. At the same time, we endeavour to develop the human resources of the organisation while struggling through the collective bargaining process. We talk of company image, of corporate identity, we use market research, we discuss social responsibility, we face rapidly changing situations which often threaten the survival

---

[3] Morrison, R. Ian (1977), "25 Years A-Growing", *Management*, May, p. 7.

of the organisation and we battle with the Prices Commission, the Civil Service, foreign competitors and changing attitudes of the younger workforce.

We enter export markets. We take risks. We make mistakes — often expensive mistakes. But we have in our minds the picture — in both qualitative and quantitative terms — of the organisation we would like to be. We suffer disappointments, all too often we find ourselves on the defensive and all too infrequently we pass a milestone of progress with a sigh of relief while tensing for the next obstacle. This is the essence of the manager's life. We keep watch for our specific span of command, we develop succession, we hope they learn from our mistakes and do not invent too many new mistakes. We shake our heads over brilliant young executives returning from business school who want to be President tomorrow. We manage imperfections to the best of our abilities, we are constantly the student and, even more so with the passing of years, we take nothing for granted and fight the cynicism which threatens to rob us of the very value system which has brought us to where we are.

Chief executives may not attend courses at the rate they did on their way to the top but their links with the Institute are close, nevertheless. Their special needs are addressed in a number of ways. A forum for chief executives established in the 1970s has continued, in one form or another, to provide a relaxed framework for the exchange of experience between them on concerns exclusive to the role. A common preoccupation is to maintain a perspective on the economic and regulatory environment in which business has to operate. Briefings are arranged with leading business thinkers, commentators and academics and others who influence national policy. The National Management Forum[4] brings together senior managers from business with the top ranks of the Civil Service, enhancing an understanding and exchange of the different perspectives. The Institute also sponsors a special — and influential — forum for CEOs of multinational companies where they can con-

---

[4] See page 258.

sider those issues of crucial interest to MNCs and, sometimes, to lobby for change.

As the reader will have noticed, early records of the Institute leave no doubt that the management domain was then presumed male. The female pronoun is absent from reports and submissions. An IMI survey[5] in the 1970s first highlighted the imbalance in the ratio of women to men in management, in fact showing that, even then, it was overwhelmingly male. Though women accounted for over 30 per cent of employees in manufacturing, less than two per cent of managers were women. They did better — eight per cent — in small firms. Most of those making it into management got as far as the lower rungs only. Of the 160 chief executives interviewed in the survey, only one was a woman. The outlook for the immediate future looked no more encouraging because, of full-time students taking business studies in the colleges of the National University of Ireland and the University of Dublin, only five per cent were women. In an International Labour Organisation study of women in administrative, executive and managerial work,[6] Ireland (5.7 per cent), although not the worst in Europe, lagged behind Europe's best, France (11.9), and far behind the world leader, the United States (17.7).

Manpower training agencies looked to address the issue. So did the IMI. Its response was a course, Women into Management — for women already in the workforce who aspired to promotion. Later came special training courses in assertiveness which enabled women acquire confidence-building skills as well as sufficient knowledge of the anatomy of management to encourage them to take that first step into an executive role. Ruth Handy, a psychologist at the IMI who has studied the problems of women in organisations and who has pioneered many IMI courses in the field, says that, even today, the situation remains out of equilibrium:

> As society changed, the case for special courses for women became questionable and *Women into Management* was discontinued. But the Institute continues to run courses for women in bigger organisations wishing to ac-

---

[5] Gorman, Liam et al. (1974), *Managers in Ireland*, Irish Management Institute.

[6] International Labour Organisation (1973) *Yearbook of Labour Statistics.*

celerate the achievement of equal opportunity. Top leadership roles remain predominately male largely because organisations have not learned to adapt to the imperatives of child rearing, still considered the province of women. Reacting to the ethos and inflexibility of large organisations, more and more women are leaving to start their own businesses.

Women attend IMI courses in greater numbers now. An example is the long-established Executive Development Programme for middle to senior managers in their thirties, already carrying a significant managerial load in their organisations. The 18-day programme is often seen as a route to the top. More than one-third of participants are women and the trend is towards fifty-fifty.

A member of the visiting faculty on the Institute's Executive Development Programme, Professor Terri Monroe of the Department of Leadership Studies of the University of San Diego, has considered the question of women in management:

> In taking up authority, there are not many models of effective female managers for young women to look to. Society presents women with a narrower range of what it judges acceptable behaviour: aggression and ambition are seen as dubious qualities in a woman. From a young age, there is a higher expectation of deference and politeness in girls. These constraints make it difficult to help women find an effective range of interpersonal skills needed when they take on a managerial role.

A survey[7] published by IBEC reported that women now account for 8 per cent of Irish chief executives, 21 per cent of senior managers and 30 per cent of middle managers. Despite this continuing imbalance in the numbers of women at the top levels of organisations, there is increasing confidence that the positive trend will, in time, prevail.

---

[7] *Women in Management in Irish Business* (2002), IBEC Research and Information Service.

For the IMI itself, what will be different about the future? The Institute puts much store in the closeness of its connection with business: its status as a creation of business *for* business and the close involvement of its faculty in the real world of its client, business. The faculty profile reflects this emphasis: recruitment policy puts a premium on practical management experience at senior level, not just on strong academic achievement.

Twenty years ago when it decided to offer degrees, the Institute had a choice: to become a business school, or to continue as a post-experience centre for management training, working exclusively with practising managers. Had it chosen the academic path, executive development programmes for practising managers would have become a subsidiary output. Other centres of management took that route. The IMI did not. It opted to continue with executive development as its main thrust: working exclusively with managers, developing their potential in the context of the actual and likely future needs of their businesses.

Most modern businesses are in continual transition. Strategies must, therefore, have built-in flexibility and nimbleness. Because of that dynamic, the demands on managers are spiralling, leading to more searching expectations of the IMI which, in response, is tending more towards a partnership, rather than supplier, relationship with its clients. A sustained association with the client company allows the faculty to focus its intervention not just on achieving optimum performance in the managers' current roles — although that, too — but on developing their capacity to contribute at ever higher levels.

The Institute distinguishes between management development and management training. The latter description applies in the main to the Institute's open (i.e. public) programmes in which it has a strong market position. Finely tuned to the needs of the manager, these courses are an important and profitable part of what the IMI does. But they cannot take account fully of the needs of a specific business operating in a turbulent world. "Management development" describes a longer-term process based on a closer knowledge of the individual and an appreciation of his/her company's strategy and goals. It addresses the full armoury of management — knowledge, skills and behaviour. It is more likely to induce lasting change. Companies are increasingly comfortable with this way of addressing their leadership needs. The Institute is, therefore, likely to be working more on a one-to-one basis with larger organisations, developing greater understanding of the nature of the performance they require of their managers and designing tailored programmes to achieve it. Chief executive Barry Kenny:

> We want our customers to see the IMI as an ongoing partner, helping them continually to develop their management teams. This is consistent with the view that our core role is management development, not just training. Training is a response to the needs of today and the next immediate phase of change. Development concerns transition — preparing organisations and individuals for the challenges of tomorrow, working with their managers to help them determine and reach the goals of the business.
>
> Our object, which is widely shared in the Institute, is to become excellent in developing management competencies that drive business performance. This has to happen to the highest standards. Our challenge is to move up the "value chain", doing more interesting, innovative work with senior managers and, maybe ultimately, ceding some of the basic programmes to others. The aim is to see the Institute universally recognised by Irish corporations as central to better business performance. We have a committed body of colleagues who would like to work to that end.

The Consortium — one of the IMI's twenty-first-century products — exemplifies this aspiration. It was originally designed for managers on their way to top positions in blue chip Scandinavian companies. "Borrowed" by Barry Kenny from the Swedish Institute of Management, the Consortium model lies somewhere between open courses and company-specific interventions. A select number of businesses — usually five — commit themselves in advance to a three-year cycle of training, assigning groups of executives to each element in the cycle. Uniquely, the companies participate in the choice of content, ensuring that it relates closely to their development strategies. The programme is run in four-week residential modules and taught by an international faculty of distinction, well published, and with considerable consulting experience. It is rated an élite programme, of equal standard to those of its genre offered by leading international centres such as the Wharton School in the US or INSEAD in France.

There is a growing international trend towards residential courses, which have two main benefits over the nine-to-five variety: by working into the evenings, managers' time away from the job is kept to a minimum; residential courses also create a deeper learning experience, because of the extended exchange between participants.

As the IMI approached the considerable milestone of its Golden Jubilee, Barry Kenny recommended to his board the construction of a residential block for which provision had been made on the Sandyford campus over a quarter century before. In 2001, the board, persuaded that the case for a residential component was cogent and pedagogically sound, sanctioned a study into the feasibility of a block of 50 study/bedrooms and a large conference suite.

Barry Kenny:

> The residential course, shorter but more intensive than the traditional model, is becoming the product of choice for today's larger client companies. The decision to go residential is not commercial but strategic. Although it will prove commercially sound as well, it is part of the wider strategy to move the Institute into even higher value work.

This latest project will at last realise the grand design for a national management centre first recommended by the Joint Committee on Education and Training for Management in 1956, 45 years earlier!

At 50, the IMI and the modern Irish economy are the same age. They broke their own trails, shaped their own ends. Both were inter-dependent. The Institute, reflecting on its journey of 50 years, contemplates an Ireland greatly different to that from which it emerged. Professional, confident managers were rare in the sparse industrial post-war Irish landscape. Ireland is now rich in this essential resource.

Would the transformation from a narrow, protectionist economy to a post-industrial showpiece have happened without the IMI's input? Distinguishing causality from correlation and coincidence is never simple, but it may reasonably be concluded that the IMI contributed to the evolution of the Irish economy in a number of respects. In its early days, it gave companies a framework for managing. It taught managers techniques they had not known before — and how to apply them. They did so, and that is demonstrable. The presence of the Institute was important to the fruition of the IDA's inward investment policy; many of the IDA's client corporations looked to the IMI to provide tailored development programmes for their management teams. In turn, of course, the presence in Ireland on MNCs in such numbers had the effect of dispersing advanced management practices and know-how through Irish business, not least through start-up industries by the Irish "alumni" of those companies or their recruitment by established local firms. The IMI also created in the wider Irish society a sense of awareness of management, of the centrality of management and management education to economic development. The record speaks to that accomplishment also. Most important, but least capable of measurement, it contributed to confidence, to the attitude of can-do that has brought Ireland's industrial economy from there to here.

Of course, it did not do so unaided. On the contrary, the readiness of the state and the European Community to assist a private body to fulfil a national role of some importance provides a model of what is achievable by public/private partnership. Without the flow of funds from successive governments and from Europe, the Institute could not have sustained its mission: the creation, from virtually zero, of a cadre of managers during a critical phase in the shaping of the modern Irish economy. Remarkably, at no time during its prolonged dependence on this external funding, did the IMI experience any interference in its autonomy.

The simply stated goal that the founders chose for the Institute — to raise the standard of management in Ireland — endures. Much has been achieved; but it is clear, also, that an abundance of challenge awaits along that continuum.

Sir Anthony O'Reilly, observing, from a global business perspective, the progress of the Institute — in which he taught work study long ago in the 1960s — says of the IMI:

The Irish Management Institute was decisive early in its
time in defining the educational process for managers, in
creating an ethos which led to the development of master's level management degrees in Ireland making it possible for practising managers to "migrate" from
management courses to full MBA immersion. It was a very
important catalyst at that educational level. When the
great Jewish Lord Mayor of Cork, Gerald Goldberg, built a
new bridge over the Lee, Corkonians immediately
dubbed it "the passover". For Ireland, the IMI was the
"passover" from a rural economy to a post-industrial society. It is a wonderful story.

The Irish Management Institute today represents the sum of the
remarkable vision, idealism, commitment and drive of many individuals who conceived it, put it in place, set its course and kept it *à
point*. The enduring tribute to those who gave part of themselves to
this story of accomplishment is that, 50 years on, it is, with Long-
fellow,

still achieving, still pursuing.

APPENDIX 1

THE CHAIRMEN AND THEIR TIMES

A chronology of the Irish Management Institute's 23 past chairmen and the issues they faced.

1952–56: Sir Charles O. Harvey

As assistant managing director of Guinness, he led one of the two groups seeking to establish a centre for management in Ireland. The groups (the other led by industrialist T.P. Hogan) joined forces in 1952 at the prompting of Sean Lemass and John Leydon. Sir Charles Harvey was the unanimous choice to lead the merged group. Elected first chairman of the new IMI in December 1952.

1956–59: Thomas F. Laurie

Tom Laurie, a Yorkshireman, was chairman of Esso Ireland. Oversaw the formation of the Management Development Unit within the IMI and also the move from Merrion Square to Leeson Park. When he retired, Esso established a foundation in his honour that allowed the Institute invite to Ireland distinguished contributors to management theory and practice.

1959–61: Denis A. Hegarty

Denis Hegarty was General Manager of the Dublin Port & Docks Board. An enthusiast for management development, he was one of the few local authority figures to involve himself with the private sector in this regard. He was close to the Organisation for Economic Co-operation and Development, helping channel its resources to Ireland and the IMI. He was the main mover in establishing the Irish National Productivity Committee.

1961–63: A.H. "John" Masser

A.H. Masser was another of those English businessmen who took a hand in setting up the IMI and as chairman oversaw the historic decision that the IMI would "grow its own timber" — recruit and train its first team of management specialists. This followed a study by the Review Committee on Education and Training for Management, a strategic work that mapped out the future of management education in Ireland.

1963–65: Jeremiah F. Dempsey

Jerry Dempsey was one of the modernisers of Ireland's economy. As long-time head of Aer Lingus, he embraced innovation in all its forms, not just the technology of his industry, but management processes as well. He was probably the first Irish chief executive to introduce a formal management development programme for his entire executive team.

1965–67: Michael Rigby-Jones

The youngest of the IMI presidents, Michael Rigby-Jones was head of Irish Ropes. The production systems he introduced there were widely admired and copied. He was generous in allowing that experience to be used freely in IMI case studies. He led the move to Orwell Road and, in 1966, presented to government the IMI's extensive study, *The Management of Irish Industry*. He died in the Staines air disaster in June 1972.

1967–69: A. Gunnar Larsen

Gunnar Larsen chaired the IMI at a time of rapid expansion in Orwell Road and led the executive committee through a review of future accommodation needs. Much media attention focused on the major issue of the period — a proposed union of the leading business organisations, including the IMI, into a "Nationwide Irish Business Organisation" (NIBO).

1969–71: Frank Lemass

Frank Lemass was general manager of CIE. Like his brother, Sean, he had a keen business brain, which he brought to bear on the work of the IMI. When chairman, he led the decision to build the National Management Centre in Sandyford. As president, he chaired the funding committee that raised £1.2 million to make it happen.

1971–73: Ronald S. Nesbitt

Ronald Nesbitt, chairman of Arnotts, was the IMI's first chairman from distribution. He presented to government the Consultative Board's report, which set the foundation for a national management education system that still endures. He was closely involved in the 1972 discussions about a possible merger with the Confederation of Irish Industry.

1973–75: Michael J. Dargan

As honorary secretary of the founding group, he was involved in the establishment of the IMI. Afterwards, he helped determine the path the IMI would follow, chairing a number of influential committees on training policy. Under his chairmanship, the Institute undertook a national research programme into the state of management in Ireland. He presided at the opening of the new National Management Centre in 1974.

1975–77: R. Ian Morrison

Ian Morrison's chairmanship coincided with the IMI's emergence from the turbulent aftermath of the mid-1970s recession. The IMI initiated a sweeping strategy review and restructuring. It moved to longer management development programmes, leading for the first time to the awarding of certificates in management.

1977–79: J. Paddy Hayes

Paddy Hayes faced difficulties not shared by his predecessors: he came to the leadership of the IMI from the southern capital, where he was head of the Ford company's Irish operation, commuting regularly to council and executive committee meetings from Cork. His term of office saw a review of the membership structures and the introduction of certified membership and fellowship.

1979–81: Mark Hely Hutchinson

Mark Hely Hutchinson was managing director of Guinness. He was appointed vicechairman 25 years after Sir Charles Harvey launched the Institute. During his term, the Institute developed its pioneering overseas work. Dr Julius Nyerere, President of Tanzania, visited the IMI in 1979 to pay tribute to the Institute's work in that country and was conferred with honorary life membership by Mark Hely Hutchinson.

1981–83: David M. Kennedy

David Kennedy was the third chief executive of Aer Lingus to lead the IMI. During his term, the Consultative Board was reconstituted and Brian Patterson was appointed director of the Institute. The Institute's first Life Fellowship was conferred on President Hillery. The Programme Development Group was appointed to advise on the training needs of industry.

1983–85: Michael Killeen

Michael Killeen viewed his appointment as IMI chairman as complementing his pioneering work in the IDA. He helped persuade Irish business leaders in stringent times to fund the Institute's research. In October 1984, he presented to government, under the title *Strengthening Ireland's Management*, the IMI's input to the White Paper on Manpower Policy. He died in 1986 while vice-president of the Institute.

1985–87: Feargal Quinn

Feargal Quinn, an innovator in the retail sector and an exemplar of what the IMI teaches about the eminence of the customer in the hierarchy of business, was only the second retailer to become chairman. In his term, the Institute established a partnership with Fordham University in New York and developed other strategies to bring it smoothly into the 1990s. He recruited Maurice O'Grady to succeed Brian Patterson as Director General.

1987–89: Howard Kilroy

Howard Kilroy bluntly told the Government in 1989 that the IMI would be better and more businesslike without state grants, at the time amounting to £430,000 per annum. Although the grant disengagement took almost a decade to complete, none would disagree that the IMI is indeed the better for it. In 1987, he presided over the opening of the Institute's information technology centre by Taoiseach Albert Reynolds.

1989–91: Tony Halpin

Tony Halpin was one of Cork's best-known businessman. He excelled at marketing and, as a member of the Southern Regional Committee, helped promote the Institute in the South. As chairman, in 1989 he approved the establishment of an IMI marketing arm in Britain to introduce the IMI to UK companies. The Institute's distance learning was also launched.

1991–93: Fergus McGovern

Fergus McGovern oversaw the implementation in the Institute of a demanding strategy, with an emphasis on financial rigour, to offset the effects of a steep decline in external funding. He chaired the *Year of the Manager* initiative in 1991, a joint project, assisted by state and EC funds, to strengthen awareness of the importance of management training.

1993–95: Dermot Egan

Dermot Egan's association with the Institute spanned most of his career. He was one of the first management specialists in the early 1960s. As deputy chief executive of the AIB group, he served as member of the council, chairman and president. As chairman, he initiated a "reorganisation and change programme" and, for an interim period, assumed the role also of chief executive, pending Barry Kenny's appointment.

1995–97: Jerry V. Liston

Jerry Liston initiated an all-Ireland conference in Belfast on the island's economy. IMI International was launched in 1996, working with governments and agencies in more than 35 countries. The National Management Forum was inaugurated to bridge the divide between the leaders of the public and private sectors. At the end of his term, Liston could report that the IMI was fully independent, operating without state or EU subsidy.

1997–99: Norman Kilroy

Norman Kilroy completed a unique family double when, a decade after his brother Howard, he also became chairman. His term saw a new focus on research, with the publication of books and papers based on the IMI's work, and a joint research initiative with the University of Limerick. In addition, the National Action Learning Programme was launched, a unique group approach to management development.

1999–2001: Kieran McGowan

Under Kieran McGowan's chairmanship, the Institute commenced a process of strategy development, building on its now sound financial base. Appropriately, because of his work in the IDA, it was in his term that the IMI created, in conjunction with NUI, Galway, the Masters Degree Programme in Information Technology. The Institute also published a significant research report into the management of knowledge employees.

Appendix 2

Life Fellows of the Irish Management Institute

Recipients of the Institute's highest honour

On 5 November 1981, Dr Patrick Hillery, President of Ireland, was elected the first Life Fellow of the Irish Management Institute. As of that date, Honorary Life Members of the Institute became *ipso facto* Life Fellows and the designation Honorary Life Member ceased.

1.	Sir Charles Harvey	1961
2.	John Leydon	1965
3.	Thomas F. Laurie	1967
4.	Denis A. Hegarty	1968
5.	James C.B. MacCarthy	1968
6.	A.H. Masser	1969
7.	Jeremiah F. Dempsey	1970
8.	A.G. Larsen	1972
9.	Colm Barnes	1973
10.	T. Kenneth Whitaker	1973
11.	Ivan Lansberg Henriques	1974
12.	Thomas P. Hogan	1974
13.	Michael J. MacCormac	1974

14.	Paul Quigley	1974
15.	Ronald S. Nesbitt	1976
16.	Michael J. Dargan	1978
17.	W.J. Louden Ryan	1978
18.	Donal S.A. Carroll	1979
19.	Julius K. Nyerere	1979
20.	R. Ian Morrison	1980
21.	Patrick J. Hillery	1981
22.	Ivor Kenny	1982
23.	J.P. Hayes	1982
24.	Tadhg O Cearbhaill	1982
25.	Koji Kobayashi	1983
26.	David Rockefeller	1983
27.	D. Donovan Coyle	1983
28.	Mark Hely Hutchinson	1984
29.	Michael W.J. Smurfit	1984
30.	David Kennedy	1986
31.	Anthony J.F. O'Reilly	1987
32.	Peter F. Drucker	1987
33.	Wolfgang Stabenow	1987
34.	Feargal Quinn	1990
35.	Howard Kilroy	1991
36.	Fergus McGovern	1994
37.	Dermot Egan	1996
38.	Jerry Liston	1998
39.	Norman Kilroy	2001

PHOTOGRAPHIC CREDITS

The Irish Management Institute commissioned many photographs over the decades, usually for *Management* magazine or for official Institute reports and publications. A number of these are reproduced in this book. For many years, the agency responsible was Lensmen, and the author and publishers are grateful to them for the wonderful record they have bequeathed of those times.

We would also like to acknowledge the other agencies and photographers whose images have been reproduced here, including Michael O'Reilly, Silver Image, Davison and Associates, Photostyle, Rex Roberts Studios, Frank Fennell, Barrys, Tony O'Malley, G.A. Duncan, Independent Newspapers, *LIFE* magazine and *The Connacht Tribune*. Every attempt has been made to trace the origins of the photographs used; if any omission has been made, the publishers would be happy to correct this in any future printings of the book.

Thomas Ryan RHA was commissioned in the 1970s to draw line portraits of the early chairmen, and these are included in Appendix 1, "The Chairmen and their Times" (pages 299–301). Jack Cudworth sketched the early homes of the IMI; his drawings are reproduced on pages 44, 54, 56 and 89. The photograph of the National Management Centre at Sandyford on page 214 is by Henk Snoek for the *Architectural Review*.

INDEX

Vermeulan, Adrianus, 104–5
vice-chairman, 1965 dispute over,
   109–20
Viney, Michael, 274
vocational education, 29, 30, 57,
   61, 123, 127, 128, 136
Vroom, Professor Vic, 147

Wade, T.C., 6, 19
Walls, Bert, 96, 247
Walsh, Ciaran, 225, 287
Walsh, John J., 15, 16, 18, 19, 25, 33
Warren, Michael, 213
Waterford Glass, 24
Waterford Iron Founders, 24, 34,
   38
Waterman, Robert H., 288n
Webb, Ivan, 174
Weirs Jewellers, 55
Wells Organisation, 201–2
Wharton School, 296
Whelan, Brian, 77–8, 79, 82, 88,
   104, 140, 159n, 167
Whelan, Dermot, 158, 237

Whitaker, Dr T.K., 2, 71–2, 74, 85,
   99, 134, 160, 164–5, 307
Whittaker, Andrew, 184, 189
Whyte, C., 15n
Wightman, S., 249n
Willis, Bob, 196
Wills, Donal, 210, 247
Wills, W.D. & H.O., 52
Winds of Change, 260, 268
women in management, 210, 290,
   292–3
Women Into Management
   Programme, 292
Woods, Michael, 232
Working Group on Co-operation in
   Business Education, 140–2, 144
Wright, Lance, 213n

Yale, 147
Year of the Manager, 259, 305
Youth Employment Agency, 162

Zambia, 247